W9-BRV-885

The Writer's Complete CRIME Reference Book

The Writer's Complete CRIME Reference Book

MARTIN ROTH

Cincinnati, Ohio

 Published by Writer's Digest Books, an imprint of F&W Publications, Inc., 1507 Dana Ave., Cincinnati, Ohio 45207. First edition.

94 93 92 6 5

Library of Congress Cataloging-in-Publication Data

Roth, Martin
The writer's complete crime reference book / Martin Roth.
p. cm.
Includes bibliographical references.
ISBN 0-89879-397-1
1. Detective and mystery stories—Authorship. 2. Detective and mystery stories—Handbooks, manuals, etc. 3. Crime—United States—Handbooks, manuals, etc. 4. Criminal justice, Administration of—United States—Handbooks, manuals, etc. I. Title.
PN3377.5.D4R6 1990 89-29422
364—dc20 CIP

Design by Joan Jacobus

To my wonderful wife, Marjorie, without whose encouragement, patience, support, and love, this book might never have seen the light of day.

Acknowledgments

I wish to express my sincere appreciation and gratitude to Barry Fisher, Director of Scientific Services Bureau, Los Angeles County Sheriff's Department; Michael Fooner, international crime expert and author on criminal justice; criminal defense attorney Arthur Lewis; and to the untold number of other experts and specialists from local, state, and federal law-enforcement agencies; the U.S. armed forces military justice systems; the private investigators, judges, and criminalists who so graciously provided me with much of the invaluable information included in this book.

One last kudo and that is to my editors, Jean Fredette and Nancy Dibble, whose knowledge, patience, and assistance helped prepare and make this book a reality.

Contents

Introduction *1*

The Criminal — **2**

The Professional Criminal *3*

The Amateur and Nonprofessional *4*

Serial Killers *4*

White-Collar Criminals *6*

The Computer Criminal *7*

Internal Crimes by Employees *8*

Organized Crime — ***10***

The Mafia *10*

The Triads *13*

Mafia Organizational Chart (An Organized Crime Family) *14*

Street Gangs *15*

Motorcycle Gangs *16*

Law Enforcement — ***18***

Local Law-Enforcement *20*

Los Angeles Police Department *21*

Los Angeles Police Department Organizational Charts *29-33*

County Sheriff's Department *28*

Los Angeles County Sheriff's Department Organizational Charts *42-50*

Cincinnati Police Division *41*

Cincinnati Police Division Organizational Chart *52*

Forensic and Police Sciences *51*

Office of the District Attorney *55*

Office of the City Attorney *56*

Department of Justice Organizational Chart *57*

The United States Department of Justice *56*

The Federal Bureau of Investigation (U.S. Department of Justice) *63*

United States Marshal's Service (U.S. Department of Justice) *67*

The Immigration and Naturalization Service (INS), Investigations Division (U.S. Department of Justice) *68*
Drug Enforcement Administration (DEA) (U.S. Department of Justice) *69*
Bureau of Alcohol, Tobacco, and Firearms (U.S. Department of the Treasury) *69*
Bureau of Alcohol, Tobacco, and Firearms Organizational Chart *71*
U.S. Customs Special Investigative Division (U.S. Department of the Treasury) *70*
Internal Revenue Criminal Investigations (IRS—U.S. Department of the Treasury) *72*
The United States Coast Guard (U.S. Department of Transportation) *72*
U.S. Postal Inspection Service *72*
Federal Air Marshals (FAMs) *73*
Bureau of Land Management (U.S. Department of Interior) *74*
Defense Criminal Investigative Service (U.S. Department of Defense—Inspector General's Office) *74*
Defense Investigative Service (DIS) (U.S. Department of Defense) *75*

National Crime Information Center Operation ________ ***76***

United States Military and Naval Law Enforcement ________ ***78***

United States Army Criminal Investigative Command (USACIDC) *78*
United States Naval Investigative Service (NIS) *79*
United States Air Force Office of Special Investigations (OSI) *79*
Military Police (MP) *79*

The Private Investigator ________ ***81***

The Courtroom ________ ***83***

Characters in a Courtroom *83*
Lawyers—Types *84*
Courts *85*
U.S. Armed Forces Courts *86*
Church Courts *86*

Special Juries *86*

Federal Bureau of Prisons — ***87***

New Facilities (list) *88*

Federal Bureau of Prisons Organizational Chart *89*

Locations of Federal Prisons (map) *90*

Percentage of Population Confined to Institutions by Offense (chart) *91*

Military Justice System — ***92***

SOFA (Status of Forces) *92*

United States Army Command and General Staff College Student Text 27-1 (excerpt) *94*

Fundamentals of Investigation — ***100***

Identifying and Locating the Criminal *100*

Tipoffs, Informers, Associates of a Suspect *101*

The First Twenty-Four Hours *102*

The Scene of the Crime *103*

Informational Sources to Investigate *105*

Surveillance — ***109***

Tailing or Shadowing *109*

Telephone Taps *110*

Electronic Surveillance Equipment *111*

Other Forms of Surveillance *111*

Police Vehicles *111*

Police Technical and Scientific Services *112*

The Police Crime Lab — ***113***

Chemical Examinations *114*

Biological *114*

Markings Identification *114*

Firearms Identification *114*

Documents Section *114*

Photographic *115*

Identification Sources — ***116***

Arson Investigation — ***118***

Motives for Arson *119*

Missing Persons 121
Steps in Attempting to Identify a Jane Doe or a John Doe *122*

Investigation of a Burglary 123
Types of Burglaries *123*

Sex Offenses 125
Attempt to Commit Rape *125*
Assault with Intent to Commit Rape *125*
Checklist for the Investigator *126*

Larceny 127
Auto Theft *127*
Confidence Games *128*

Robbery 131
Types *131*
Types of Weapons Used in Armed Robbery *132*
Methods *132*
Objects *132*
Crimes Committed in Addition to Robbery *132*

Smuggling 133
Concealment of Objects *133*
Concealment of Individuals *134*
Suspicious Persons *134*
Among Aircraft and at Airfields *135*
At Marinas or on the Water *136*
At Checkpoints *136*

Weapons Used in Commission of a Crime 138

Explosives 140

Firearms and Manufacturers 141
Terms Used in Firearms Identification *144*

List of Crimes 151
Crimes Associated with Politics *153*
Crimes Associated with Business and Professions *153*
Domestic Crimes *154*
Crimes Associated with Racketeering (Nonorganized) *154*

Crime Glossary 156

Cons, Dupes, and Trickery — *162*
Devices to Aid in Conning, Duping, and Trickery *163*

Narcotics and Drug Addiction — *164*
Drug Addiction *164*
Narcotics *164*
Synthetic Analgesics *165*
Tolerance and Dependency *165*
Use and Effect *165*
Drug Trafficking *165*
Points of Origin *165*
Narcotics (chart) *166-167*
Some Substances Not Used for Medical Purposes (chart) *168-171*
Possession *172*
Selling *173*
Narcotics—Packaging and Distribution *173*

Crime Drugs — *175*
Drugs of Addiction and Intellect Influence—Representative *175*

Slanguage — *178*
Underworld Slang with Emphasis on Drug Culture *178*
Street-Gang Slanguage *194*
Prison Slanguage *198*
Police Slanguage *199*
On-the-Road Slanguage *203*
General Crime Slanguage *203*

Crime — *213*
Methods of Escape *213*
Means of Execution *214*
Unusual Means of Disposing of Body *214*
Acts of Violence, Torture, Cruelty *215*

Police Codes — *218*
Ten Code *218*
Police Codes and Traffic Violations *221*

Correctional Institutions — *224*
California's Correctional Institutions *224*

United States Penitentiary — *238*
Visiting Instructions *238*

Parole — *241*
What Is Parole? *241*
How Long Does Parole Last? *241*
When Are Inmates Released to Parole? *242*
What Happens on Parole? *243*
What Are Conditions of Parole? *243*
Where Is the Parolee Placed? *244*
Can Parole Be Revoked? *244*
Reentry Programs *245*
Parole Officers *247*

Criminal Law — *248*
Sentencing *249*
Criminal Law Defined *249*

Legal Terminology — *262*

Evidence — *271*
Admissibility of Evidence in Criminal Cases *276*

Criminal Procedure — *283*

Arrest — *286*

Homicide — *291*
Motives for Homicide *289*
Types of Homicides *289*
Investigator's Arrival on Scene *290*

Bibliography — *295*

Index — *297*

Introduction

Crime pays! At least it does for the writer who can spin a good mystery yarn or crime story. That is evidenced by the overwhelming number of television shows, motion pictures, and novels dealing with crime and the number of crime and mystery fans who hungrily devour these stories the moment they're produced or published.

Assuming, of course, that you intend to write about crime and mysteries, you'll find this book an essential tool in helping you add credibility to your story or script: a substantial amount of crime-related information is now literally at your fingertips. This reference source includes information and facts dealing with the fundamentals of investigation, as well as with the wide variety of law-enforcement agencies and investigative services and their responsibilities and jurisdictions. Criminal motives, escape methods, weapons, rules of evidence, and slanguage are just a small portion of research and reference material within the covers of this book.

Much of the material that can be found herein came from the personal files, research, and reference material I collected during my forty years as a professional writer working on such shows as "Hawaii Five-O," "Hart to Hart," "Vegas," "Barnaby Jones," "Mannix," "Ironside," and many others as well as a few theatrical films.

This reference-and-research book can't write your story for you, but it can save you many, many hours of research in aiding you to create, commit, and solve your own crime story. It took a lot of years to compile and assemble all the information you now have at hand. It is the only book of its kind. I know how much it helped me to make my stories more credible and how often just looking up a particular subject gave vent to a new idea or a new direction to take. I hope the information in this book serves you as well and as successfully as it did me.

1

The Criminal

What makes an individual commit criminal acts is something far better left to those dealing in criminal psychology—especially when such a criminal habitually continues to live outside the law with total disregard for the lives, safety, and possessions of others—than for the author to attempt such a complicated explanation.

When dealing with an individual who willfully commits a crime, there are no hard-and-fast rules as to what brought that individual to that point. The basis could be purely psychological, going far back into the individual's childhood. Then again, the criminal act could be brought about at the spur of the moment. It is also conceivable that the perpetrators believe in their own minds that the acts they are committing are totally justified, or with respect to certain crimes, are unaware that what they are doing is unlawful.

One thing is certain, however, that links the professional and nonprofessional criminal together and that is motive. People do not commit a crime without a motive, even the individual who bears no grudge against society or another individual, or was not committing a crime out of passion or for personal gain or profit. Committing a crime just for the sheer thrill of it is in itself a motive. Crimes are committed for a reason, and the writer must firmly and foremost decide that reason before beginning the development of the plot, even though the writer may choose not to reveal the criminal's true motive until the very end of the story. (See section on motives to aid you in selection.)

In helping you determine the motive for the individual who is to commit a criminal act or series of such acts, it is important that you develop an association with that individual, motive and the background of that character to help justify some underlying basis for the eventual act(s). (See section on character development, jobs and professions, education, hobbies, family origin, etc.) The professional writer already knows that all characters are important and should be fleshed out as much as possible; accordingly, it is essential that the writer thoroughly provide the *victim* with a well-fleshed-out background, not only to help explain the perpetrator's motive, but also to provide something deep enough for the police to delve into during their investigation. Although real-life criminal investigators usually go through long, laborious, and often tedious days, weeks, and even months before turning up a decent lead, to heighten the drama, the more the police officer's personal as well as professional backgrounds are brought into play, the more interesting those in pursuit of the culprit will become.

In an *open story*, that which immediately identifies the criminal and possibly reveals exactly how, when, and where the crime took place, there is little need for those *red herrings*, or other possible suspects that must be investigated before the real perpetrator is revealed. In a *closed story*, however, the red herrings become extremely important, and the writer must painstakingly develop those red herrings so they are not easily dismissed by the reader or the viewer or by those characters involved in unraveling the crime and identifying the criminal responsible for the crime.

These red herrings must not only be well-developed characters, but each should have an excellent motive, in addition to opportunity, for having committed the crime.

THE PROFESSIONAL CRIMINAL

The professional criminal, as the term *professional* implies, is one who derives his living by performing criminal acts primarily for gain. I say "primarily" because, although the professional criminal does seek to gain and profit from criminal enterprises, there are many criminals who also enjoy living a life of crime. Some derive great satisfaction by attempting to outwit the police and to prey upon innocent victims. Others are sadistic in their nature and enjoy the pain, terror, and injuries they inflict upon their victims. Similarly, some criminals enjoy the fear they impose upon others and the momentary power they wield over their victims, and many times, their underling associates. Then there are the professionals who, because of a lack of formal education or some means of employable training, turn to crime as a profession because they do not believe they can succeed in the world any other way. And lastly there are those who consider themselves maladjusted to or rejected by society at large and thus turn to crime as a profession. Most professional criminals have records or "rap sheets," although some professionals have managed to escape prosecution for lack of evidence or because of mistrials.

THE AMATEUR

Amateur criminals fall into three categories. One is the criminal who is mentally and legally ill and is unaware of the crime he or she is committing. The second is one judged as temporarily insane. And the third is one who commits a crime for the thrill of it or for any of the reasons listed under "motives," which include revenge, jealousy, ambition, profit, mercy, etc. Opposed to most professional criminals who have an M.O. (modus operandi), when dealing with the amateur, the police have no M.O. to refer to, and unless they have some clue, identity, or motive for the crime, the investigative procedure can be difficult. On the other hand, crimes committed by amateurs can often be sloppy and reveal the perpetrator's identity much more readily than that of the professional criminal. This is by no means meant to minimize the cleverness and planning that some nonprofessionals bring to their criminal acts.

SERIAL KILLERS

According to recent studies about serial killers, most cases do not indicate that the serial killer suffers from a medical problem but more from cultural and sociological problems. According to a substantial number of researchers, serial killers usually seek celebrity status, venting their aggression and hostile feelings in order to gain admission to the higher levels of society because of their cultural obstacles and total frustration. Serial killers usually act sane, and in many, but not all, cases, are not considered to be psychiatric freaks, but are generally sociopaths or those suffering from personality disorders. Studies reveal that most serial killers are white males between twenty-five and thirty-five and are usually products of working- or lower-middle-class families. Except for sociopaths, serial killers usually seek victims from upper-middle-class backgrounds. Although it is not a hard-and-fast rule, a large number of serial killers supposedly have charm; are innately selfish, impulsive, and ambitious; seek to gain admission into upper-middle-class lifestyles; and many come from broken homes or homes where they had been abused. Most serial killers have suffered rejection, which causes them to experience frustration and psychological emasculation. Few serial killers express any feelings of guilt or remorse for their crimes.

Most serial killers, using some ruse to gain control of their victims, target upper-middle-class females. Their patterns usually call for sexual contact followed or proceeded by murder and mutilation to help the killer achieve that desired and much-needed celebrity status. One violent act makes it easier for the serial killer to continue seeking, murdering, and mutilating successive victims. Criminological motivations have been broken down by researchers into four major categories.

The first and the only one that could be considered mentally insane is called the *visionary type*, who claims to have heard voices belonging to demons or God ordering him to kill. The *sociopath* is one with a goal, usually the elimination of certain people existing within our society. This type believes that he is helping society by purging it of those he believes to be destructive to that society.

Another serial killer-type is one whose only gratification comes from exercising power over his victim, more often than not, having sex with his victim, the control of the victim bringing greater satisfaction than the sexual act itself.

Last is the *pleasure-seeking killer*, whose thrill comes from performing a knowingly perverted act, which is his gratification. In all, most serial killers are sexually motivated even if the act itself is not the ultimate gratification. In a majority of cases, the serial killer's primary mission is to a secret fantasy of sorts, and the killings carry with them any one or a combination of the following: cannibalism, torture, mutilation, dismemberment, and in some cases, necrophilia.

Although behavioral sciences have yet to completely identify what *episodic aggressive behavior* would mark a person as a serial killer in the making, such behavior still is a common factor among people who later become serial killers. Following are examples of episodic aggressive behavior:

Deviant sexual behavior
The inability to tell the truth

Chronic drug or alcohol abuse
Extreme cruelty to animals, pets
Feelings of inadequacy, rejection, being misunderstood
Being the victim of parental abuse in childhood
Arson
Being the result of an unwanted pregnancy
Compulsiveness
Suicide attempts
Chemical imbalance
Physical or neurological impairment
Feelings of persecution
Disrupted thought patterns
Drastic changes in moods
Hyper- or hyposexuality
Religiously obsessive
Prolonged or continued sequences of depression
Hallucinations
Egocentricities or feelings of grandiosity
Desire to be a loner; isolation
Withdrawal from friends, parents, society
Chronic insecurity

WHITE-COLLAR CRIMINALS

One of the fastest rising areas of crime today is that which is taking place within corporate America, various banking institutions and brokerage houses dealing in stocks, bonds, and commodities. Much of the white-collar crime fighting is being done by the Federal Bureau of Investigation, the U.S. Attorney's Office, the Internal Revenue Service, the Federal Trade Commission, the Postal Inspector's Office, the Securities and Exchange Commission, and the DCIS, the Defense Criminal Investigating Service, created in 1982 by the U.S. Department of Defense to investigate corporate corruption in the defense industry.

White-Collar Crimes

Bank frauds
Insider trading
Fraudulent billing in defense contracts
Manufacturing or distributing faulty parts
Fraudulent loans

Fraudulent bankruptcy
Stock manipulations
Overcharging for auto repairs
False or misleading advertising
Shortchanging in retail stores
Overcharging on government contracts
Product substitution on government contracts
Kickbacks
Bribery
Bank misappropriation of funds
Boiler-room investment scams
Tax and anti-trust violations
Computer thefts
Embezzlement
Arson-related insurance frauds
Medicare and medical insurance frauds
Staged accident insurance fraud
Excessive interest charges
Fraudulent billings
Corporate-raider manipulations
Political- or business-related improprieties
Tax-shelter frauds
Inferior merchandise

THE COMPUTER CRIMINAL

With the advent of the computer, a new brand of criminal has come upon the scene to take advantage of modern technology's latest means of recording transactions, developing plans and systems, transferring funds, and communicating and disseminating all sorts of valuable information which offer staggering rewards from the electronic revolution.

Today's computer criminal can use a computer to embezzle funds, transfer bank accounts, create a means of diverting funds, payments, obtain credit, eavesdrop on confidential data being transmitted, bill for nonexisting merchandise, steal programs, commit sabotage, erase existing programs, etc. Offenders commit computer crimes for various reasons: the thrill of pulling it off, greed, theft for profit, industrial or military spying, extortion, blackmail, etc. Computer criminals have even been known to hold a stolen program or one that they are capable of destroying for hostage, demanding a substantial ransom for the program's release or return.

Computer criminals work in a variety of ways. Some gain access to correct codes simply by experimentation, while others may scrounge through office trash baskets or discarded printouts, or merely observe an authorized computer operator at work and note the access code to a program. Computer crime investigators often require expert consultants to assist investigators in addition to the investigator's having a good working knowledge of computers and an awareness of the various schemes used by computer criminals.

INTERNAL CRIMES BY EMPLOYEES

Not all thefts are committed by professional criminals or those addicted to drugs. Many crimes in the home or at a place of business are committed by employees for a multiplicity of motives. In many cases, the employee feels justified for the criminal act he or she commits, unlike the criminal who commits his or her act purely out of greed. At times, however, crimes are committed in the home or office by nonprofessionals for the same motive as that of the common criminal.

Crimes Committed Against an Employer at Home or Office

Theft of cash
Theft of personal possessions
Theft of company checks
Theft of company books, records, or documents
False doctoring of company books or records
Theft of equipment or office supplies
Theft of company products or merchandise
Falsifying signatures on checks, documents, letters, etc.
Theft of company's plans, research, technical information
Theft of computer programs
Arson, flooding, or otherwise destroying company property or records
Trading on inside information
Blackmail
Physically attacking an employer, supervisor, company employee
Sabotaging company's plant, factory, office, plans, equipment
Selling company secrets

Misappropriating company funds
Assisting professional criminal in committing a criminal act against an employer's home or place of business
Using company equipment for personal gain
Padding or falsifying expense accounts
Diverting company funds to self
Forging signatures

Motives for Internal Crimes Against Home or Place of Business

Employee feels grossly underpaid
Employee believes he or she has been unfairly treated
Revenge against employer, supervisor, other employee for firing, treatment, being passed over for promotion or raise
Employee sees opportunity to blackmail company for profit or revenge
Employee has been offered substantial gain for selling company secrets, destroying or sabotaging company
Employee is addicted to drugs or alcohol
Employee is deeply in debt
Employee seeks better lifestyle
Jealousy or envy
Personal dislike of employer
Personal greed
Disagreement with social or political ideals
Bigoted or prejudiced against employer
To draw attention to a specific issue
Labor disagreement
To gain control over employer or company
Disagreement with company policy

2

Organized Crime

The term *organized crime* applies primarily to criminal gangs that are structured either in local, state, federal, or international criminal activities such as but not limited to South American organizations, Mexican networks, Sicilian Mafia, national outlaw motorcycle gangs, and Oriental organized crime groups who are involved in corruption of public officials, illegal infiltration of legitimate businesses, gambling, loan sharking, laundering of illicit funds, gangland slayings, labor racketeering, extortion, counterfeiting, prostitution, and drug trafficking.

THE MAFIA

The Mafia is probably the singularly most familiar name associated with the term *organized crime*. Sometimes dubbed "the Mob" or "La Cosa Nostra" ("Our Thing") it is believed to have had its roots in Palermo, Italy, in 1282, when Sicilian Vespers revolted against the French Angevins, who were then ruling Sicily.

Although today's Mafia is unquestionably one of the strongest groups identified with organized crime, it actually began as a secret society, originally formed to protect the poor, oppressed, and mistreated Sicilians from their invading rulers. Once freed of the French domination, however, the secret Mafia began to increase both in number and in the power it wielded. In 1417, however, the Italian states once again found themselves under foreign domination, this time by the Bourbons, who had spawned the birth of another secret organization in Seville. Called "The Camorra," this organization began with no altruistic ideals. It was composed of out-and-out criminals. Transported to Sicily and neighboring states by the Bourbons, the Camorra and the Mafia soon began to merge, the Mafia's once altruistic aims now giving way to more profitable ventures: that of gaining control of all criminal activities. The Camorra maintained headquarters in Naples, the Mafia, in Sicily. The Mafia reached the pinnacle of its power around the turn of the nineteenth century, and it was then that both the Mafia and the Camorra began their migration to the United States to prey upon the Italian population who had emigrated to America.

Once here, however, bad blood often led to feuds between the Camorra and the Mafia. Although the bonds were often sealed between the two, feuds continued to plague both organizations. Wars erupted frequently as the two competed for the total supremacy of criminal power in the new land. In the years that came to pass, the Mafia grew stronger and became the dominant force in the United States. Although the Camorra still exists to some small extent in this country, the Camorra N'Drangatta still reigns in Naples, while some remnants of the old Mafia still preside in Sicily.

The New Mafia

Sworn to obedience to their chief, known simply as "The Boss" (see organizational chart), members of the Mafia have no appeal to legal law enforcement, but only to those powers within their own organization, for justice. It is an unwritten law that any offense commited against one is to be considered against all. Members are bound by "Omerta," the code of silence. It is simply a way of saying, "If you talk—you die!"

The Mafia in the United States is dedicated to subverting and infiltrating all branches of the government so as to corrupt and bribe those who would benefit their purpose. Its aim is to control every profitable and productive area of crime and to convert legitimate enterprises so they are controlled and dominated by organized crime. Members are committed to murder and all forms of mayhem against any member or outsider who informs on them or is in any way a threat to their existence and their goals. It is essential that they show respect and complete obedience to those of greater authority within their organization. Should there be a disagreement or dispute, those involved may request a *sit-down*, where decisions are made by a council as to who is right and who is wrong and how peace may be achieved between the opposing parties.

When the Mafia first settled in the United States, they were often referred to as "The Black Hand," their hands often stained with the black tar that came from the tarpaper in which they wrapped the remains of those who opposed them so as to prevent blood spillage.

As time passed, the machine-gun activities of the Mafia became more and more muffled. The Families of the Mafia began to spread out, each Family given its own territory in which to operate. Soon, the Mafia had ensconced itself in almost every major city in the United States. In time, another transition was to take place—one that would transform the "Mob" and the "Mustache Petes" from pinstriped-suited racketeers and gangsters into black-mohair and gray-flannel-suited "businessmen" who could disguise much of their criminal activities behind the guise of legitimate business enterprises and labor unions. Their profile lowered; they had learned how to further increase their profit taking from a criminal genius by the name of Meyer Lansky.

In the early years of the Mafia in the United States, competition arose not only from the Camorra but also from those of non-Italian extraction, namely the Irish, German, and Jewish gangs who nibbled at the heels of the Mob. As the Mafia refused to permit the merging of outsiders into their Italian organization, Lansky proposed a mutual working agreement that would not only put an end to gang wars, but that would also greatly increase the coffers of organized crime. It was to become what is now known as the Syndicate.

The Syndicate stood to gain greater strength in unity as well as greater profits if it expanded its control over prostitution, gambling, and a variety of other criminal activities. Syndicate members concealed much crime under the guise of legitimate enterprises, but also engaged in and sought the means to put their combined wealth and power to use in infiltrating the labor movement and a host of many "legitimate" enterprises that could launder their illegal gains; much of their profits were stashed away in foreign banks and invested in the political powers of foreign government officials and in real estate both here and abroad. Of course, this was during the days when drugs were but a small part of organized crime's empire.

This situation would soon change, and so would the meaning of the term *organized crime*. It took the Korean and Vietnam conflicts to introduce drugs as probably the most profitable activity known to organized crime. Unfortunately for the Mafia as well as for law enforcement in the United States, little attention had been paid to other organized crime enterprises outside of our own borders. However, the effect was soon felt, as the Triad, spawned from ancient Chinese Tongs, began to expand into the world marketplace along with the Japanese underworld known as the Yakuza, Colombia's Medellin and Cali Cartels, and the Jamaican Posses. Although the Mafia still holds a substantial position in drug trafficking, it no longer holds the distinct title as leader in this worldwide drug epidemic.

THE TRIADS

One of the fastest rising criminal organizations in the United States are the Chinese Triads. Much like the Sicilian Mafia, Triad societies were first founded as patriotic secret societies, one of whom was The Eight Trigrams Sect of Fists of Harmony and Justice, later referred to as Boxers when leading the Boxer Rebellion against the European "White Devils." Represented by an equilateral triangle, each side signifying one of the three basic Chinese concepts, Earth, Man, and Heaven, most Triads have long since abandoned their original purpose in favor of lucrative criminal endeavors, including murdering-for-hire, prostitution, extortion, and drug trafficking.

The Chinese organizations control most of the world's supply of heroin from the Golden Triangle, which covers parts of Burma, Thailand, and Laos, earning more in one year than the total of U.S. currency now in circulation. The actual size or numbers of Triads and members is not known. However, Hong Kong's 14K Triad is only one of fifty separate Triads in the British colony, and 14K supposedly has fifty subgroups of its own. Hong Kong alone boasts some 300,000 Triad members, as opposed to only 2,000 known members of the American Mafia. You can see the enormity of the Triads on a worldwide basis. The United States is said to contain five major Chinese Tongs, the largest of which is New York's "On Leong Tong," followed by San Francisco's "Hip Sing." The "Ying On Tong" covers Los Angeles and the southwestern portion of the United States. The "Hop Sing" and "Suey Sing" Tongs operate on the Pacific Coast but also have locations on the East Coast as well. Although many Tong members in the United States are basically law-abiding citizens, the influence of the Triads and their manipulation of some of the Tongs have given the Triads a deep cover.

Due primarily to the staggering profits of their drug trade, the Triads have been able, like the Mafia, to infiltrate the legitimate business community, permitting themselves to launder the rewards of their

An Organized Crime Family

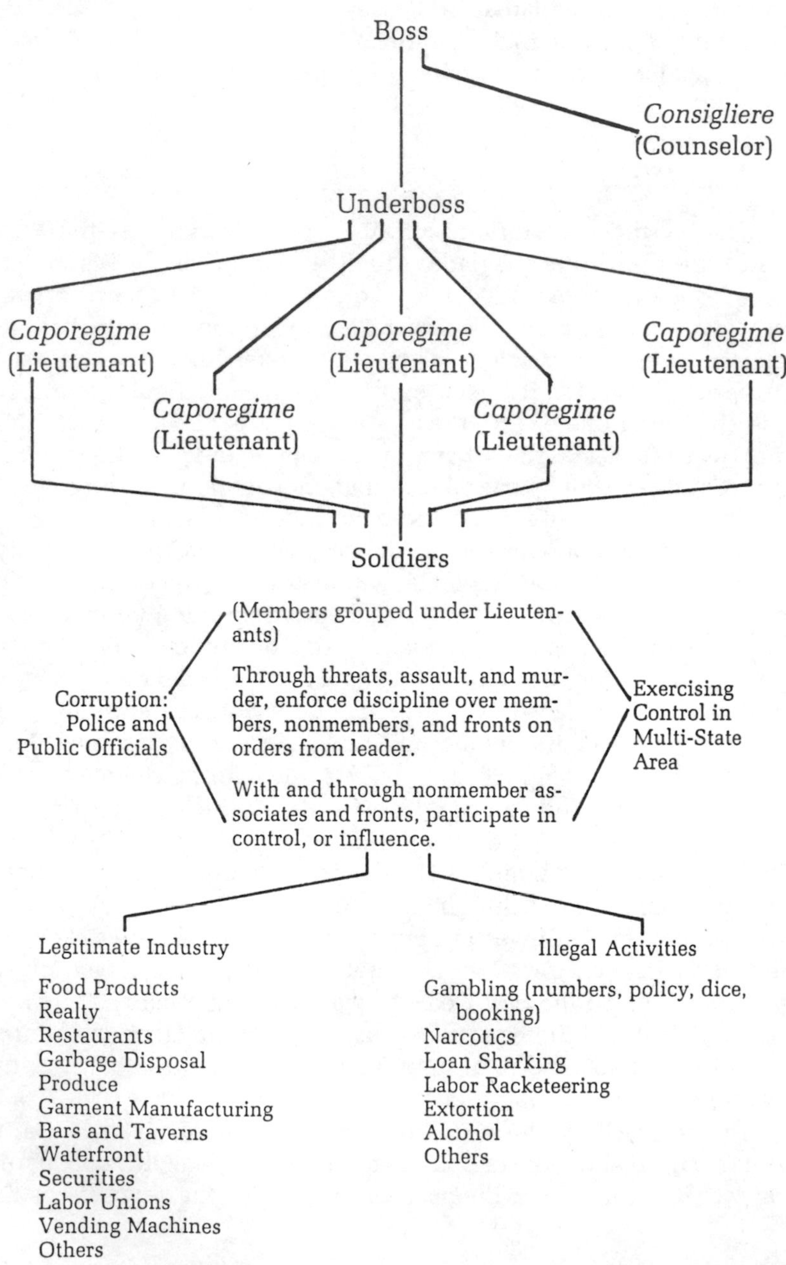
Boss
Consigliere
(Counselor)
Underboss
Caporegime
(Lieutenant)
Caporegime
(Lieutenant)
Caporegime
(Lieutenant)
Caporegime
(Lieutenant)
Caporegime
(Lieutenant)
Soldiers
(Members grouped under Lieutenants)
Through threats, assault, and murder, enforce discipline over members, nonmembers, and fronts on orders from leader.
With and through nonmember associates and fronts, participate in control, or influence.
Corruption: Police and Public Officials
Exercising Control in Multi-State Area
Legitimate Industry
Food Products
Realty
Restaurants
Garbage Disposal
Produce
Garment Manufacturing
Bars and Taverns
Waterfront
Securities
Labor Unions
Vending Machines
Others
Illegal Activities
Gambling (numbers, policy, dice, booking)
Narcotics
Loan Sharking
Labor Racketeering
Extortion
Alcohol
Others

criminal activities, and to reap even greater profits, power, and control over society. As opposed to their Asian counterparts, Chinese street gangs in the United States are almost always members of a Triad subgroup, such as the Wah Ching, which is supposedly one of the largest Chinese youth gangs on the West Coast; only San Francisco's Hip Sing rivals it in size. In New York, the On Leong use the youth gang known as the Ghost Shadows for their street muscle, while the Flying Dragons provide the necessary violence for the Hip Sing Tong.

Supposedly, the Triads' national syndicate inside the United States is run to some extent much like the Mafia: it has a council of its own based in New York. While the Colombians are little concerned with their notoriety, the Triads, much like their Sicilian counterparts, have learned, if not inaugurated, a policy of maintaining as low a profile as possible while continuing to expand their criminal horizons. However, following the Vietnamese conflict, law enforcement has discovered a new dimension to the already complex Asian crime problem arising in the United States: Tongs now employ newly formed Vietnamese gangs whom they call upon to do their violent and deadly work.

Amongst these new additions to the Triads are former South Vietnamese Special Forces soldiers called the Frogmen, who are specially trained in the use of explosives and assassination. Because Hong Kong is soon to be taken over by Mainland China, U.S. law enforcement expects to see an even greater rise in Triad members migrating from Hong Kong to the already crime-infested United States.

STREET GANGS

The term *street gang* once referred to neighborhood toughs who banded together to protect their neighborhood turf from members of bordering neighborhood gangs. Although these gangs committed criminal acts such as stealing hubcaps, tires, mugging, and occasionally stealing a parked vehicle, most of their time was spent warring with rival gangs. But today, the term *street gang* has taken on a much more sinister meaning primarily due to the tremendous increase in drugs. Whereas a set of stolen hubcaps might bring a few dollars, the infiltration of many street gangs by organized crime and Colombian, Mexican, and Jamaican drug kingpins have taught these gangs that trafficking in drugs is a much more profitable business.

With that came competition, as in any business, and street gangs now battle over who sells the drugs and where. Whereas the street gangs of bygone days were once made up primarily of teenagers, today's street-gang members range from age ten on up into their thirties and forties. Whereas street gangs once went to war armed with chains, bats, knives, and zip guns, today's weaponry, which includes automatic weapons, machine pistols, shotguns, high-powered rifles, bazookas, and even hand grenades, compares almost to that of the armed forces; quite often their firepower exceeds that of law enforcement.

Although street gangs do not necessarily qualify as organized crime, having no political clout or corrupt connections as with the more sophisticated criminal organizations, street gangs do have their leaders and lieutenants, however, and follow their orders. Gangs such as California's Crips and Bloods have grown into such mighty numbers, reports indicate they have sent cadres out into other cities thus awarding them the dubious description "organized."

To distinguish themselves from rival gangs, most street gangs have adopted either colors such as the Crips (Blue) and the Bloods (Red), while others set themselves apart by the type of clothing their gang wears or the manner in which they wear it. Many gangs have devised their own secret codes, handshakes, slanguage, and signals to ensure their individuality. What was once a neighborhood nuisance has now become a national menace, and with the ever-increasing flow of aliens into this country come more gangs and secret criminal societies. Many of these alien gangs begin by preying solely on their own ethnic groups. But as the profitability of drug trafficking continues to increase, more and more of these gangs seek the opportunity to break out of their own turf looking for greener pastures.

MOTORCYCLE GANGS (BIKERS)

Although most motorcycle or biker gangs are to some extent organized, they, like their street gang counterparts lack discipline, leadership, political, and corrupt connections. Most bikers travel in smaller packs compared to the members of the street gang, although some larger biker gangs have chapters all across the United States, such as the famed notorious Hell's Angels, who wear their insignia on leather jackets or tattoed on their arms or chests.

Unlike street gangs, the motorcycle gangs don't usually carry armament and automatic weapons, nor do bikers usually lay down any specific barriers as their turf. Bikers lay claim to their turf wherever they are at the time. Bikers are also known to carry their women with them, and in most cases their women are treated practically as slaves, quite often being passed around from one biker to another. Most illegal motorcycle gangs are involved in drug trafficking and dealing, although some have resorted to mayhem, robberies, rapes, murder, and an assortment of other crimes.

Bikers operate clandestine drug labs, favoring the illicit manufacture of methamphetamine (speed).

3

Law Enforcement

Law enforcement must be broken down to the jurisdictional area they are involved in, and the writer must determine the jurisdiction of the crime that has been committed and whether or not the perpetrator has left the scene, thus entering another law enforcement agency's jurisdiction, i.e., leaving a city or town and entering another city or state. Should the criminal move from one state to another, it is possible in some types of crimes that it then becomes a federal crime, as it has become interstate.

Each law-enforcement agency, whether local or city police, a sheriff's department, state police, military, or one of the many federal law-enforcement agencies, has its own table of organization, jurisdiction, and operating procedures. The writer should check out the law-enforcement agency he or she intends to employ in his or her story for information dealing specifically with that law-enforcement organization, as well as the laws governing that crime in that particular jurisdiction, as the laws relating to certain crimes vary from city to city and state to state.

As diverse as these various law-enforcement agencies are with respect to their jurisdictions and organizations, so are the weapons, equipment, and scientific technologies available to them; even so, most of these law enforcement agencies cooperate with one another whenever possible. It should be noted, however, that there are times when these organizations for various reasons do not alert one another as to their own particular ongoing investigations, as many of these investigations are covert operations.

When developing the process of an investigation, it is imperative that the writer be as authentic as possible as to the type of law-enforcement agency employed; to the officers involved in the investigation; and the methods, equipment, weapons, and scientific technologies that are available to them.

Should the writer wish a law-enforcement officer to "not go by the book" or to go "above the law" in attempting to investigate and apprehend the guilty party, the writer must know what "the book" and "the law" are that the law-enforcement character is breaking so as to establish conflict with those working by the book or within the law.

It is also important for the writer always to remember that law-enforcement officers, regardless of what agency or department they are employed by, are human beings. They have their own personal problems; there are good ones and bad ones; they may become frustrated and disillusioned; they live in a world all of their own, much of their lives spent with fellow officers and their families. Furthermore, they have spent most of their days and nights with the dregs of society and have a much different outlook on life and on crime and society than those not involved in day-to-day law enforcement.

More often than not, police work is oversimplified by the writer, who will justify a superficial presentation by claiming he or she has just so much time to set the stage, begin the investigation, quickly ascertain enough clues to put the investigator on the trail of the culprit, get into a hot chase, and catch the perpetrator or kill the guilty party in an action-packed shootout. Unfortunately, the writer seldom allows for a true insight into the criminal investigator's problems, for there is much more to determining the identity of the perpetrator and catching the criminal. *Catching the criminal who committed a crime and seeing that criminal convicted is another story.*

All law-enforcement officers, whether local police, small-town sheriffs, or federal officers, must contend with the law in order to gain a conviction, and that means they must not only apprehend the criminal responsible for the crime, but also be able to prove legally and conclusively the case against the perpetrator.

The letter of the law *must* be adhered to for the professional police officer to protect an individual's constitutional rights. One mistake—a technicality found by the defense forcing the court to declare a mistrial or even dismissing the accused altogether—and the law can suddenly work against the innocent or in favor of the criminal, thus frustrating those law-enforcement people who see their quarry go free because of a legal technicality. It is essential to be aware of what the law-enforcement officer must contend with in order to bring about a satisfactory conclusion, should that be your aim.

Many times the drama can be heightened by making these problems work for you. Use your creativity and ingenuity to help that investigator accomplish his goal by using the law rather than going around or above it.

Almost every law-enforcement agency has a public affairs or public relations section, and you will find them most cooperative in answering questions related to their agency and in aiding you to lend authenticity to your work. Many times they will put you in direct touch with an officer or an agent in the specific area of law enforcement that you're interested in, and it is advisable that you develop a list of such contacts for further use. It might be wise to send a letter to the officer or agent who assisted you, expressing your appreciation for his or her help. It will be remembered the next time you call for assistance.

Remember that law-enforcement jargon and acronyms vary from one area to another, as do criminal code numbers. In the movie *Robocop,* for instance, the script used California codes over the police radio for Detroit, Michigan, police.

LOCAL LAW ENFORCEMENT

Overview

For the purpose of identifying local law enforcement, let us refer to all city, county, and state police law-enforcement agencies as "local" as opposed to the federal law-enforcement agencies, which operate under one government, taking into consideration that these federal agencies still have their own separate jurisdictions and areas of responsibility.

Because laws and law-enforcement agencies vary from city to city, county to county, and state to state, it is quite impossible to provide you with information regarding each and every local law-enforcement agency in the United States. The local agencies presented in this book are described primarily for the purpose of illustrating local law enforcement. It is recommended that you contact the local law-enforcement agency in the location that you are writing about to confirm or to further research the specifics of the local agency involved in your particular story.

The Los Angeles Police Department (LAPD) and the New York Police Department (NYPD) are two of the largest local police departments in the nation. Although both of them undoubtedly share the same areas of responsibility in their respective communities, the breakdown of the organizational structures differs in numerous areas. For example, inasmuch as both police departments function under police commissioners with a chief of police in charge of the force operating out of police headquarters, the further breakdown of their bureaus and departments, as well as the nomenclature of special units, personnel, etc., may differ in many respects. Whereas LAPD operates out of what they refer to as divisions, NYPD operates out of station houses often referred to as *Precincts*. Neither LAPD nor NYPD has a police title such as lieutenant colonel, though the Cincinnati, Ohio, Police Department does. These are only two examples of learning to use the proper identification when you are writing about a particular city's law-enforcement agency, so before you write about a particular city, county, or state law-enforcement agency, check it out!

Note that the various divisions of local, state, federal, and military law enforcement may be (and often are) in conflict with one another over which has jurisdiction and that any may be critical or at odds with another over the handling of a given case. Individuals within or among these agencies may also have personal or professional differences, dislikes, and grudges. Therefore, it would be a mistake to assume that all these agencies, dedicated alike to law enforcement, operate at all harmoniously in daily practice. Opportunities for conflict—and dramatic storylines—are virtually unlimited.

LOS ANGELES POLICE DEPARTMENT

Organization and Functions

The organization and functions of the investigative branches of the LAPD are presented so as to provide a more definitive example of the operation of a major city's police force. It should be noted that all police department organizations do not necessarily function exactly the same way nor do they all separate their departments and responsibilities in the same mannner. When writing about a particular city, be sure to verify the organizational and functional procedures of that specific city's police department.

The Detective Support Division is responsible for investigating suspected conspiracies directed toward educational institutions; investigating specified bomb-related crimes; investigating, arresting, and processing certain felony fugitive and out-of-state misdemeanor fugitive suspects; monitoring gang-related activities and gang-related crimes; maintaining surveillance of known criminals engaged in unlawful activities; and responding to subpoenas and legal processes directed to sections of the Detective Support Division.

The Criminal Conspiracy Section is responsible for investigating criminal conspiracies directed toward the various educational institutions in the city; all bombings, attempted bombings and bomb threats; extortion or threats of extortion not investigated by Robbery-Homicide Divisions involving adult and juvenile victims or suspects when extortion elements involve or imply an explosive device or nuclear material; investigating all written and verbal threats against the mayor, City Council members, city attorney, City Comptroller, and persons designated by the Commanding Officer, Detective Services, Headquarters Bureau, along with maintaining records of all incidents motivated by hatred or prejudice in the city.

The Fugitive Section investigates, arrests, and processes felony fugitives, out-of-state misdemeanor fugitive suspects, and out-of-state juveniles wanted on criminal charges.

The Gang Activities Section is responsible for investigative patrols monitoring gang-related activities, including those who are gang members, as well as photos of and vehicles of gang members.

The Special Investigations Section maintains a mobile force of investigators to assist other divisions in locating and maintaining surveillance of active, known criminals and to effect arrests.

Bunco-Forgery is responsible for investigating auto repair frauds; offers of bribes; consumer frauds; Corporate Securities Act violations; any crime committed through use of computer-stored information or sabotage of same; manufacturing, distribution, or wholesaling of pirated recordings; capping; fraudulently printed checks; counterfeit currency; forged airline tickets; burglaries and thefts of blank checks and checkwriting equipment; fraud by worthless checks or credit cards, or forgery; and forged prescriptions. Bunco-Forgery also maintains a Pickpocket Detail.

Headquarters Detective Services Group, Robbery/Homicide Division is composed of a Robbery Special Section, Bank Robbery, Hijack-Cargo Theft Section, Homicide Special Section, Rape and Domestic Violence Section, Major Crimes Section, and Officer-Involved Shooting Section.

The Robbery Special Section is responsible for investigating extortions or threats of extortion when a prolonged investigation is required, when the extortion does not involve a juvenile as a victim or suspect, and when the suspect has threatened to do unlawful injury to the person or property. This section investigates selected kidnappings that are for the purpose of robbery.

The Bank Robbery, Hijack-Cargo Theft Section investigates robberies of banks, bank employees and messengers, insured credit unions, savings and loans, and armored cars; thefts of commercial vehicles transporting merchandise when cargo is the object of attack; and extortions by any means, including explosives when directed against a bank, employee, etc.

Homicide Special Section is responsible for investigating abortions, certain major homicide cases, attending coroner's autopsies involving homicide or suspected homicide victims, and reviewing all deaths, arrests, and crime reports pertaining to homicides.

Major Crimes Investigation Section is responsible for investigating major selected crimes at the direction of the commanding officer and for providing personnel to accompany VIP's visiting the city.

Officer-Involved Shooting Section is responsible for investigations when an officer has discharged a firearm causing a gunshot wound to be inflicted on any person; when an officer receives a gunshot wound; when a staff or command officer is involved in a shooting in which no gunshot wound was inflicted on any person; when death or serious injury results from an officer-related incident (except those involving traffic officers); and in incidents involving the death of a person in department custody.

Rape and Domestic Violence Section is responsible for investigating selected sex crimes and insuring proper collection of evidence in sexual assault cases.

The Burglary/Auto Theft Division is responsible for investigating all vault and safe burglaries except where the safe has been removed from the premises or lacks evidence of forced entry; burglaries where business machines are the primary object and reported loss is in excess of $20,000; all burglaries or thefts where fine art is the objective; hotel-room thefts and burglaries in major hotels; telephone-booth burglars; shop lifters; and major receivers of stolen property.

Commercial Auto Theft Section investigates stolen trucks (in excess of five tons); theft of commercial trailers, tractors, heavy-duty equipment; secondhand auto-parts dealers; car, truck, and motorcycle thieves.

Pawn Shop Section investigates and ensures compliance with laws, rules, and permits pertaining to antique dealers, junk collectors and dealers, pawnbrokers, secondhand stores, and swap meets.

Headquarters, Detective Services Group, Juvenile Division is composed of a Commanding Officer, Administrative Section, Operations Section, Juvenile Narcotics Section, and Child Protection Section. It provides information, training, and evaluations of juvenile policies and procedures; implements modifications of same; ensures that departmental policies are being followed; audits and processes all juvenile arrest dispositions; conducts follow-up investigations of cases in which a parent, stepparent, legal guardian, or common-law spouse appears responsible for depriving a child of the necessities of life to the extent of physical impairment; physical or sexual abuse of a child; homicide when the victim is under eleven years of age.

This division conducts any child-abuse case directed by the Commanding Officer of the Juvenile Division; investigates violations of state and federal laws pertaining to sexual or commercial exploitation of children when under sixteen years of age (e.g. child prostitution rings); assists fire department in processing of juvenile arson cases; investigates narcotics cases when suspect or victim is a juvenile; conducts counseling and provides dispositions for juvenile narcotics violators; conducts undercover juvenile narcotics investigations; and maintains liaison with the Juvenile Justice System's Probation Department, Youth Authority, Juvenile Court, District Attorney, and Public Defender in the processing of juvenile cases.

Organization and Functions of the Office of Operations

The Office of Operations is responsible for stimulating mutual understanding between the police and the community in order to prevent crime; patrolling the streets to deter crime; identifying, arresting, and cooperating in the prosecution of criminal offenders; recovering lost or stolen property to its lawful owner; enforcing traffic laws; and advising the public in emergency situations.

The Commanding Officer, Operations Headquarters Bureau, under the Director, Office of Operations, exercises command over operations of Operations-Headquarters, coordinating matters concerning uniformed and investigative services. The Commanding Officer, Air Support Division, under the Commanding Officer, Headquarters Uniformed Services Group, exercises command over the operation of the Air Support Division.

Organization and Functions of the Office of Special Services

The OSS is under the direction of the Director, Office of Special Services, under the direction of the Chief of Police, and exercises line command over the OSS. The OSS is composed of (1) The Internal Affairs Division; (2) Organized Crime Intelligence Division; (3) Bureau of Special Investigations; (4) Narcotics Division; and (5) Administrative Vice Division. Responsibilities include:

Recording and investigating complaints against department employees and processing disciplinary cases.

Collecting and disseminating intelligence information relative to organized crime.

Monitoring narcotic and vice enforcement efforts and investigating major occurrences involving narcotics and dangerous drugs and drugs illegally manufactured, supplied, or distributed.

Monitoring labor disputes and investigating selected related crimes.

Maintaining the Undesirable Informant File.

Issuing consular identification cards.

Maintaining records of aggravated incidents involving consular officers and members of their families.

The Administrative Office—Special Duties prepares correspondence; conducts research and surveys; makes required recommendations; reviews information or material of official position of the department that will disclose procedures, case events, or other confidential matters. It conducts background investigations of persons applying for employment with the city and maintains and monitors a master file of all narcotics reports.

The Internal Affairs Division is responsible for investigating personnel complaints involving staff and command officers except as directed by the chief of police. It records and investigates selected complaints against other department personnel. In serious disciplinary matters, it reports findings and makes recommendations to concerned commanding officers, the Chief of Police, and the Director, Special Services. It represents the department in disciplinary cases.

The Organized Crime Intelligence Division is responsible for gathering, recording, and investigating information concerning individuals and organizations whose backgrounds, activities, or associates identify them with or are characteristic of organized crime. The division also provides information concerning organized crime to concerned units of the department and to other law-enforcement agencies. It maintains a detail at the airport for the purpose of observing and reporting arrivals and departures of persons known to be associated with organized crime, a master index file containing data and information concerning persons investigated by the division, press clippings concerning racketeers and criminals indexed to the master file, a file of telephone numbers checked by the division in connection with investigations, a record of telephone toll bill search-and-warrant information, and a file of arson involving organized crime.

Organization and Functions of the Bureau of Special Investigations

The responsibilities of the Bureau of Special Investigations include monitoring narcotic and vice enforcement; investigating major occurrences involving narcotics and dangerous drugs that are illegally manufactured, supplied, or distributed; and monitoring labor disputes and related crimes and those duties that are the responsibility of the Public Affairs Section. The Bureau is composed of (1) the Narcotics Division; (2) the Administrative Vice Division; (3) the Labor Relations Division; (4) the Public Affairs Section; and (5) the Drug Abuse Resistance Education (DARE) Division.

The Narcotics Division is responsible for the enforcement of narcotics laws when the violations are committed by adults. It obtains, exchanges, and coordinates information concerning narcotics suspects and drug traffic. It develops narcotics statistics, including department enforcement efforts and the availability of drugs. It investigates major suppliers and distributors of narcotics and dangerous drugs who engaged in illegal activities on an organized commercial basis. These duties include evaluating the circumstances of each case to determine the advisability of seizing a conveyance and initiating formal forfeiture proceedings, and providing advice on geographic location of storage and maintenance of vehicles, boats, and airplanes seized. Directing and preparing necessary documents for presentation to the district attorney for completion of a petition for forfeiture.

It disposes of any seized asset related to controlled substance trafficking, and when appropriate, conducts investigations on a state university campus. It exchanges and coordinates information concerning narcotics suspects and drug traffic with Narcotics Information Network, (N.I.N.), and other agencies concerned with control of drug abuse. It obtains, records, and coordinates use of information concerning suspects and drug traffic. It administers the activities of the department's Undercover Buy Program. It reviews and coordinates all requests for pretrial destruction of excessive quantities of controlled substances and maintaining such files. It maintains the following files: narcotics information inquiries, N.I.N. investigations, department undercover buy locations, narcotic expertise certification card files, narcotics arrest and seizure statistics, narcotics resource materials, narcotics arrests and dispositions, narcotics suspects moniker information, border crossings of suspects. It maintains liaison with the state's tax board for possible state tax violations by narcotics suspects and the undercover and narcotics sting operations.

The Administrative Vice Division is composed of (1) an Administrative Section; (2) Gaming Section; (3) Pornography Section; and (4) Prostitution Section. The responsibilities of this division include monitoring and auditing geographic vice units' enforcement efforts to ensure uniformity and effectiveness; investigating vice activities of an organized nature; assisting geographic vice units, upon request, with operations exceeding their own resources or geographic jurisdictions; correlating and maintaining intelligence information related to organized vice activities; and coordinating, procuring, returning, and maintaining a file of undercover driver's licenses on a department-wide basis.

This Division's Administrative Vice Section is specifically responsible for securing complaints from the District Attorney's Office on all felony vice arrests and crime reports made in the metropolitan area; researching proposed and new legislation and developing procedures to assist maintaining effective vice control; storing, maintaining, and disseminating the division's electronic equipment; maintaining intelligence information related to organized vice activities; conducting electronic investigations and ensuring that standard procedures and policies are adhered to; identifying problem establishments suitable for abatement proceedings and providing assistance and functional supervision to vice/narcotic personnel in abatement proceedings; and maintaining files on bookmaking arrestees, mugs of all vice arrestees suspected of being connected with organized crime, and pimping arrestees.

The Gaming Section is responsible for investigating violations of gambling and bookmaking laws when violations are of an organized nature; maintaining liaison with Department of Animal Regulations regarding dog and cock fighting; maintaining liaison with Bingo Division of Social Services Department for investigation of licenses and with the State Lottery for lottery-related crimes within the city.

The Prostitution Section investigates violations of pimping, pandering, prostitution, and prostitution-related crimes; violations of Alcoholic Beverage Control laws when violations are of an organized nature; and monitors live stage acts when performance is generally of a sexually related nature.

The Pornography Section is responsible for investigating violations of pornography and obscenity.

The Labor Relations Division is responsible for maintaining liaisons with labor and management groups and monitoring labor disputes; and investigating crimes arising from labor disputes except homicides; bombings, kidnappings, and bomb threats.

The Public Affairs Section is responsible for providing news releases and public service announcements to the news media; establishing guidelines for public relations material by the department; preparing the department's magazine and annual report; answering requests for information; preparing Department Commendations and arranging for the formal presentation of all department awards to employees; preparing Police Commission Citations for private citizens, Certificates of Appreciation and Recognition; handling arrangements for visiting VIP's and law-enforcement personnel; maintaining the department's archives; conducting tours; and processing requests for speaking engagements.

The Anti-Terrorist Division operates solely under the direction of the chief of police and is responsible for gathering intelligence, as well as investigating and maintaining records and information on terrorists and terrorist organizations known to be in the city while maintaining liaison with other local, state, and federal agencies involved in anti-terrorist activities.

COUNTY SHERIFF'S DEPARTMENT

The sheriff is the chief law enforcement officer of the county and, as such, is responsible for general law enforcement in all unincorporated areas of the county and in those cities that contract for the services of the Sheriff's Department to avoid the cost of outfitting their own departments, equipment, personnel, and investigative expertise.

Duties and Responsibilities

The California Government Code and the California Penal Code authorize the sheriff of a county to perform certain duties and assign him the responsibility for certain actions within his county. The following is a list of duties and responsibilities:

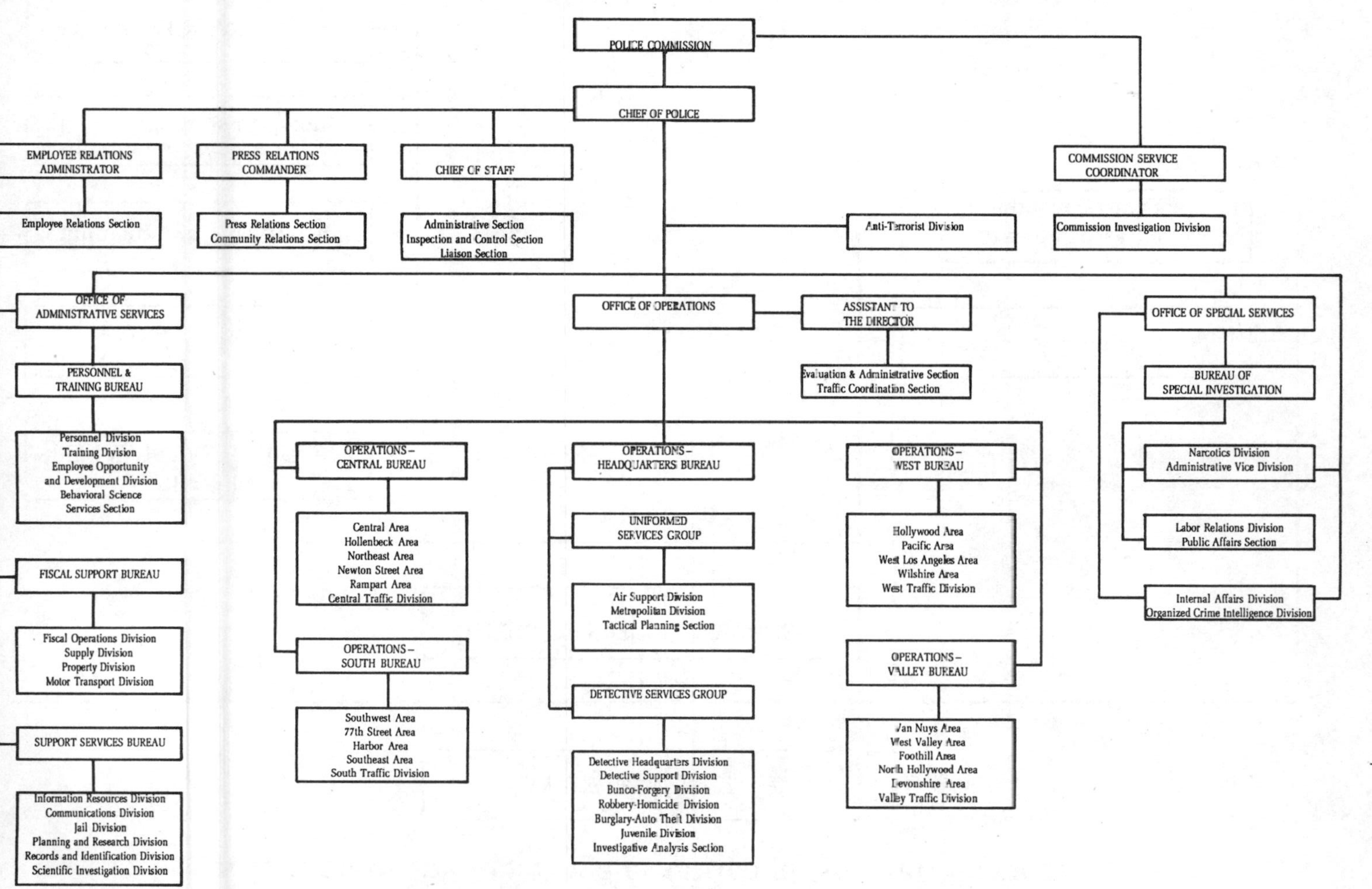

POLICE COMMISSION
CHIEF OF POLICE
EMPLOYEE RELATIONS ADMINISTRATOR
Employee Relations Section
PRESS RELATIONS COMMANDER
Press Relations Section
Community Relations Section
CHIEF OF STAFF
Administrative Section
Inspection and Control Section
Liaison Section
Anti-Terrorist Division
COMMISSION SERVICE COORDINATOR
Commission Investigation Division
OFFICE OF ADMINISTRATIVE SERVICES
PERSONNEL & TRAINING BUREAU
Personnel Division
Training Division
Employee Opportunity and Development Division
Behavioral Science Services Section
FISCAL SUPPORT BUREAU
Fiscal Operations Division
Supply Division
Property Division
Motor Transport Division
SUPPORT SERVICES BUREAU
Information Resources Division
Communications Division
Jail Division
Planning and Research Division
Records and Identification Division
Scientific Investigation Division
OFFICE OF OPERATIONS
ASSISTANT TO THE DIRECTOR
Evaluation & Administrative Section
Traffic Coordination Section
OPERATIONS–CENTRAL BUREAU
Central Area
Hollenbeck Area
Northeast Area
Newton Street Area
Rampart Area
Central Traffic Division
OPERATIONS–SOUTH BUREAU
Southwest Area
77th Street Area
Harbor Area
Southeast Area
South Traffic Division
OPERATIONS–HEADQUARTERS BUREAU
UNIFORMED SERVICES GROUP
Air Support Division
Metropolitan Division
Tactical Planning Section
DETECTIVE SERVICES GROUP
Detective Headquarters Division
Detective Support Division
Bunco-Forgery Division
Robbery-Homicide Division
Burglary-Auto Theft Division
Juvenile Division
Investigative Analysis Section
OPERATIONS–WEST BUREAU
Hollywood Area
Pacific Area
West Los Angeles Area
Wilshire Area
West Traffic Division
OPERATIONS–VALLEY BUREAU
Van Nuys Area
West Valley Area
Foothill Area
North Hollywood Area
Devonshire Area
Valley Traffic Division
OFFICE OF SPECIAL SERVICES
BUREAU OF SPECIAL INVESTIGATION
Narcotics Division
Administrative Vice Division
Labor Relations Division
Public Affairs Section
Internal Affairs Division
Organized Crime Intelligence Division

Organization of the Los Angeles Office of Special Services

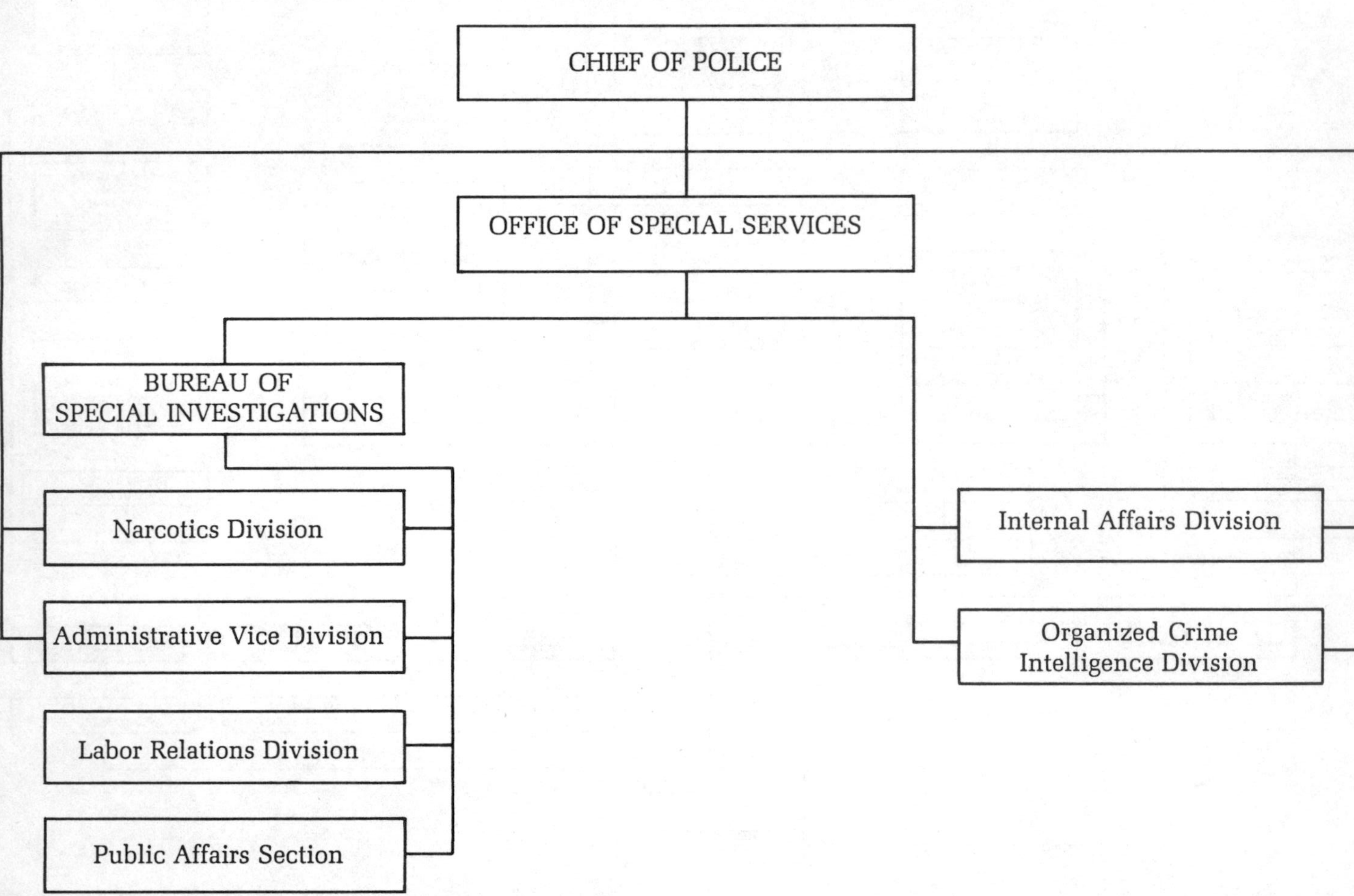

Organization of the Los Angeles Office of Special Services

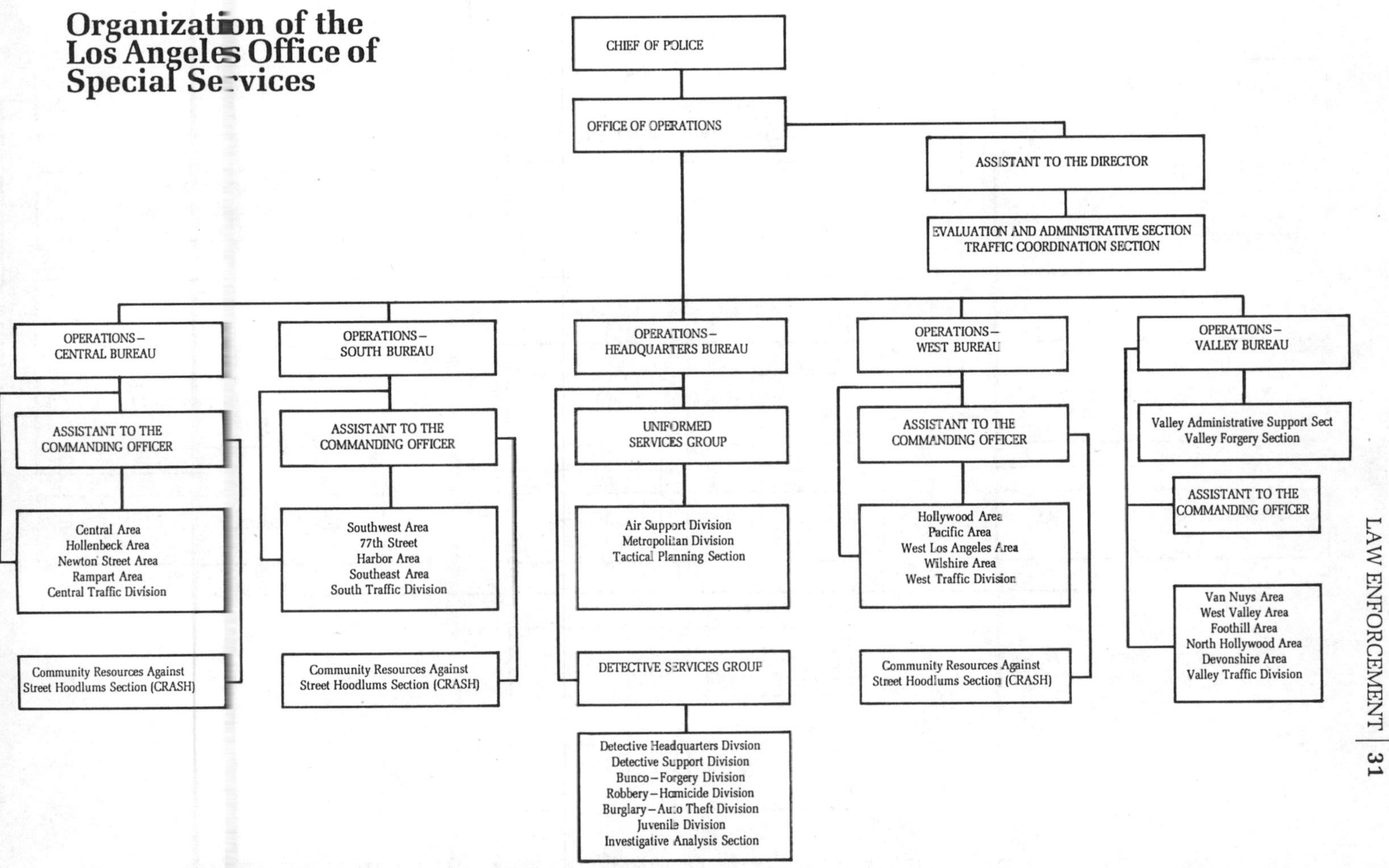
CHIEF OF POLICE
OFFICE OF OPERATIONS
ASSISTANT TO THE DIRECTOR
EVALUATION AND ADMINISTRATIVE SECTION
TRAFFIC COORDINATION SECTION
OPERATIONS–
CENTRAL BUREAU
ASSISTANT TO THE
COMMANDING OFFICER
Central Area
Hollenbeck Area
Newton Street Area
Rampart Area
Central Traffic Division
Community Resources Against
Street Hoodlums Section (CRASH)
OPERATIONS–
SOUTH BUREAU
ASSISTANT TO THE
COMMANDING OFFICER
Southwest Area
77th Street
Harbor Area
Southeast Area
South Traffic Division
Community Resources Against
Street Hoodlums Section (CRASH)
OPERATIONS–
HEADQUARTERS BUREAU
UNIFORMED
SERVICES GROUP
Air Support Division
Metropolitan Division
Tactical Planning Section
DETECTIVE SERVICES GROUP
Detective Headquarters Divsion
Detective Support Division
Bunco–Forgery Division
Robbery–Homicide Division
Burglary–Auto Theft Division
Juvenile Division
Investigative Analysis Section
OPERATIONS–
WEST BUREAU
ASSISTANT TO THE
COMMANDING OFFICER
Hollywood Area
Pacific Area
West Los Angeles Area
Wilshire Area
West Traffic Division
Community Resources Against
Street Hoodlums Section (CRASH)
OPERATIONS–
VALLEY BUREAU
Valley Administrative Support Sect
Valley Forgery Section
ASSISTANT TO THE
COMMANDING OFFICER
Van Nuys Area
West Valley Area
Foothill Area
North Hollywood Area
Devonshire Area
Valley Traffic Division

Organization of the Los Angeles Office of Administrative Services

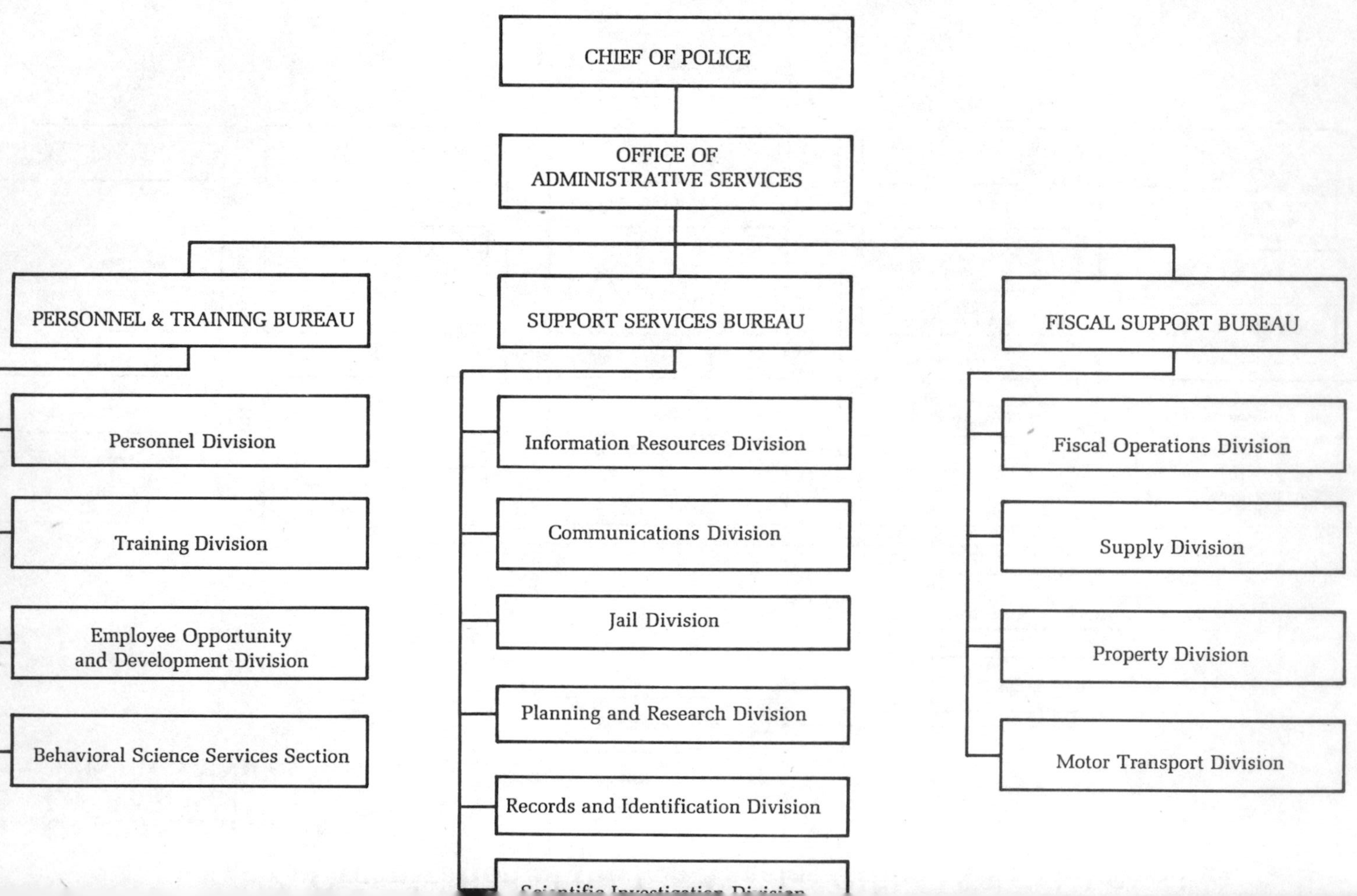

Organization of the Los Angeles Office of Special Services

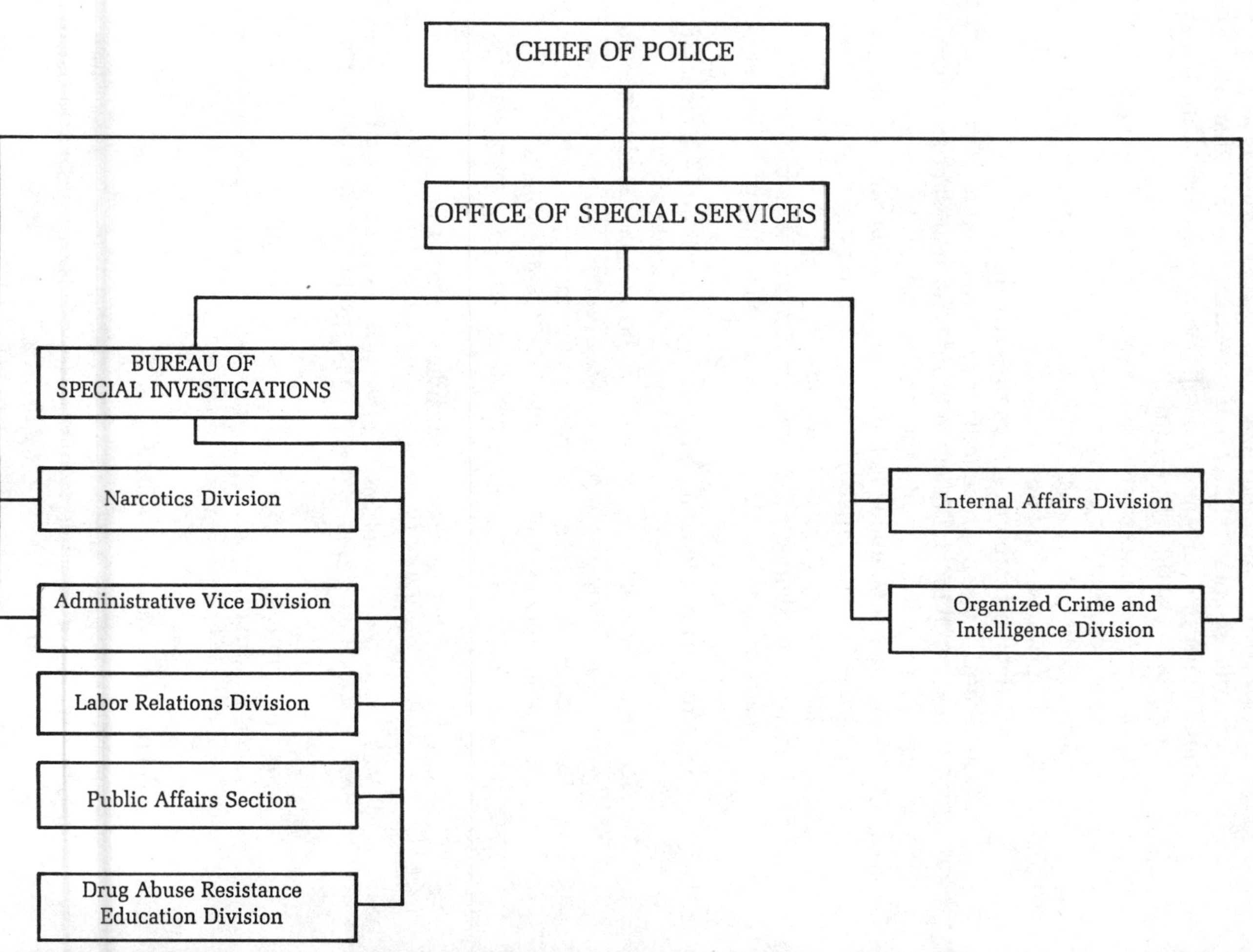

Preserve the peace.
Arrest all persons attempting or committing public offenses.
Prevent and suppress affrays and investigate public offenses.
Attend superior courts and obey all lawful orders and directions of all courts within the county.
Take charge of and keep the county jail and the prisoners in it.
Release attachments or garnishments of property.
Endorse receipts of process and issue certificates of delivery.
Serve all processes and notices.
Act in attendance upon court as the crier thereof.
The Sheriff may supply ambulance service; enforce the Vehicle Code; search for and rescue persons who are lost or are in danger of their lives within the county; command the aid of all adult male inhabitants in the county to accomplish his duties.
Hold ex-officio the Office of County Director of Emergency Services and carry out the duties thereof.
Transport and deliver prisoners committed to state prisons.
Transport prisoners to hospitals or to the custody of an officer of another jurisdiction.
Upon request of the court, may have responsibility for care and custody of minors charged with or convicted of felonies.
Execute writs and transport persons who are narcotics addicts and sexual psychopaths to places of confinement.
Execute search warrants and arrest warrants.
Sit as a member of the Board of Parole Commissioners.
Take possession of, appraise, and keep safely found or wrecked property.
May be directed to remove intruders from waste or ungranted lands of the state.
May serve all writs, notices, or other processes issued by superior, municipal, or justice courts, and lawful orders of the state government.
May be required to serve processes or warrants issued by any court-martial officer, labor commissioner, or insurance commissioner to a person within the county.

Administrative Organization

The Sheriff of Los Angeles County is elected to a four-year term of office and is responsible to the electorate. He is subject to fiscal control by the Los Angeles County Board of Supervisors.

The sheriff's department is a quasi-military organization. All sworn personnel are deputy sheriffs, regardless of rank, and are subordinate in order of rank to the sheriff. The rank structure is as follows:

Sheriff
Undersheriff
Assistant Sheriff
Chief
Commander
Captain
Lieutenant
Sergeant
Deputy

The undersheriff, an appointed position, is second in command and subordinate only to the sheriff. He commands the department in the sheriff's absence and otherwise conducts the affairs of the department as directed by the sheriff.

The third level of command is that of assistant sheriff. This department has two assistant sheriffs, each with separate areas of responsibility. In the absence of the sheriff and the undersheriff, the designated assistant sheriff assumes full command of the department.

Other major staff executives are the eight division chiefs, who command the activities of their respective divisions in accordance with the policies of the sheriff.

Departmental Organization

The sheriff's department is composed of eight divisions, each of which is commanded by a chief. These divisions operate on a twenty-four hour schedule to provide full services whenever needed. The divisions are:

Administrative
Court Services
Custody
Detective
Field Operations Region I
Field Operations Region II
Field Operations Region III
Technical Services

Administrative Division. This division functions as the major coordinating unit for the department's overall operations. It is responsible for providing administrative staff services to the entire department. These services include recruiting, training, coordinating retirements, maintaining personnel and payroll records, conducting pre-employment background investigations, researching problem areas, and analyzing legislation. Through its Internal Investigations Bureau, this division investigates citizen complaints and other cases involving departmental personnel.

Court Services Division. This division is responsible for carrying out part of the mandated duties of the sheriff as set forth in the Government Code. Primary among these is the requirement to act as the Chief Ministerial Officer of the Los Angeles County Superior Court. The Court Services Division serves and enforces civil and criminal processes submitted by the court, attorneys, and litigants, and provides bailiffs to the superior and justice courts. This division is also responsible for transporting prisoners to and from court and between custodial facilities.

Custody Division. This division is responsible for the operation of the sheriff's custody system, which includes incarceration of all sentenced and pretrial inmates detained in sheriff's facilities. Medical services are also provided for the approximately 17,500 inmates housed in custody facilities.

Detective Division. This division has the responsibility for investigating, among others, the major crimes of arson, forgery, fraud, robbery, flight from prosecution, and homicide. Specialized bureaus within this division have responsibility for the investigation of narcotics and vice operations. The Hazardous Materials Team is also part of the Detective Division.

Field Operations Regions. Three Field Operations Regions provide general law enforcement, patrol, and investigative services to unincorporated areas of the county. In addition to these services, contract cities are also provided with traffic law enforcement. When major or specialized crimes occur, follow-up investigations are conducted by the Detective Division. The department's jurisdiction extends to inland waters.

To supplement and improve the effectiveness of field operations, specialized units have been established as separate bureaus within the Field Operations Regions. These include Aero, Emergency Operations, Special Enforcement, and Juvenile Operations Bureaus.

Technical Services Division. This division is responsible for providing the specialized technical services necessary for the efficient operation of the department's line units and for maintaining the official activity records of the department. Other services include maintaining the department's vehicles, operating the telecommunications system, operating the criminalistics and photographic laboratories, and preparing the department's statistical reports on jail population and criminal activity.

This division is also responsible for operating the department's Communications Center and coordinating the Justice Data System (JDS).

Specialized Investigations

Two highly specialized bureaus, Special Investigations and Inspectional Services, operating from the office of the undersheriff, conduct sensitive staff-support functions.

The Inspectional Services Bureau was established in 1975. This bureau conducts specialized inspections on a department-wide basis to ensure uniformity of procedures, to maximize efficiency, to project future problems, and to recommend solutions to identified problems.

The Special Investigations Bureau was organized to investigate known or suspected organized crime, prison gang activity, and individuals or groups involved in terrorist-type conduct.

Emergency-Services Detail

The Emergency Services Detail is recognized as one of the finest emergency-services groups in the nation.

Deputies from this detail were the first lawmen in the country to earn the title *paramedic*. To achieve this distinction, deputies completed a rigorous 1,000-hour training course at the University of Southern California Medical Center. Once certified, and acting under the supervision of a licensed medical doctor, these deputy-paramedics are able to provide immediate medical aid in the field. This extra care for the injured has saved many lives.

In addition to paramedic training, these deputies are trained extensively in search-and-rescue techniques, mountain rescue, helicopter evacuation of the injured, and underwater search and recovery.

Technological Advances

To adequately serve an area the size of Los Angeles County, the sheriff's department must have a fast, accurate, and dependable communications system. This system uses decentralized command and control with centralized dispatching. There are twenty patrol stations located throughout the vast 4,083-square-mile county, and each station operates as a self-contained law-enforcement unit. The key element in the communications system is the centralized radio center, which coordinates all two-way radio communications with mobile units. These include patrol and investigative vehicles, helicopters, airplanes, buses, trucks, jeeps, boats, and assorted mobile support equipment.

To provide countywide coverage, the communications system utilizes transmission and reception sites on fourteen mountain-top and nineteen local sites connected to the centralized dispatching center by a county-owned microwave system, which is one of the largest private microwave systems in the world. The system uses 55 frequencies operating through one or more of the 116 base transmitters, 344 receivers, and more than 1,000 mobiles. Over 61 million transmissions are generated within a single year.

In 1975, the Sheriff's Radio Communications Center computerized its capabilities. This highly flexible communications computer maintains a bookkeeping operation of the workload and distributes incoming traffic equally among all the radio-dispatching positions.

The computer senses an incoming digital message from a station, assigns a console within fifty milliseconds, and activates a bank of relays that provides the dispatching console with all of the transmitters, receivers, telephone lines, and status signals necessary to handle the transmission. The relays, located in a central equipment room, can be accessed by all consoles; thus, every console in the facility can be considered a master console, able to handle any frequency at any transmitter/receiver location.

The computer also monitors and records the status of on-duty units, the calls assigned to them, and whether or not the call has been handled within a preset time. When the mobile unit finishes an assignment, clearance for the call is manually entered into the computer, which is programmed to print out a complete log of each original call and its clearance, as well as various other reports.

A primary part of the communication system is the Justice Data System (JDS). This system was developed to handle the booking and court information on all persons who enter the criminal justice system. Pertinent information on identification, charges, and court appearances on adults and juveniles detained in police custody for more than one hour is entered into this system. JDS now includes sixteen other police agencies, including the Los Angeles Police Department. Future plans are to include all law-enforcement agencies in Los

Angeles County and to become the data base for information on persons going through the criminal justice system.

Justice Data System also serves as a central information source for all criminal justice agencies within the county area. Information is processed into the Automated Index, which itself is organized into two groups of information—the Personal History Index and the Event Index. The Personal History Index provides data to attain a positive identification of each individual as well as his arrest and conviction recap. The Event Index provides information relevant to a particular criminal offense. The two indexes retain enough information to satisfy approximately 90 percent of all inquiries from the various justice agencies.

One of the many advantages of JDS is the ability of each sheriff's station to obtain complete criminal information immediately. In cases where there is limited information regarding an individual under investigation, the Event Index enables the recall of information contained in reports by a number of criteria, such as victim's/witness's name, vehicle license, and other identifiers.

In addition, the department will be able to perform special searches on partial fingerprint classifications. These searches will fulfill information needs on types of arrest, names under investigation, name of officer, date of occurrence, and report status.

Using computerized systems pioneered and developed by this department, they have achieved a truly innovative, efficient, and reliable communications network. An important phase of this network is the Justice Data Interface Controller (JDIC). This system replaced the FAST (Fully Automatic Switching Teletype) system formerly used by most law-enforcement agencies in the county to gain access to law-enforcement agencies and criminal-justice-system data banks.

Aero Bureau

The use of aircraft, with its unprecedented degree of flexibility and mobility, has added an entirely new dimension to law-enforcement patrol.

Originally started in 1929 by volunteers, it was not until 1966 that modern airborne law enforcement came into its own, with the establishment of the Sky Knight program.

The department's Aero Bureau fleet has been increased with the most modern and varied equipment available. Currently, the rotary fleet consists of five Hughes 300's, five Hughes 500's, three Bell 47G3B's, one Bell 20 GL, one Sikorsky S-58, and three Sikorsky CH38 helicopters. Fixed wing aircraft include two Cessna 210's.

Based at Long Beach Airport, Aero Bureau provides services for over 3,100 square miles of Los Angeles County, including many of the incorporated cities, which contract with the sheriff's department for police services. Within this jurisdiction, there is a great variety of terrain: high mountains, rugged wild canyons, vast desert areas, large ocean stretches, and offshore islands. Because of this, Aero Bureau also maintains helicopters at strategic locations throughout the county to minimize response times and increase efficiency. The Aero Bureau flies numerous medical evacuation missions, surveillance missions, prisoner transfers, hazardous materials investigations, photo flights, and investigator transportation flights.

Search and Rescue is another facet of the Aero Bureau. There were 718 rescue missions flown during fiscal year 1984-85. Search-and-rescue teams from various sheriff's stations are frequently assisted by paramedic-equipped helicopters able to reach areas inaccessible by ground crews. In addition to the paramedic crews, who are available twenty-four hours a day, medical doctors from the Sheriff's Department's Reserve Forces volunteer their services to the citizens of Los Angeles County. Aero Bureau assigns rescue helicopters staffed with these doctors and paramedics primarily on weekends in strategic areas, where their lifesaving services are frequently needed.

Aero Bureau employs one Hughes 500, chiefly to locate illegal hazardous materials disposal sites, as well as to conduct surveillances of suspected unlawful disposals. Aero Bureau also investigates aircraft accidents and thefts of aircraft parts, and it performs any mission requiring the use of aircraft as directed and approved by the sheriff.

Harbor Patrol

Since its construction in 1962, Marina del Rey has become the world's largest small-craft harbor. Anticipated population growth in the Marina del Rey community, as well as plans to increase the number of channels and slips, led to the establishment of the twentieth station facility there in 1984. That same year, the Los Angeles County Harbor Patrol merged with the sheriff's department, resulting in more streamlined law-enforcement service to the citizens in the marina.

The Sheriff's Harbor Patrol enforces both California State Statutes and Los Angeles County Codes, placing an emphasis on boating and marine laws. It also performs search-and-rescue missions, as well as provides services to boaters in the marina.

The many years of nautical experience accumulated by former

harbor patrolmen still benefit the citizens of Los Angeles County, as each of them are now deputy sheriffs. Each deputy sheriff assigned to the Sheriff's Harbor Patrol has received 895 hours of specialized training in addition to the standard Sheriff's Academy curriculum. This training includes instruction in marine firefighting, navigation, diving, and search and rescue. All Harbor Patrol Deputies have also received 120 hours of emergency medical technician training.

The Sheriff's Harbor Patrol maintains a fleet of six specialized boats. Facilities include several hundred feet of dock, a boat maintenance center, and a haul-out yard.

The sheriff's department also has a contingent of harbor patrol deputies. Their mission is the same as that of deputies—enforcing of boating laws and ensuring the safety of the water-faring public.

CINCINNATI POLICE DIVISION

The Cincinnati, Ohio, Police Division consists of four bureaus: Operations Bureau, Investigative Bureau, Technical Services Bureau, and Personnel Resources Bureau.

The Operations Bureau consists of five police districts and the Operational Support Section. These five districts are charged with the responsibility of patrol covering general criminal activities along with community relations. The Operational Support Section as part of the Operations Bureau is responsible for the SWAT Coordination Unit, the Crime Prevention Unit, the Traffic Unit, Youth Aid, and a new unit called the Alarm Enforcement Unit, which is charged with reducing the number of false alarms requiring police response.

The Investigations Bureau (I.B.) is charged with the responsibility for drug, vice, and criminal investigation and enforcement; it comprises the Criminal Investigation Section (C.I.S.), Central Vice Control Section, Intelligence Section, and Narcotics Liaison. Under the C.I.S., the Youth Squad is assigned the function of investigating child abuse, child neglect, custody, and missing persons. The Homicide Squad is responsible for investigating all homicides, questionable deaths, aggravated assaults where death may occur, rape and sex-motivated offenses where the victim is eighteen or older, all police interventions in shootings or death, kidnapping and abductions, and patient-abuse offenses. Also under the I.B. is the Robbery Unit; the Major Offender Project, which coordinates cases involving serious and repeat career criminal offenders; The Criminalistics Squad, which responds to the crime scene. There, they assist the district investigators in handling

Los Angeles Administrative Division

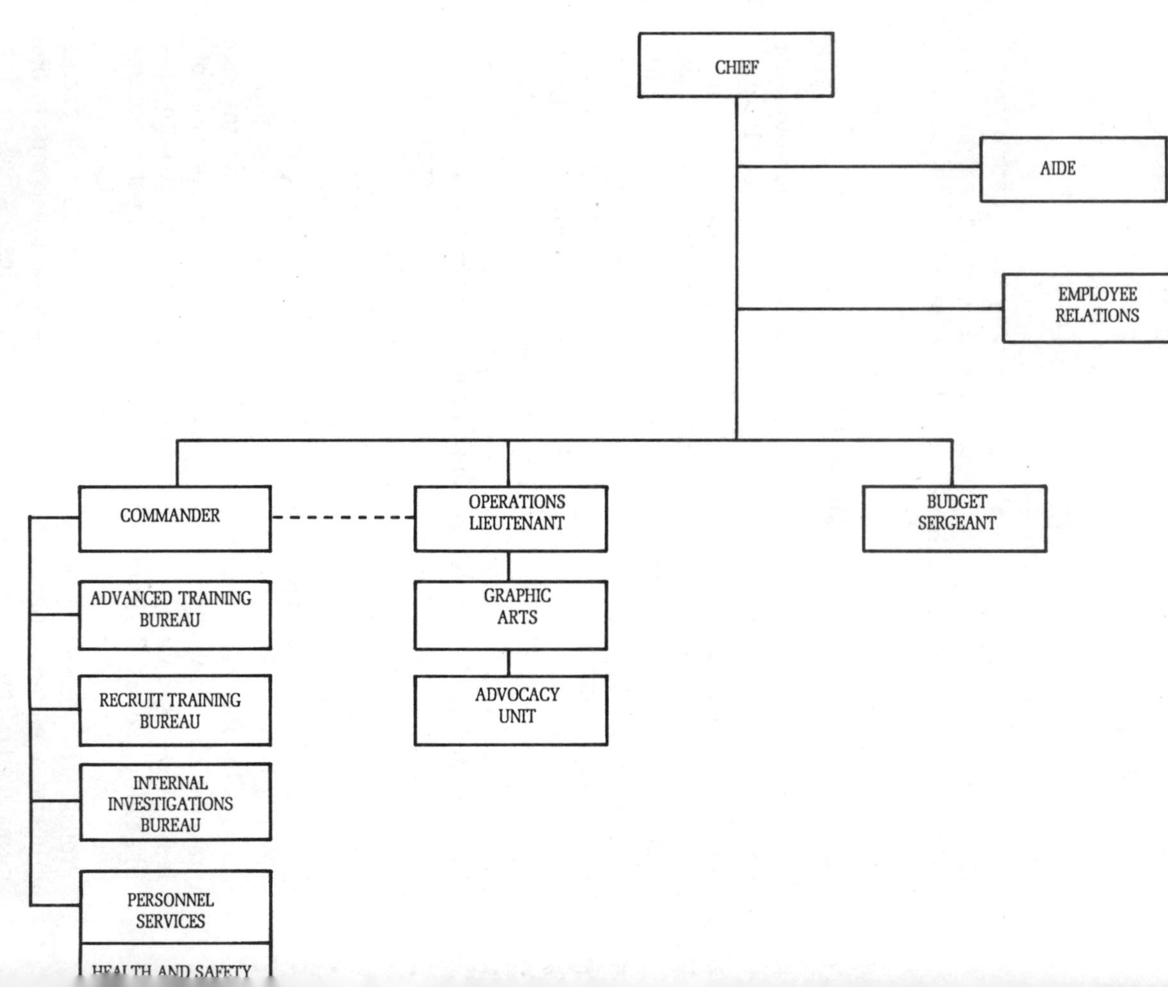

Los Angeles Field Operations Region I

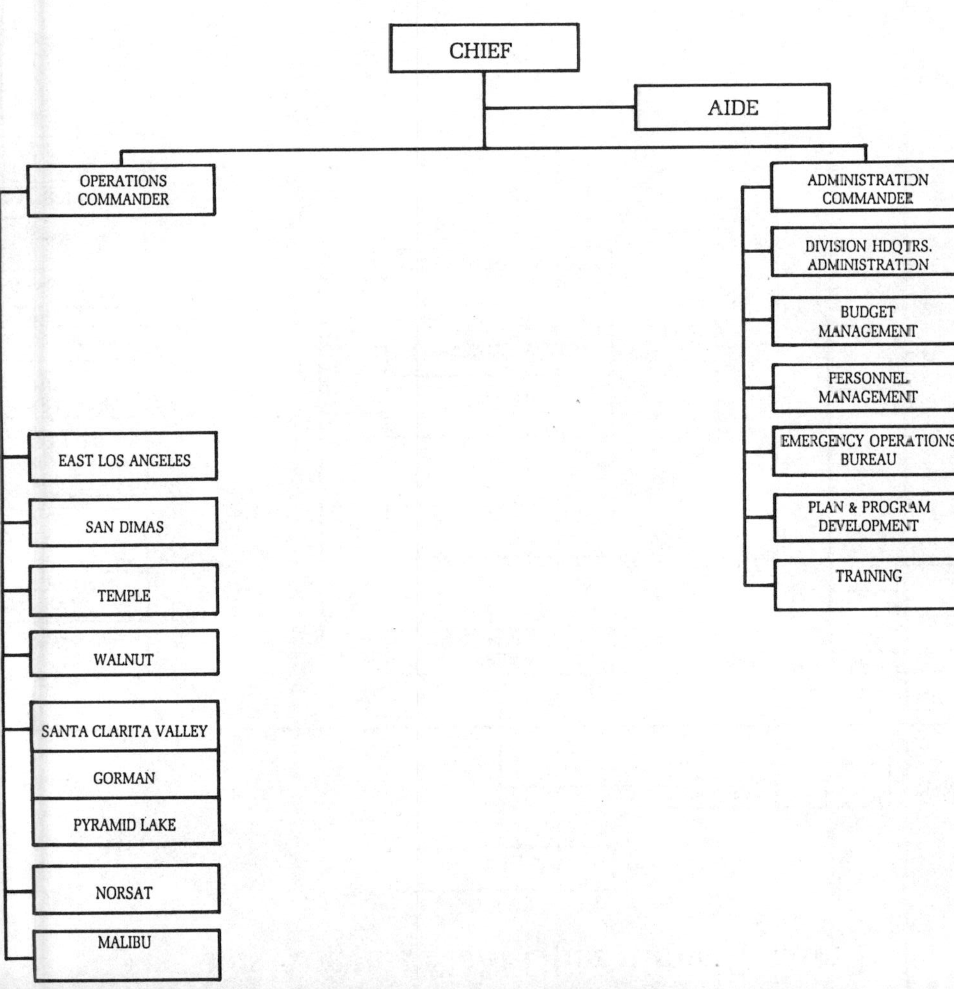

Los Angeles Field Operations Region II

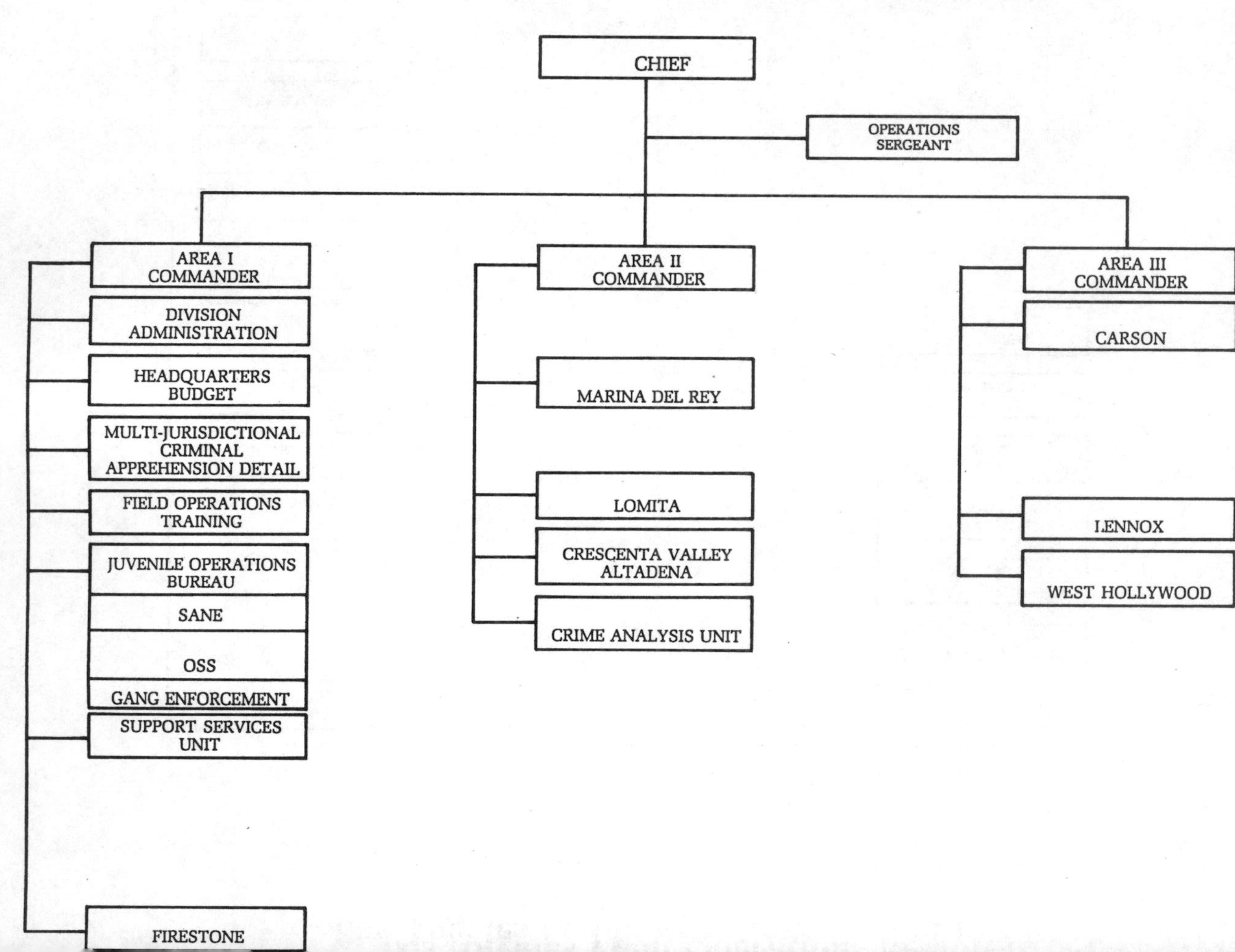

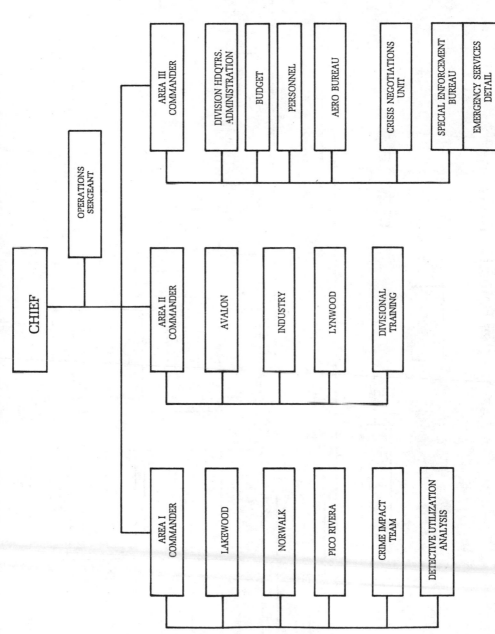

- CHIEF
  - OPERATIONS SERGEANT
  - AREA I COMMANDER
    - LAKEWOOD
    - NORWALK
    - PICO RIVERA
    - CRIME IMPACT TEAM
    - DETECTIVE UTILIZATION ANALYSIS
  - AREA II COMMANDER
    - AVALON
    - INDUSTRY
    - LYNWOOD
    - DIVISIONAL TRAINING
  - AREA III COMMANDER
    - DIVISION HDQTRS. ADMINISTRATION
    - BUDGET
    - PERSONNEL
    - AERO BUREAU
    - CRISIS NEGOTIATIONS UNIT
    - SPECIAL ENFORCEMENT BUREAU
      - EMERGENCY SERVICES DETAIL

Los Angeles Detective Division

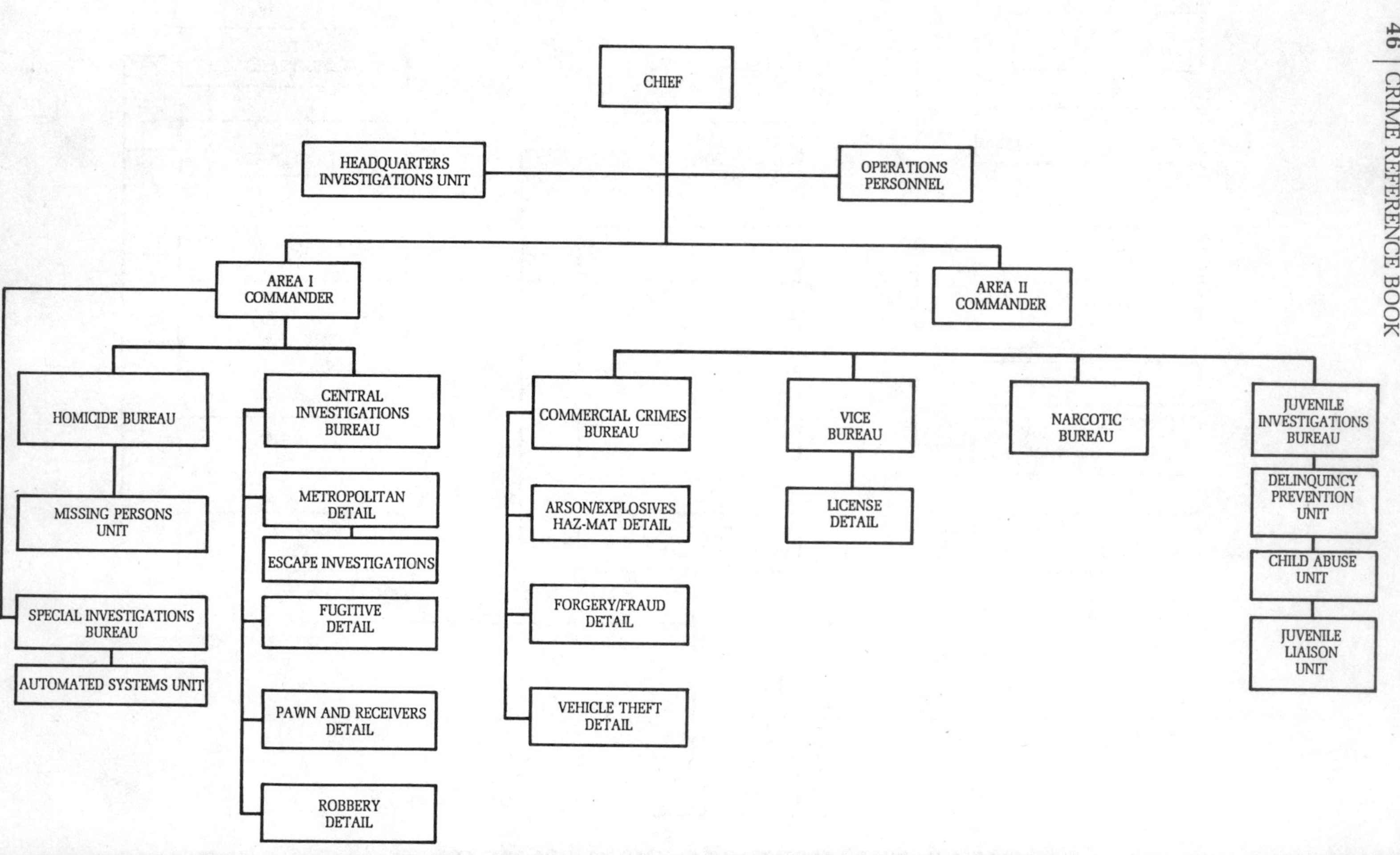

- SHERIFF
  - EXECUTIVE ASSISTANT
  - UNDERSHERIFF
    - INSPECTIONAL SERVICES BUREAU
      - MANUALS & ORDERS
      - PROPERTY & EVIDENCE
    - ASSISTANT SHERIFF
      - EXECUTIVE OFFICES COMMANDER
        - CONTRACT LAW ENFORCEMENT
          - TRAFFIC SERVICES DETAIL
        - RESERVE FORCES BUREAU
          - OFFICE OF SPECIAL PROGRAMS
          - INDUSTRIAL RELATIONS DETAIL
          - CRIME PREVENTION DETAIL
        - INDUSTRIAL RELATIONS BUREAU
      - DETECTIVE DIVISION CHART 2
      - FIELD OPERATIONS REGION I CHART 3
      - FIELD OPERATIONS REGION II CHART 4
      - FIELD OPERATIONS REGION III CHART 5
    - ADMINISTRATIVE DIVISION CHART 6
    - ASSISTANT SHERIFF
      - MEDICAL SERVICES
      - COURT SERVICES DIVISION CHART 7
      - CUSTODY DIVISION CHART 8
      - TECHNICAL SERVICES DIVISION CHART 9
    - EXECUTIVE PLANNING COUNCIL
      - LEGAL ADVISORY
      - LEGISLATIVE UNIT
    - PSYCHOLOGICAL SERVICES
    - FISCAL SERVICES
    - SHERIFF'S INFORMATION BUREAU
      - INTERNATIONAL LIAISON
    - FACILITIES PLANNING SERVICES UNIT

Los Angeles Court Services Division

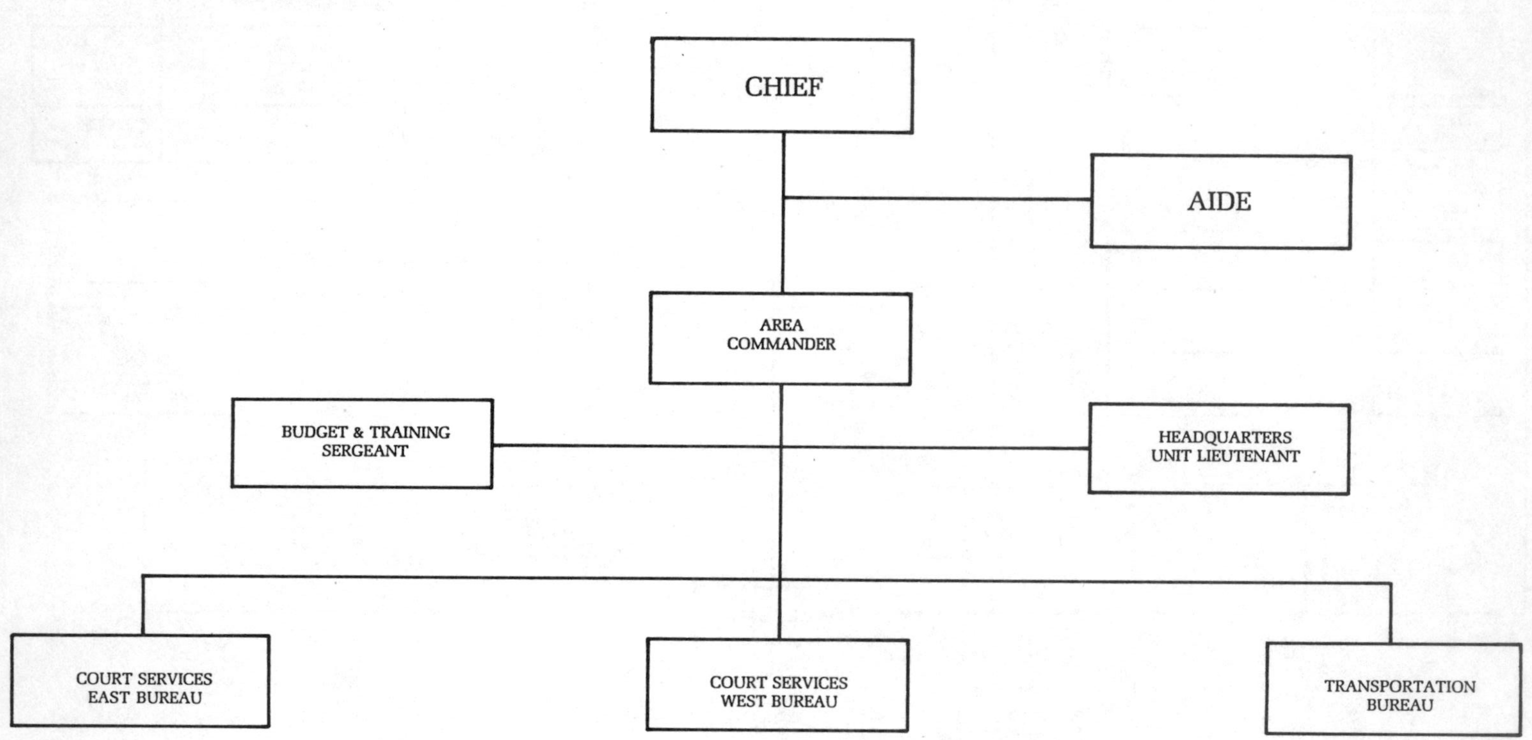

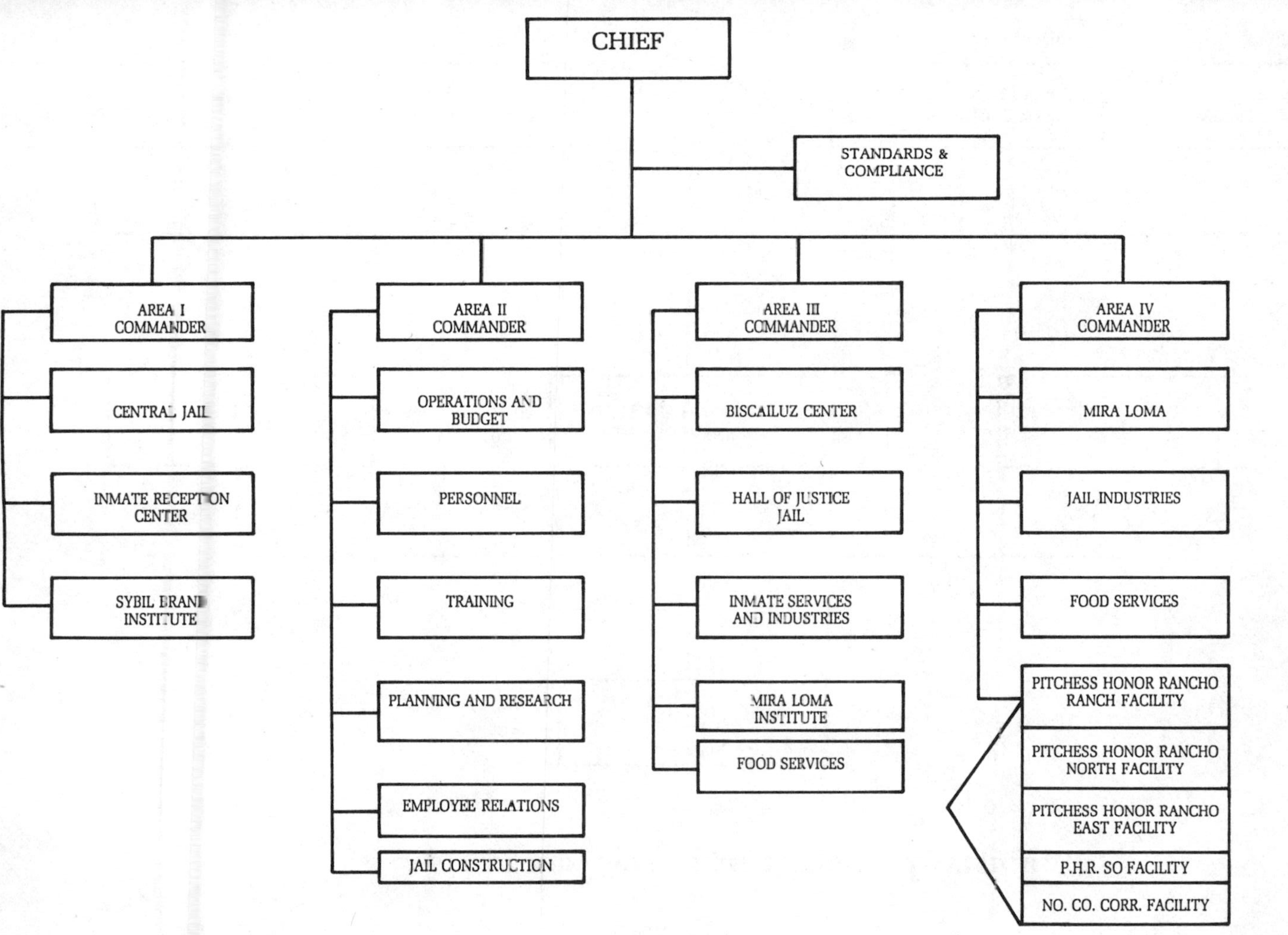
CHIEF
STANDARDS & COMPLIANCE
AREA I COMMANDER
CENTRAL JAIL
INMATE RECEPTION CENTER
SYBIL BRAND INSTITUTE
AREA II COMMANDER
OPERATIONS AND BUDGET
PERSONNEL
TRAINING
PLANNING AND RESEARCH
EMPLOYEE RELATIONS
JAIL CONSTRUCTION
AREA III COMMANDER
BISCAILUZ CENTER
HALL OF JUSTICE JAIL
INMATE SERVICES AND INDUSTRIES
MIRA LOMA INSTITUTE
FOOD SERVICES
AREA IV COMMANDER
MIRA LOMA
JAIL INDUSTRIES
FOOD SERVICES
PITCHESS HONOR RANCHO RANCH FACILITY
PITCHESS HONOR RANCHO NORTH FACILITY
PITCHESS HONOR RANCHO EAST FACILITY
P.H.R. SO FACILITY
NO. CO. CORR. FACILITY

Los Angeles Technical Services Division

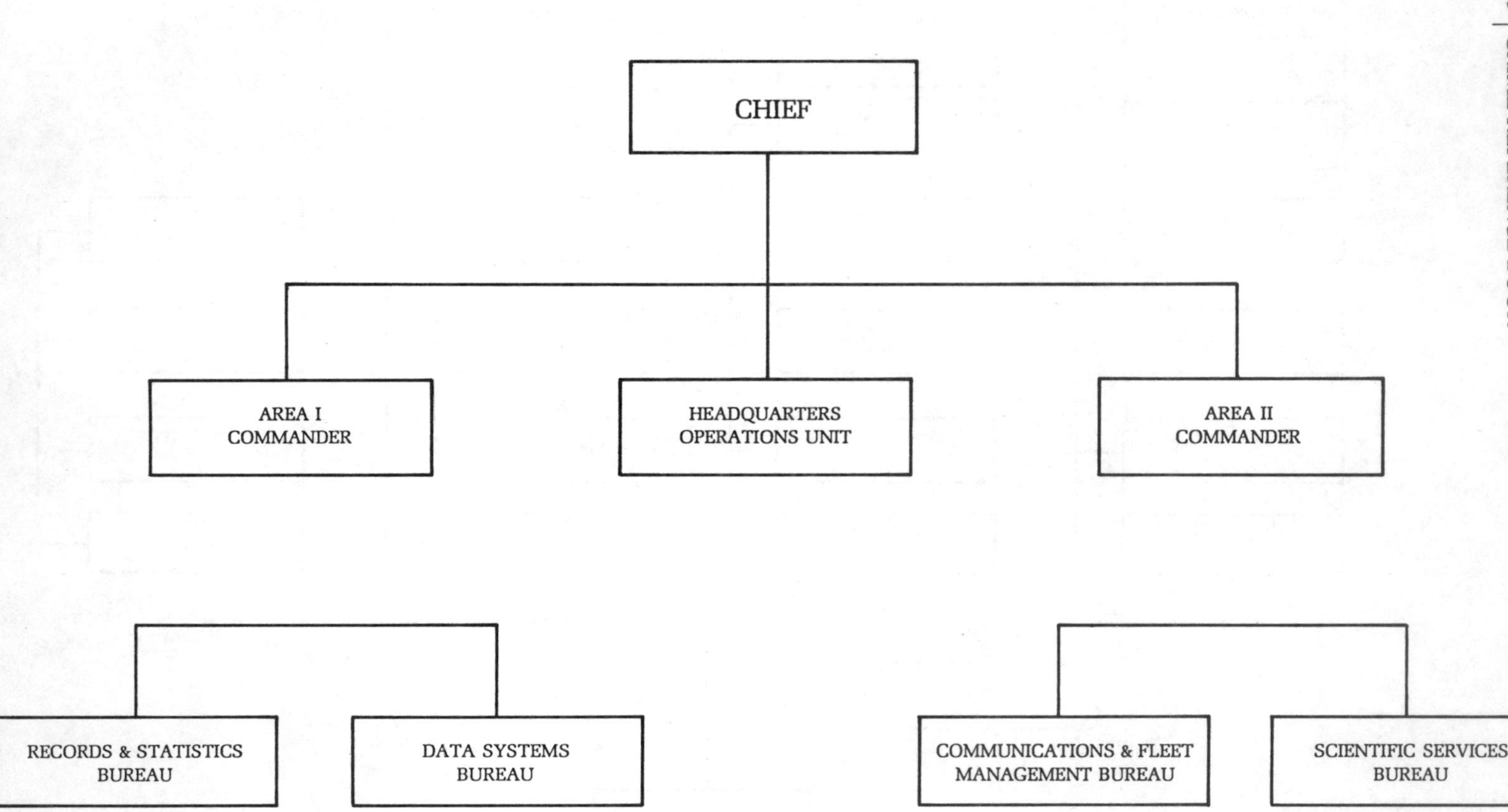

the identification of suspects through fingerprint comparison, utilizing photography and video recording, and in handling the collection of crime-scene material and evidence. All this is then routed by the squad to various laboratories, such as the Hamilton County Coroner's Office, the Ohio Bureau of Identification, and the Federal Bureau of Investigation for processing. Also operating under the Investigations Bureau are Burglary and Auto Theft, the Pawn Shop Unit, the Polygraph Unit, and the Fraud Unit.

The Central Vice Control Section is charged with enforcing laws and controlling criminal conduct in the areas of drugs, prostitution, gambling, liquor law enforcement, and pornography.

The Intelligence Section develops information and initiates investigations into cults, gangs, and terrorists, and conducts in-service training for division personnel.

The Narcotics Liaison Section provides investigative and supervisory personnel to the Regional Enforcement Narcotics Unit (RENU). In 1988, personnel in this unit were assigned to the newly formed DEA Cincinnati Task Force, a multi-agency drug enforcement unit composed of Cincinnati police, DEA Agents, and Hamilton County Sheriff's officers.

The Technical Services Bureau comprises three sections: the Police Communications Section; the Equipment Management Section, which includes the Impoundment Unit, responsible for all vehicles in custody, the Transportation Unit, which oversees the division's motor fleet, and the Supply Unit, which fields all supplies and equipment requests; and the Court/Records Services Section, the last of which operates four units; Court Administration, County Property, Warrant/Identification, and Records.

Personnel Resources Bureau comprises the Personnel Section, the Police Academy, the Inspection Section, and the Internal Investigations Section. These sections provide Recruit Training, Maintenance of Personnel Records, Investigation of Citizens' Complaints, Processing of Employment Records, and liaison with organizations represented in the Police Division.

The Office of Coordination, Planning, and Budget provides administrative assistance and staff to the police chief by reviewing and expediting official business, budgeting, planning, conducting research, and generally developing the department.

FORENSIC AND POLICE SCIENCES

Modern forensic and police sciences in major cities throughout our country cover all areas dealing with the commission of a crime

Cincinnati Police Division

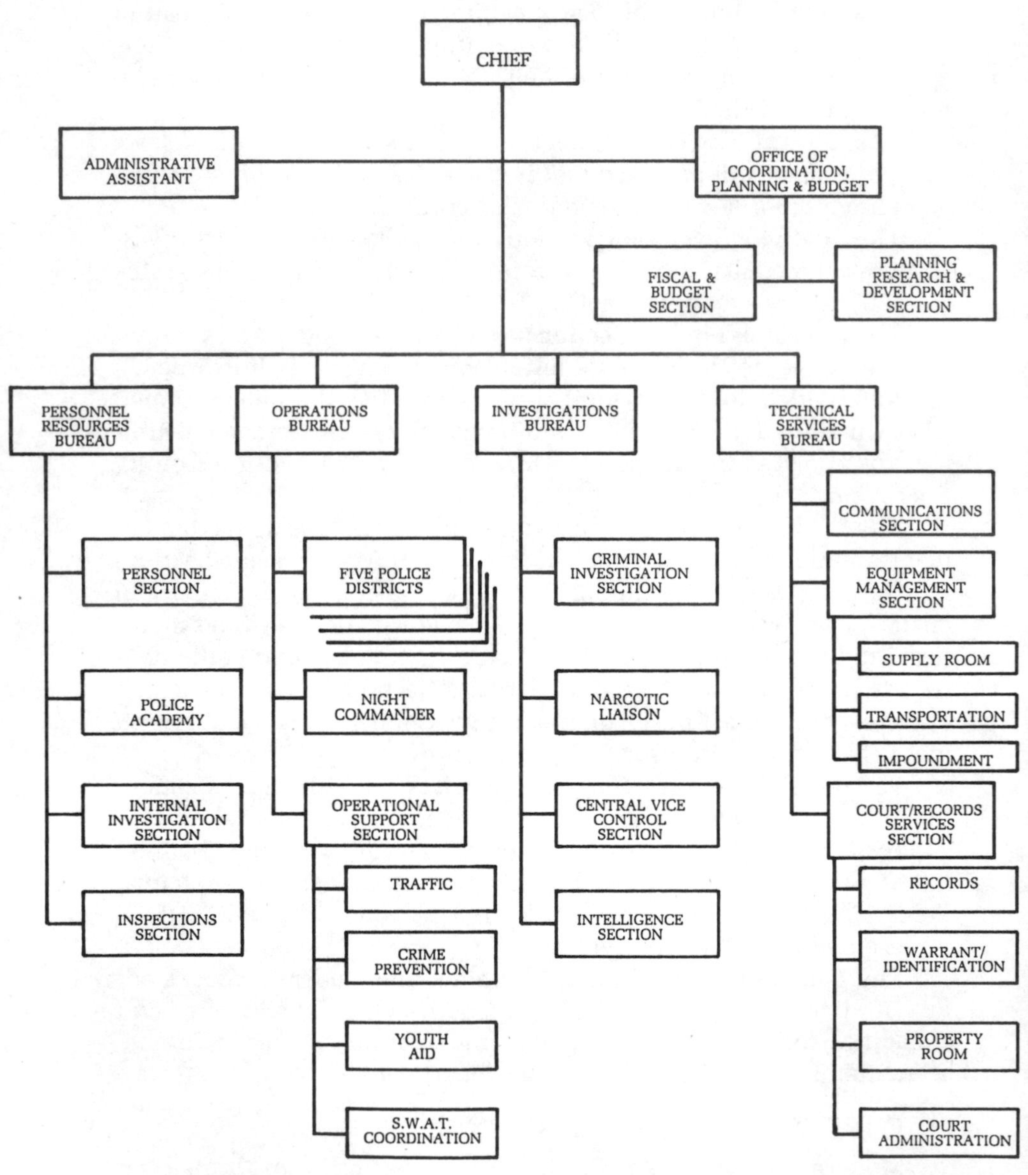

through their lab, forensic, and behavioral sciences departments. The deductive process of Sherlock Holmes days is long gone. It has been replaced with highly skilled technicians and criminalists, many of whom are civilians working for law-enforcement agencies.

Police sciences include a number of sections, such as toxicology, identification, serology, blood-alcohol testing, narcotics, physical evidence, firearms, questioned documents, polygraph, behavioral sciences, and photographic sciences.

Firearms deals with bullet comparisons, tool mark examinations, gun makes, and serial numbers restoration.

Questioned Documents deals with the analysis of written documents or those from a dubious source, including bad checks, forgeries, typewriter and computer analysis, and indented writings.

Identification is involved in fingerprint comparison and field work, including the collection of latent prints on various surfaces using chemical and mechanical means.

Physical Evidence works on comparison of hair and fiber evidence, shoe prints, tire prints, physical matches, arson and explosives, and gunshot-residue analysis.

Serology deals with identification and subsequent grouping of blood and other body fluids such as semen and saliva in major crimes, primarily homicide and sexual assault.

Narcotics analyzes bulk narcotics evidence.

Toxicology analyzes drugs and their metabolites in blood and urine.*

Blood Alcohol Testing Section analyzes blood-alcohol levels in blood and urine for testimony of at what level of alcohol in an individual's blood has impaired the driving of a vehicle.

Polygraph handles administration and interpretation of the polygraph test.

Behavioral Science Section is usually separate from the crime laboratory. Most agencies, except the FBI, don't have a formal behavioral science unit. More often, police officers assigned to detective functions will have had specialized training in this area.

Photographic produces crime-scene photography, microphotography, infrared and ultraviolet photography.

---

* *Toxicology for the purpose of determining poisoning, etc. is done by the coroner's office.*

New Equipment and Technology in Forensic and Police Sciences

We've come a long way since the days of Sherlock Holmes and his brilliant deductive processes, as evidenced by the application of a wide variety of computer sciences that have been adapted by police sciences and crime investigation technology. The following equipment and technology are among the latest available to law enforcement:

Laser: Laser is used to better visualize fingerprints, fibers, semen evidence, and other trace material in the field and in the lab.

Electrostatic Detection Apparatus (ESDA): This instrument allows sensitive analysis of indented writing, sometimes as deep as fifteen to twenty sheets in a pad of paper.

CAL ID is a computer system that has all criminal fingerprints on file from the state of California. A check of other major sheriff's and police departments will determine if a similar computer system exists in their state. This system enables a possible match of a single latent print of an individual from a data base of all convicted criminals. The generic for CAL ID is AFIS: Automated Fingerprint Identification System, which is operational in many states.

High Pressure Liquid Chromatography (HPLC): This specific separation technique can positively identify drugs and other organic compounds for toxicology or narcotic examinations.

Gas Chromatography—Mass Spectroscopy (GCMS): This separation technique can positively identify a substance (narcotic, poison, etc.) and compare the spectra of its mass against a computer library for a comparison to a standard.

Liver Temperature Reading: Used by the coroner or medical examiner at the scene of the murder by making an incision in the abdomen and inserting a probe with a thermometer into the victim's liver, one can almost pinpoint the time of death.

DNA Identification: The various techniques and probes work on the same essential theory: that the unique genetic factors in our chromosomes (DNA—Deoxyribonucleic acid) can be identified from body fluids (blood, semen) and hair, and can be compared to known standards (samples from a suspect or victim) to make a positive identification. This genetically based form of identification was at first widely applauded on the presumption that it was 100 percent accurate, with no meaningful possibility of mistake, since no two individuals can have exactly the same genetic makeup, with the possible exception of identical twins. However, there seems to be more overlap and common factors than was originally thought, and experts differ on how reliable

DNA identification can be assumed to be. Therefore, DNA identification is no longer universally accepted as sufficiently foolproof to meet court standards for reliable evidence. Further refinement of the procedures, though, may again restore the high credibility of such evidence. As with all rapidly changing technologies, check on the current status of this procedure before making it a crucial element in a story.

Currently, only a few agencies have DNA typing capability. Most contract such work out to private labs or send evidence to the FBI lab.

OFFICE OF THE DISTRICT ATTORNEY

The size of the staff and the extent of the responsibilities of the district attorney may vary depending upon the location. The Los Angeles District Attorney's Office, which has nearly 2,000 support personnel, is the largest such office in the United States and has been chosen to best illustrate the full capacity of such an office.

The Los Angeles District Attorney's Office is primarily responsible for prosecuting felonies under state law, although it also prosecutes misdemeanors in Los Angeles County and for cities in the county that do not wish to retain their own city attorney.

The administration of the district attorney's office is composed of the district attorney, his chief deputy, and the assistant district attorney. Reporting directly to the Administrative Section are two Deputy DA's, one in charge of Organized Crime and the second in charge of Special Investigations, primarily the investigations of public officials.

Reporting to the administrative command is the Director of Central Operations, which oversees Career Criminals, Special Trials, and Central Trials; the Director of Special Operations, which oversees major frauds, hard-core gangs, consumer protection, environment, and COPOS (crimes against police officers), the Special Crimes Division, Special Legal, and the Juvenile Division; the Director of Branch and Area, which supervises the large number of Deputy District Attorneys in the district attorney's office.

A Family Support Section has its own deputy, called the deputy in charge, along with its own director and support staff. Its mission is investigation and prosecution with regard to family violence, child abuse, and related situations.

The Bureau of Investigation is the investigative arm of the District Attorney's Office, and its personnel are assigned to the various sections and divisions as required.

OFFICE OF THE CITY ATTORNEY

The Los Angeles City Attorney's Office is the largest municipal law office in the nation, divided among the Civil Branch, the Criminal Branch, and the Special Operations Branch. The city attorney is the legal advisor to all city departments and agencies, including the office of the mayor, city council, police and fire departments, city commissions, and other city departments.

Under the direction of the city attorney, attorneys from this office appear in all courts of the state, the federal courts, and the U.S. Supreme Court, as well as before a large number of state and federal regulatory and administrative agencies.

The Special Operations Branch of the City Attorney's Office deals with the Consumer Protection Section, the Environmental Protection Section, and the Housing Enforcement Section.

The Criminal Branch, headed by the senior assistant attorney, handles all infraction and misdemeanor cases within the city, including consumer fraud, labor law violations, battery, theft, burglary, assault with a deadly weapon, vice, drunk driving, election compliance, and air pollution violations. A special section of the Criminal Branch is the Gangs Unit (COPE), dealing with youth-gang problems.

The Civil Branch is headed by a senior counsel and handles everything from land use, contracts, personal injury, and zoning, to the Harbor and Airports departments and the Department of Water and Power.

THE UNITED STATES DEPARTMENT OF JUSTICE

Headed by the attorney general of the United States, the Department of Justice exists to provide legal advice to the president, representation of the executive branch in court, investigation of federal crimes, enforcement of federal laws, operation of federal prisons, and provision of law-enforcement assistance to states and local communities.

Organizations of the U.S. Department of Justice

Office of the Attorney General
Office of the Deputy Attorney General
Office of the Associate Attorney General
Office of the Solicitor General
Antitrust Division
Bureau of Prisons

Department of Justice

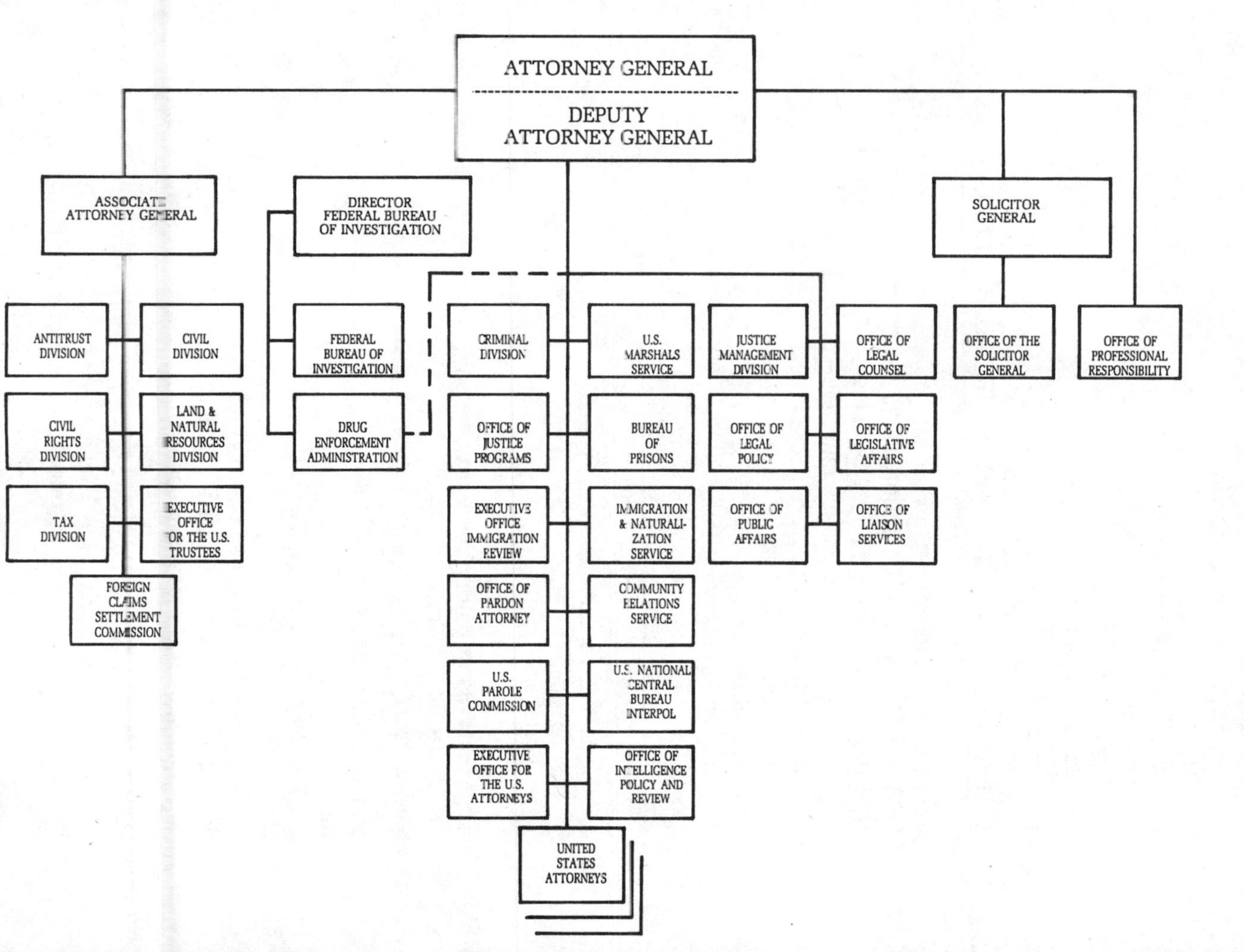
ATTORNEY GENERAL
DEPUTY ATTORNEY GENERAL
ASSOCIATE ATTORNEY GENERAL
DIRECTOR FEDERAL BUREAU OF INVESTIGATION
SOLICITOR GENERAL
ANTITRUST DIVISION
CIVIL DIVISION
CIVIL RIGHTS DIVISION
LAND & NATURAL RESOURCES DIVISION
TAX DIVISION
EXECUTIVE OFFICE FOR THE U.S. TRUSTEES
FOREIGN CLAIMS SETTLEMENT COMMISSION
FEDERAL BUREAU OF INVESTIGATION
DRUG ENFORCEMENT ADMINISTRATION
CRIMINAL DIVISION
U.S. MARSHALS SERVICE
JUSTICE MANAGEMENT DIVISION
OFFICE OF LEGAL COUNSEL
OFFICE OF THE SOLICITOR GENERAL
OFFICE OF PROFESSIONAL RESPONSIBILITY
OFFICE OF JUSTICE PROGRAMS
BUREAU OF PRISONS
OFFICE OF LEGAL POLICY
OFFICE OF LEGISLATIVE AFFAIRS
EXECUTIVE OFFICE IMMIGRATION REVIEW
IMMIGRATION & NATURALIZATION SERVICE
OFFICE OF PUBLIC AFFAIRS
OFFICE OF LIAISON SERVICES
OFFICE OF PARDON ATTORNEY
COMMUNITY RELATIONS SERVICE
U.S. PAROLE COMMISSION
U.S. NATIONAL CENTRAL BUREAU INTERPOL
EXECUTIVE OFFICE FOR THE U.S. ATTORNEYS
OFFICE OF INTELLIGENCE POLICY AND REVIEW
UNITED STATES ATTORNEYS

Civil Division
Civil Rights Division
Community Relations Service
Criminal Division
Drug Enforcement Administration
Executive Office for Immigration Review
Executive Office for U.S. Attorneys
Federal Bureau of Investigation
Federal Prison Industries
Immigration and Naturalization Service
International Criminal Police Organization—United States National Central Bureau
Foreign Claims Settlement Commission
Justice Management Division
Land and Natural Resources Division
Office of Intelligence Policy and Review
Office of Justice Programs
Office of Legal Counsel
Office of Legal Policy
Office of Legislative Affairs
Office of Liaison Services
Office of Professional Responsibility
Office of Public Affairs
Office of Pardon Attorney
Tax Division
United States Attorney's Office
United States Marshal's Service
United States Parole Commission
United States Trustee's Offices

The Attorney General supervises and directs the administration and operations of the boards, divisions, and bureaus of the Department of Justice.

The Deputy Attorney General advises and assists the attorney general.

The Associate Attorney General advises and assists the attorney general and the assistant attorney general.

The Solicitor General is responsible for conducting and supervising all aspects of government litigation in the U.S. Supreme Court.

The Office of Legal Counsel assists the attorney general.

The Office of Legislative Affairs helps formulate and coordinate legislative policy among organizations within the department and maintains the department's liaison with the Congress.

The Office of Liaison Services is an outreach service to governors, state legislators, and the law-enforcement community.

The Office of Legal Policy is a strategic legal "think tank" serving the Attorney General's policy development staff.

The Office of Professional Responsibility reviews, and where appropriate, investigates allegations of misconduct against the department's employees.

The Justice Management Division controls and oversees department management issues and the department's liaison on budgetary matters; it includes such staffs as Procurement, Audit, Security, Equal Opportunity, General Counsel, Policy and Planning, Comptroller, Budget, Information Technology, Computer Technology and Telecommunications, Information Systems, Library, Litigation Systems, Personnel and Administration, and General Services.

The Office of Intelligence Policy and Review helps ensure that the national security-related activities of the United States are consistent with relevant law.

The U.S. Parole Commission is an independent agency in the department whose primary function is to administer a parole system for federal prisoners. It is responsible for developing a federal parole policy and is authorized to grant or deny parole to eligible federal prisoners.

The Office of Pardon Attorney. Although the president exercises the pardon power, the pardon attorney receives and reviews all petitions for executive clemency, initiates investigations, and prepares recommendations to the attorney general.

Federal Bureau of Investigation. See FBI

Drug Enforcement Administration. See DEA

The Criminal Division establishes federal criminal law-enforcement policies and facilitates their implementation. It is responsible for the general supervision of all federal criminal laws except for those assigned specifically to Antitrust, Civil Rights, Land and Natural Resources, or Tax Division. Operating as part of the Criminal Division is the Organized Crime and Racketeering Section, which develops and coordinates nationwide enforcement programs to reduce the influence of organized crime groups in the U.S., working primarily through twenty-six Strike Forces and field offices throughout the nation.

The Public Integrity Section is responsible for independent counsel matters, investigations and prosecution of federal judges, major federal corruption and misconduct investigations, election and campaign financing crimes, and significant state and local corruption cases.

The Office of Policy Management Analysis studies and recommends positions on policy and management issues of concern to both the division and the department.

The Fraud Section deals primarily with economic crime, especially in the areas of waste, fraud, and abuse in government programs and contracts.

The General Litigation and Legal Advice Section develops and implements enforcement programs in key statutory areas, including terrorism, pornography, intellectual property, and nuclear safety.

The Appellate Section handles cases and renders advice to the U.S. Attorney's offices, especially with regard to the Comprehensive Crime Control Act of 1984.

The Internal Security Section is responsible for enforcing criminal statutes affecting national security and foreign relations. It also administers and enforces the Foreign Agents Registration Act, supervising investigations and prosecution of offenses involving espionage, sabotage, treason, violations of the Atomic Energy Act, neutrality statutes, Trading With the Enemy Act, Arms Export Control Act, and Export Administration.

The Office of Internal Affairs is responsible for formulating, supervising, and executing international, criminal-justice-enforcement policies and procedures, including the following: negotiating international agreements and treaties related to criminal law enforcement (extradition and prisoner transfers); preparing and litigating requests for international extradition, obtaining evidence for foreign jurisdictions, and coordinating requests to and from foreign countries to obtain evidence in connection with investigations and prosecutions in the United States and abroad.

The mission of the **Office of Special Investigations** is to investigate and take legal action against anyone in the United States who incites, participates, or assists in the persecution of persons based on race, religion, or political beliefs.

The Narcotics and Dangerous Drugs Section's activities are primarily to prosecute and convict major drug traffickers involved in the importation, manufacturing, shipment, and distribution of illicit drugs and narcotics.

The Office of Legislation is responsible for developing and supporting the Criminal Division's legislative program. The Office of Administration provides the Division's administrative services through its Personnel Unit; Fiscal Unit; Mail, File and Records Unit; Procurement, Security, Safety, and Space Unit; and the Information Systems Unit.

The Office of Enforcement Operations uses the most sensitive investigative tools at the Department's disposal; electronic surveillance, hypnosis in the interrogation of witnesses, etc. It is also responsible for the authorization of witness immunity and witness relocation. This office supervises all aspects of the Witness Security Program for the Criminal Division and oversees all electronic and consensual monitoring efforts pursued within the federal justice system.

The Asset Forfeiture Office reduces criminal activity by depriving criminals of the profits obtained by their illegal acts.

The Executive Office for U.S. Attorneys provides general executive assistance and nonlitigative oversight to the ninety four offices of the U.S. Attorneys. Under this office function the Office of Administration and Review, the Office of Legal Education, the Office of Legal Services, the Office of Management Information Systems and Support, the Law Enforcement Coordinating Committee Staff, and the U.S. Attorneys, who are the chief law-enforcement representatives of the Attorney General.

The Executive Office for U.S. Trustees supervises the administration of all cases filed under chapters 7, 11, and 13 of Title I of the Bankruptcy Reform Act.

The Bureau of Prisons has forty-seven institutions and is responsible for the operation of federal correctional facilities and their inmates.

The U.S. Marshal's Service. See U.S. Marshal

The Office of Justice Programs works to improve the treatment of victims of crime and family violence and administers the Crime Victims Fund.

The Bureau of Justice Assistance administers state and local justice assistance programs to improve justice-system operations.

The Bureau of Justice Statistics collects, analyzes, publishes, and disseminates statistical information on crime, victims, and criminal offenders as well as on the operations of justice systems at all levels of government.

The National Institute of Justice is the primary federal sponsor of research on crime and justice.

The Office of Juvenile Justice and Delinquency Prevention develops and implements programs to respond to the mandate of the 1984 Missing Children's Assistance Act.

The Executive Office for Immigration Review is responsible for the ongoing improvement of the immigration adjudication process and is independent of the INS (Immigration and Naturalization Service), which is responsible for the enforcement of immigration laws. This office contains the Board of Immigration Appeals and the Office of the Chief Immigration Judge.

The Antitrust Division investigates, detects, and prosecutes price fixing and related restraints of trade.

The Civil Division has four basic missions: to defend or assert programs and initiatives of the federal government, including the President's foreign and domestic policies; to bring suit and collect monies owed the United States by delinquent debtors and to recover sums lost to government by waste, fraud, and corruption; to defend government, officers, and employees seeking damages from the U.S. Treasury or from its employees, personally; and to enforce federal consumer-protection laws, the nation's immigration laws, and other program initiatives.

The Civil Rights Division enforces eight major civil rights sections prohibiting discrimination in education, employment, credit, housing, public accommodations and facilities, voting, and certain federally funded and conducted programs, along with identifying and eliminating sexual discrimination.

The Tax Division is responsible for representing the United States and its officers in all litigation arising under the internal revenue laws other than proceedings in the U.S. Tax Court. This division is involved in both civil and criminal proceedings at the trial and appellate levels. Its principal client is the Internal Revenue Service, but it also represents other federal departments and agencies in matters involving immunity from state and local taxes.

The Land and Natural Resources Division represents the United States, its agencies, and its officers in matters relating to environmental quality, natural resources, public lands, Indian lands and native claims, and wildlife and fishery resources. Its clients include the departments of Agriculture, Commerce, Defense, Energy, Interior, and Transportation, and the Environmental Protection Agency.

The Immigration and Naturalization Service carries out federal laws, regulations, and policies governing immigration, naturalization, refugees, and asylum. It is responsible for all activities related to the temporary or permanent admission of people into the United States and for the exclusion of illegal entries and residents. Its Enforcement Division is primarily its Border Patrol, whose agents patrol U.S. borders, detain and deport illegal aliens. This office also is heavily involved in marriage frauds, smuggling, narcotics, and black-market-baby operations from foreign countries. The INS also maintains an

Intelligence Office, which is heavily involved in American and Asian organized crime and Mexico's illegal migration; a data base on potential and alien terrorists; a data base on smugglers, perpetrators of fraud, and other immigration violators. In addition, it cooperates with other agencies involved in national anti-drug efforts.

INTERPOL—United States National Central Bureau. USNCB is the U.S. liaison to 142 nation members and to the General Secretariat of the International Criminal Police Organization, headquartered in Paris, France. The goal of USNCB and INTERPOL is the mutual assistance between international law-enforcement authorities in the prevention and suppression of international crime. INTERPOL's constitution prohibits intervention and investigation by its members of matters concerning any military, religious, racial, or political character.

THE FEDERAL BUREAU OF INVESTIGATION (U.S. DEPARTMENT OF JUSTICE)

The primary function of the FBI is to investigate violations of certain federal statutes and to collect evidence in cases in which the United States may be an interested party. The FBI also performs other duties specifically imposed by law or presidential directive and conducts a number of service activities for other law-enforcement agencies. In the field of organized crime, the FBI seeks to eradicate large-scale intrastate gambling, loansharking, gangland infiltration of legitimate business, and interstate travel in aid of racketeering. Other statutes often applied are those dealing with pornography, arson-for-hire, extortion, thefts from interstate shipments, and labor racketeering.

It costs approximately $1 billion to operate the FBI and its fifty-eight field offices throughout the United States and Puerto Rico in a given year. The office employs more than 21,000 employees, 9,000 of whom are Special Agents. Although the FBI has authority to operate only in the United States and its possessions, by certain grants of Congress, the FBI does on occasion have jurisdiction on the high seas. The FBI also has foreign counterintelligence responsibilities inside the United States and its possessions. In addition to working with other law-enforcement agencies both local and federal, the FBI maintains a master fingerprint identification center and the Criminalistics Laboratory Information System (CLIS), a communications network for local, state, and federal agencies to use, allowing them access to scientific reference information contained on the CLIS data base. The CLIS is currently composed of a General Rifling Characteristics file that is used to identify the manufacturer and type of weapon that may have been used to fire a bullet or cartridge.

The FBI has jurisdiction in crimes against U.S. citizens in foreign countries. For example, if a terrorist murders a U.S. citizen elsewhere in the world, the FBI may investigate and bring the defendant to trial in the United States.

The FBI also maintains at its headquarters in Washington, D.C., other types of files, primarily of a technical nature, that are helpful in criminal investigations by city, state, and federal agencies such as:

The Anonymous Letters File
Bank Robbery Note File
National Fraudulent Check File
The National Automotive Paint File
The Hair and Fiber Reference File
The National Automotive Altered Number File
The National Stolen Property File

These files contain copies of or records about evidence as well as reference samples for comparison purposes.

Fingerprint and Index Files

The subject matter and names of individuals and organizations are indexed at FBI headquarters in alphabetical order, and at the end of 1986 there were more than 178 million fingerprints on file. Ninety-two million contain criminal history data, and 84 million civil print identifications covering federal employees, alien registration, military personnel, and individuals requesting their prints be on file for identification purposes.

The fingerprint section is broken down into three divisions: identification of arrests and applications, posting of wanted and parole/probation notices, and examination of physical evidence of latent prints for court testimony.

The Federal Bureau of Investigation maintains records of missing persons and handles identification of amnesia victims and deceased persons.

In addition to the FBI's automated data processing for accounting, statistical, administrative, and investigative control operations, in 1967 a fully automated system, Automated Identification Division System (AIDS) was instituted and today the advanced phase three of that system, which can process the required information within twenty-four hours, is in full operation. Although computer data systems do most of the work, the final identification is made by an analyst within the FBI.

FBI Case Classifications

Admiralty Matters
Alien Property Custodian Matters
Antiracketeering
Antitrust
Applications for Executive Clemency and for Pardon After Completion of Sentence
Ascertaining Financial Ability
Assaulting or Killing a Federal Officer
Assaulting the President of the United States
Automobile Information Disclosure Act
Bank Robbery, Burglary, and Larceny
Bills of Lading Act
Bond Default
Bribery and Conflict of Interest
Civil Rights
Civil Rights Act of 1964
Contempt of Court
Contract Settlement Act
Copyright Matters
Court of Claims
Crime Aboard Aircraft
Crimes on the High Seas
Desertion, Harboring Deserter, Enticing to Desert
Destruction of Aircraft
Election Laws
Escaped Federal Prisoners, Parole, Probation and Conditional Release Violations
Extortion
False Entries in the Records of Interstate Carriers
Falsely Claiming Citizenship
Federal Housing Administration Matters
Federal Lending and Insurance Agencies
Federal Tort Claims Act
Federal Train Wreck Statute
Foreign Police Cooperation
Fraud Against the Government

Government and Indian Reservation Matters
Harboring Fugitives
Hydraulic Brake Fluid Act
Illegal Wearing of Uniform and Related Statutes
Illegal Use of Railroad Pass
Impersonation
Interstate Transmission of Wagering Information
Interstate Transportation in Aid of Racketeering
Interstate Transportation of Fireworks
Interstate Transportation of Gambling Devices
Interstate Transportation of Lottery Tickets
Interstate Transportation of Obscene Matter
Interstate Transportation of Stolen Cattle
Interstate Transportation of Stolen Motor Vehicles or Aircraft
Interstate Transportation of Stolen Property
Interstate Transportation of Strikebreakers
Interstate Transportation of Unsafe Refrigerators
Interstate Transportation of Wagering Paraphernalia
Irregularities in Federal Penal Institutions
Kickback Racket Act
Kidnapping
Labor-Management Relations Act
Labor-Management Reporting and Disclosure Act of 1959
Mail Fraud
Migratory Bird Act
Motor Vehicle Seat Belt Act
Narcotics
National and Federal Firearms Acts
National Bank and Federal Reserve Acts—Banks
National Bank and Federal Reserve Acts—Federal Credit Union
National Bank and Federal Reserve Acts—Savings and Loan
National Bankruptcy Act
Obstruction of Justice
Passports and Visas
Perjury
Railway Labor Act
Red Cross Act
Renegotiation Act
Selective Service Act of 1948
Sports Bribery
Switchblade Knife Act

Theft, Embezzlement, or Illegal Possession of Government Property
Theft From Interstate Shipment
Unauthorized Publication or Use of Communications
Unlawful Flight to Avoid Prosecution, Confinement, or the Giving of Testimony
Veterans Administration Matters
Welfare and Pension Plans Disclosure Act

UNITED STATES MARSHAL'S SERVICE (U.S. DEPARTMENT OF JUSTICE)

The U.S. Marshal's Service (USMS) is the nation's oldest federal law-enforcement agency. The U.S. Marshal is a presidentially appointed agent of the Department of Justice whose activities are supervised and coordinated by the Director of the U.S. Marshal's Service under the authority of the Attorney General. Almost every federal law-enforcement initiative involves the USMS, including the custody, care, and transportation of federal offenders and the tracking and apprehension of federal criminals who jump bail, violate parole, and escape prison.

USMS is also responsible for the protection of the courts, judges, attorneys, and witnesses, through the Federal Witness Protection and Relocation program, enforcement of court orders, management of assets seized or forfeited as a result of their acquisition from profits of certain criminal activities. Also included in the USMS's duties are the receipt and processing of federal prisoners, the custody of unsentenced federal prisoners, and the apprehension of fugitives wanted by foreign nations believed to be in the United States. This service accepts custody and escorts extradited or expulsed prisoners from foreign nations to the United States. USMS provides security assistance to the Department of Defense and the Air Force during the movement of missiles between military facilities. The Missile Escort program is part of USMS's Special Operations Group (SOG), which also includes the USMS Air Operations Branch. This branch responds to emergency situations, such as civil disturbances, terrorist incidents, or hostage situations where there is a violation of federal law or where federal property is endangered.

THE IMMIGRATION AND NATURALIZATION SERVICE (INS), INVESTIGATIONS DIVISION (U.S. DEPARTMENT OF JUSTICE)

Special Agents of the INS plan and conduct investigations of persons and events subject to the administrative and criminal provisions of the Immigration and Nationality Act and other statutes under the United States Code. These officers carry firearms, make arrests, prepare investigative reports, present cases to the U.S. Attorney for prosecution, and give testimony in judicial and administrative proceedings. Special Agents' missions are diverse, ranging from background studies to determine an alien's eligibility for benefits under the Immigration and Nationality Act to investigations of large-scale international organizations that smuggle aliens or perpetrate other fraudulent or criminal actions against the United States.

The INS, located in Washington, D.C., is under the supervision of the Commissioner of the Immigration and Naturalization Service and is its chief executive officer. The Commissioner is assisted by a Deputy Commissioner; an Executive Assistant; General Counsel; and Associate Commissioners for Enforcement, Examinations, Management and Operations Support; the Assistant Commissioners; and other staff members.

Field Service

The Field Service comprises four regions; within each region are district offices headed by district directors. Border Patrol functions are administered by Border Patrol Sectors within each region, supervised by Chief Patrol Agents. Each district is divided into sections to facilitate operations. The Investigations Section investigates aliens and citizens whose actions fall within the jurisdiction of the INS and make arrests in the enforcement of the act and other laws related to the immigration and naturalization of aliens.

The Examinations Section adjudicates various petitions submitted for alien benefits and inspects aliens seeking entry into this country. The Detention and Deportation section controls the movements of aliens after they have been placed under Service proceedings.

Investigations Program—Central Office

Under the direction of the Deputy Commissioner and the Associate Commissioner, the Assistant Commissioner for Investigations is responsible for the guidance, management, and direction of the Investigations Program. Service investigative activities *not* under the Assistant Commissioner for Investigations are the Anti-Smuggling Unit and the Employer and Labor Relations Unit. Anti-Smuggling is under the direction of the Associate Commissioner for Enforcement implemented by Border Patrol Sectors. The Assistant Commissioner for Employer and Labor Relations is charged with education of employer sanctions provisions of the Immigration Reform and Control Act of 1986 and the administration of the Systematic Alien Verification Entitlement Program. Special Agents of the INS are trained at the Federal Law Enforcement Training Center (FLETC) and at the Immigration Officer Academy for basic training, both at Glynco, Georgia.

DRUG ENFORCEMENT ADMINISTRATION (DEA) (U.S. DEPARTMENT OF JUSTICE)

The primary mission of the DEA is to enforce the drug laws and regulations of the United States. It is charged with investigating those organizations involved in the illegal growing, manufacturing, and distribution of controlled substances in the United States, along with regulating those individuals and companies who are legitimate handlers or manufacturers of controlled substances. The DEA is divided into enforcement and regulatory operations. Criminal investigations are handled by Special Agents (GS-1811) empowered to make arrests, perform search-and-seizures, and carry firearms. Regulatory matters are handled by Division Investigators (GS-1810).

DEA Special Agents (GS-1811) conduct criminal investigations, conduct criminal surveillance, infiltrate, identify, confiscate, and arrest violators in criminal drug activities. They prepare evidence, write reports, testify, and cooperate with municipal, state, and federal law-enforcement organizations. The DEA maintains its own training academy, sharing facilities on the FBI's training grounds in Quantico, Virginia.

BUREAU OF ALCOHOL, TOBACCO, AND FIREARMS (U.S. DEPARTMENT OF THE TREASURY)

The Bureau of Alcohol, Tobacco, and Firearms, known as the ATF, is headquartered in Washington, D.C. The ATF has a multimission responsibility to enforce federal laws on firearms, explosives, arson, alcohol, and cigarette smuggling. With the alarming rise in criminal activities, terrorism, and international conflicts, arms smuggling has become an ATF priority. In addition to these responsibilities, the ATF is charged with regulating the alcohol, tobacco, firearms, and explosives industries. Special Agents of the ATF undergo eight weeks of training at the Criminal Investigative School in general law enforcement and investigative techniques at the Federal Law Enforcement Training Center in Glynco, Georgia.

Investigative ATF agents are involved in surveillance, participate in raids, interview suspects and witnesses, obtain search warrants seeking physical evidence, and make arrests. Team composition and support in criminal bombings or arson incidents call for four teams, each composed of ten special agents, a forensic chemist, and an explosives expert from ATF's Explosives Technology Branch. Supported by technical, scientific, legal, and intelligence sources, they conduct the investigation, seek explosive tracings, perform lab analysis and case link analysis, provide legal counsel, and work in device reconstruction and classification.

U.S. CUSTOMS SPECIAL INVESTIGATIVE DIVISION (U.S. DEPARTMENT OF THE TREASURY)

Of the many missions it is responsible for, the U.S. Customs Service is empowered to prevent frauds and smuggling, to intercept illegal high-technology exports to Soviet-bloc nations, to cooperate with other federal agencies in suppressing illegal narcotics and pornography, and enforcing some 400 provisions of the law on behalf of 40 federal agencies. This division is the principal border-enforcement agency of the United States. Among its many units, the U.S. Customs maintains: an Organized Crime Strike Force; a National Patrimony Unit to protect national antiquities; a Steroid Investigative Unit; a Child Pornography and Protection Unit; currency investigations primarily with respect to the laundering of currency; Operation Exodus, which tightens controls on illegal exports; Technology Investigations and an Extraterritorial Investigative Group.

The U.S. Customs Service also conducts Tactical Operations involved in the smuggling of narcotics and maintains the Customs Office of Aviation Operations, an airborne detection unit. Its Enforcement Support section includes Communications Security, a Research and Development Division for electronic surveillance and detection equipment, boat detection systems, and border surveillance systems. The U.S. Customs Service Intelligence Program supports all major operational, inspection, and enforcement priorities for collection, analysis, and dissemination.

Department of the Treasury Bureau of Alcohol, Tobacco, and Firearms

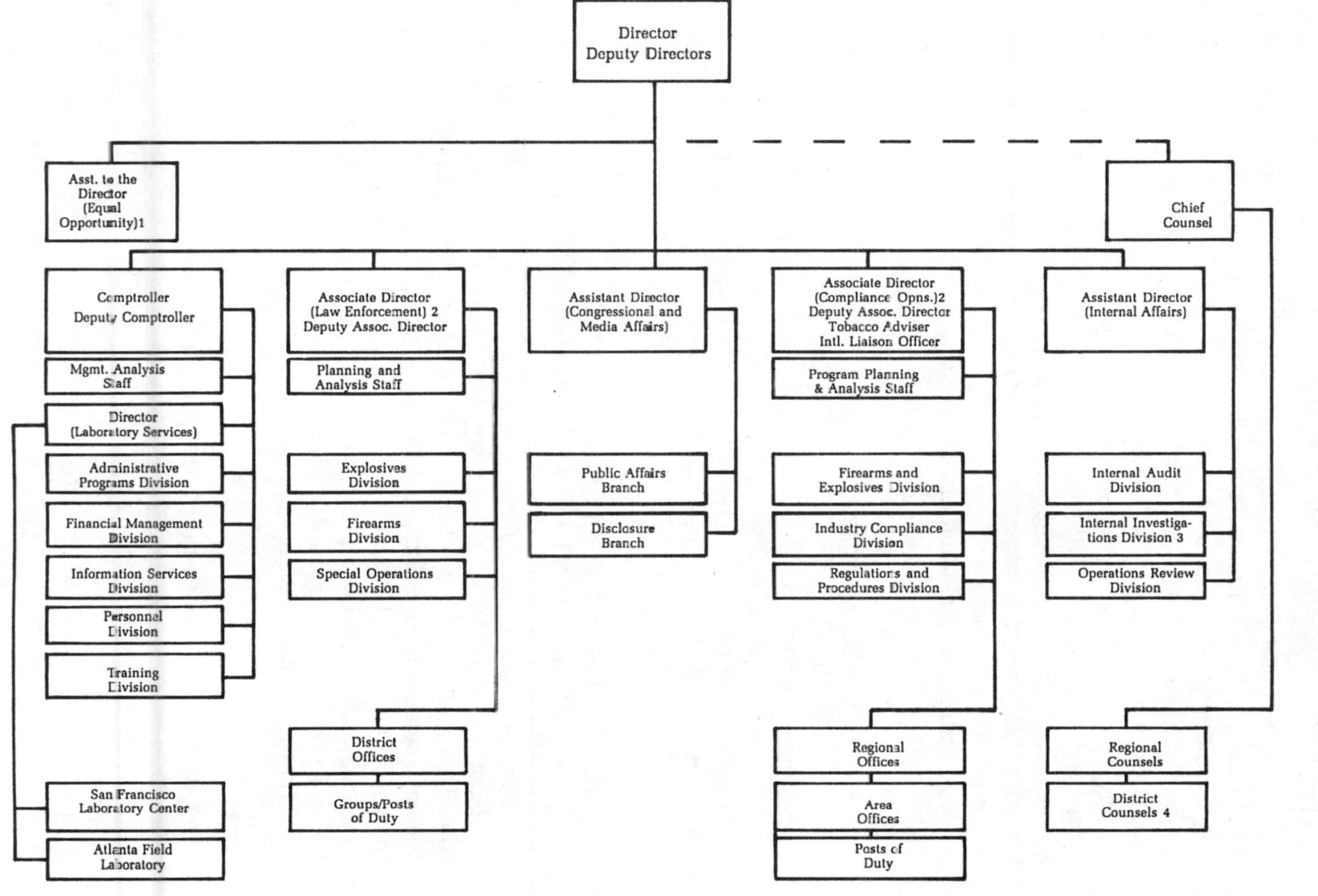

1. Field equal opportunity offices located in New York, Atlanta, Chicago, and San Francisco.
2. Associate Directors serve concurrently as Deputy Directors.
3. Field personnel stationed in Washington, DC, Chicago, and San Francisco.
4. Cincinnati and Philadelphia only.

INTERNAL REVENUE CRIMINAL INVESTIGATIONS IRS (U.S. DEPARTMENT OF THE TREASURY)

The IRS maintains an Office of Criminal Investigations and the Automated Criminal Investigations Project Office under an Assistant Commissioner, who serves as head of Criminal Investigations. The mission of Criminal Investigations is to encourage the highest possible voluntary compliance with Internal Revenue Laws by conducting quality investigations and recommending criminal prosecution when warranted. Criminal Investigation Special Agents target their efforts against organized crime, narcotics traffickers, money laundering, questionable refund schemes, tax shelters, and other domestic and international violations.

The Automated Criminal Investigations system is an extensive automation effort whose primary purpose is to improve the efficiency and effectiveness of all Criminal Investigation employees. The IRS works closely with other federal agencies in combating organized crime through the Department of Justice Strike Force. The IRS is also a significant participant in the Organized Crime Drug Enforcement Task Force. The IRS also investigates cases not connected to any special emphasis of organized crime, narcotics trafficking, etc., such as "skimming" and abusive tax shelters.

THE UNITED STATES COAST GUARD (U.S. DEPARTMENT OF TRANSPORTATION)

The U.S. Coast Guard is assigned the task of enforcing all applicable federal laws on the high seas and waters subject to U.S. jurisdiction. This includes the interdiction of illegal drugs and migrants, and the enforcement of U.S. Economic Zone laws and regulations extending 200 miles off the U.S. and territorial waters, as well as of a myriad of laws and regulations on safety issues. At times, Coast Guard Law Enforcement Detachments (LEDETS) serve aboard navy vessels and perform the actual boarding and arrest.

U.S. POSTAL INSPECTION SERVICE

The Postal Inspection Service, the law enforcement arm of the U.S. Postal Service, is headed by the Chief Postal Inspector, who oversees three divisions: Mail Investigations, Financial Investigations, and Administrative Investigations. Postal inspectors are responsible for protecting the mail, postal facilities, and employees from criminal attack and for protecting the American public from mail fraud, pornography, and other postal-related crimes.

Investigations are conducted into internal crimes such as mail theft, mistreatment, financial, and compensation abuses, and various miscellaneous internal crimes. In the area of external postal crimes, investigations are conducted into mail theft, burglaries, robberies, mail fraud, prohibited mailings such as pornography, narcotics, and bomb and explosive materials sent through the mail. The Postal Inspection Service maintains its own fully equipped, state-of-the-art crime laboratories, which investigate questioned and known documents, fingerprints, audio tapes, firearms, tools and tool marks, forensic photography, suspected controlled substances, poisons, and biological and unknown substances.

In the 1970s, the Postal Inspection Service established the Office of Security, a newly created uniformed Security Force designed to patrol major postal facilities, escort shipments of valuable mail, and provide security for postal employees. The U.S. Postal Inspector's Office is our country's oldest law-enforcement agency. Inspectors and investigative agents possess statutory power of arrest, apprehend violators, and work closely with U.S. Attorneys in prosecuting cases in court.

There are approximately 1,900 Postal Inspectors in the U.S. and Puerto Rico who also participate with Department of Justice national strike force teams. Postal Inspector trainees undergo an eleven-week basic training course in firearms, legal matters, search-and-seizure, arrest, court procedures, and postal operations, as well as a detailed study of federal laws pertaining to their jurisdiction.

FEDERAL AIR MARSHALS (FAMs)

Federal Aviation Administration—U.S. Department of Transportation known also as sky marshals, these Federal Air Marshals are assigned to U.S. Air Carriers on selected flights operating in sensitive or threatened areas around the world. The enactment of Public Law 99-83 established a basis for the FAA's FAM program. Authorized by the Secretary of Transportation and with the approval of the Attorney General and the Secretary of State, civilian aviation security Federal Air Marshals are empowered to carry firearms and to make arrests without warrants for any offense against the United States in their presence if they have reasonable grounds to believe the person to be arrested has committed a felony.

FAMs are recruited as civilian aviation security specialists (Special Agents) and when not on FAM missions, perform a wide variety of aviation security functions. As FAMs, they receive high-intensity, specialized law-enforcement training at the Federal Law Enforcement Training Center (FLETC).

BUREAU OF LAND MANAGEMENT (U.S. DEPARTMENT OF INTERIOR)

The Bureau of Land Management (BLM) is the caretaker of more than 300 million miles of public land and is charged by law to manage and protect these vast resources, including timber, minerals, livestock, forage, historic artifacts, and wild horses, and others associated with them. BLM has highly trained special agents and uniformed rangers to enforce applicable laws on federal land and to work closely with federal and state agencies and the Sheriff's Departments.

BLM special agents are responsible for enforcing federal laws and regulations relating to public lands and resources; they conduct criminal investigations and arrest violators. BLM special agents investigate numerous cases of archaeological thefts of cultural artifacts, pottery, ornaments, and even bones of American Indians who once inhabited the great West. Treating free-roaming or adopted wild horses and burros in an inhumane manner or selling them to slaughterhouses or other misuse is a federal violation investigated by BLM special agents, as are destruction, vandalism, or pollution of streams and lakes; starting fires, and growing marijuana.

Rangers are a law-enforcement arm of BLM who drive clearly marked patrol vehicles. Preventing law violations, rangers enforce laws, conduct search-and-rescue operations, eliminate hazards, and investigate accidents.

DEFENSE CRIMINAL INVESTIGATIVE SERVICE (U.S. DEPARTMENT OF DEFENSE—INSPECTOR GENERAL'S OFFICE)

The Defense Criminal Investigative Service (DCIS) is directly under the Department of Defense and the Office of The Inspector General and is responsible for criminal investigations. Working in conjunction with the military's CID, OSI, and NIS, this service is involved in combating and prosecuting fraudulent acts perpetrated against the U.S. Department of Defense, i.e., product substitution, overcharging, false charges, etc. Investigators working for DCIS are called special agents and are under the supervision of the Director of DCIS, who is also the Assistant Inspector General for Investigations.

DEFENSE INVESTIGATIVE SERVICE (DIS) (U.S. DEPARTMENT OF DEFENSE)

Headquartered in Washington, D.C., and supervised by the Director of DIS, the DIS and its Special Agents are responsible for investigating personnel for security clearances, investigating the unauthorized disclosure of classified government information, and administering industrial security programs for the Department of Defense and for eighteen other government agencies.

Other Federal Law-Enforcement Agencies that conduct investigations:

Fish and Game Commission
Securities and Exchange Commission
Defense Logistics Agency
Central Intelligence Agency
National Parks Service
General Accounting Office
Office of the Special Prosecutor (appointed by the president)
Federal Reserve Board
Maritime Commission
Office of the Inspector General

4

National Crime Information Center Operation

The National Crime Information Center (NCIC) is a nationwide criminal-justice information teleprocessing network that provides documented criminal-justice information to the entire criminal-justice community. NCIC contains records on stolen property, i.e., vehicles, license plates, guns, securities, boats, and serialized articles; wanted persons for whom arrest warrants are outstanding; unidentified persons; and missing persons meeting specific entry criteria; as well as criminal histories on persons arrested for serious offenses. An NCIC Advisory Policy Board made up of federal, state, and local justice officials furnishes advice to the FBI Director on policy matters concerning NCIC operations and thereby allows the users a voice in overall management of the system. Users of NCIC include the fifty states, all federal law-enforcement agencies, the Royal Canadian Mounted Police, the Police of the Commonwealth of Puerto Rico, and the United States Virgin Islands—all on a cost-free basis.

MISSING-CHILDREN FILE

The juvenile category of the NCIC Missing-Person File responds to inquiries within seconds. A missing-child record may be entered simply by a parent, legal guardian, or next of kin filing a missing-persons report with any local or state law-enforcement agency. The record should contain all available descriptive and identifying data, such as nicknames, birthplace and date, height, weight, scars, marks, blood type, dental information, etc. When a positive identification is made, the record of the child is promptly removed from the system.

FOREIGN-FUGITIVE FILE

Implemented in 1987, this file contains both Canadian warrants and new wanted-persons records for foreign fugitives entered by the United States Central Bureau of the International Police Organization (INTERPOL).

5

United States Military and Naval Law Enforcement

UNITED STATES ARMY CRIMINAL INVESTIGATIVE COMMAND (USACIDC)

Often referred to as the CID or Criminal Investigation Division (CID), this section of the Army is an investigative, fact-finding agency. Although CID has arrest powers, it does not prosecute, but instead turns its suspects and investigation reports over to the proper branch of service for prosecution.

Trained by the army at the FBI Academy in Quantico and often at Great Britain's Scotland Yard, the CID and its agents exist to conduct criminal investigations on military bases involving both military personnel and those civilians employed by the army or Department of Defense. Additional responsibilities include conducting crime-prevention surveys and providing protective services to the Secretary of Defense; Chairman, Joint Chiefs of Staff; Secretary of the Army; Chief of Staff, Army; and other dignitaries as directed. CID also plays an important role in terrorism counteraction, hostage negotiations, supplying protective services, security vulnerability assessments, criminal information collection, hostage negotiation, and narcotics investigations.

CID operates three crime laboratories and the Army Crime Records Center and maintains liaison with other police and investigative agencies. CID agents, who almost always operate in civilian clothes, consist of noncommissioned officers, the highest-ranking of whom is a Chief Warrant Officer.

UNITED STATES NAVAL INVESTIGATIVE SERVICE (NIS)

Working in civilian clothes, NIS Special Agents conduct criminal, narcotics, and complex fraud investigations; counterintelligence and undercover operations; and hostage negotiations. They also provide protective services and investigate infractions of military law governing naval personnel and civilians contracted or employed by the navy or the marine corps. NIS is part of the Naval Security and Investigative Command (NSIC), headquartered in Washington D.C., and commanded by a rear admiral, who reports directly to the secretary of the navy and the chief of naval operations.

UNITED STATES AIR FORCE OFFICE OF SPECIAL INVESTIGATIONS (OSI)

The OSI operates very much like the NIS in that it, unlike the CID, conducts counterintelligence operations. OSI Special Agents work in mufti and are trained at the OSI's Academy at Bolling Field AFB. Like its sister agencies NIS and CID, OSI conducts criminal investigations and serves as a fact-finding arm that turns over apprehended military and Defense Department civilian employee suspects to the Judge Advocate's Office for prosecution. Like CID, OSI maintains its own forensic police-science laboratories and criminal-records center.

MILITARY POLICE (MP)

The Department of the Army Officer Branch Code 31 is for commissioned officers in the Military Police Corps, which is responsible for the army's law enforcement in both war and peace.

In combat operations, the military police are the tactical commander's primary response force against terrorists and saboteurs; they carry on their regular military duties as well. Military police provide area security operations, oversee and evacuate enemy prisoners of war, and provide security for special ammunition. In peace and in war, military police officers, trained in methods and techniques of management and police sciences, advise and assist army commanders to establish discipline, enforce laws, and prevent crimes.

MP officers plan for the security of VIP's, military banks and hospitals, material storage areas, airfields, ports, harbors, inland waterways, railroads, and petroleum pipelines. When normal processes of government are disrupted, military police may be called upon to help restore order. Military police conduct criminal investigations and are responsible for the humane treatment of prisoners, be they army personnel or POWs. The major training site for MP officers is Fort McClellen, Alabama.

6

The Private Investigator

Contrary to the writer's and the public's concept of a private investigator (P.I.) or private eye, most private investigators seldom work on a murder case or one that involves acts of violence as they often appear in novels and on the screen. Most P.I.'s are employed by industry and in family and marital disputes. However, the fictional image of the private eye has and will continue to be highly successful in crime and murder stories.

If one were to adhere to the actual work done by private investigators (most of whom do not carry weapons), the private eye as we know him and her would vanish from all literary and screen works. (Perish the thought!) However, one thing the writer must be aware of to bring some semblance of honesty and logic to his or her works should be the fact that almost no law-enforcement agency takes kindly to private investigators who interfere with official investigations, with the possible exception of those private investigators working for insurance companies affected by the crime.

As to presenting fictional private investigators, there are no special rules to adhere to except to be aware of the attitude taken by law-enforcement agencies. With that in mind, remember that the P.I. must have a legal permit for carrying a concealed weapon, and that in chases, he or she is vulnerable to arrest for driving at excessive speeds, breaking and entering, assault, harassment, firing a weapon when not using it to defend his or her own life or the lives of other innocent people, for trespassing, and for generally breaking or interfering with any and all laws governing all other people not bearing the credentials of a law-enforcement officer in pursuit of his duty. It should also be noted that whenever a P.I. does investigate a case and does apprehend the guilty party, the same rules of evidence apply, and they must be just as conclusive as those adhered to by officers of the law in order to make an arrest and gain a conviction in a court of law.

7

The Courtroom

Many crime dramas wind up in courtrooms, and it is also conceivable that much of a crime story can be played out in a courtroom with occasional trips to other locations for investigative purposes or with the tried-and-true and often trite use of flashbacks. One of the most famous television series that played out most of its crime drama inside the courtroom was Erle Stanley Gardner's *Perry Mason*.

It is essential that the writer be familiar with the courtroom and its procedures, especially the type of courtroom to be used, e.g., pretrial, grand jury, superior court, appellate court, and sentencing court.

Although this book does contain some information on the various courts and judges, it is advisable to consult a legal expert when using legal terms, procedures, legal movements, presence of a jury, etc.

CHARACTERS IN A COURTROOM INCLUDE:

Judge
Bailiff
Court stenographer
Jury (where applicable)

Prosecuting attorney or attorney for the plaintiff
Defense attorney or attorney for the respondent
Witnesses (for defense and prosecution, where applicable)
Witnesses (expert, where applicable)

Generally, with the exception of a military court, most courtrooms all look alike and contain the *bench*, at which the judge is seated; the court stenographer's typing stand, which can be located on either side of the judge's bench; an American flag and the state flag on each side of the judge's bench; the table at which the prosecuting attorney is seated (or in a civil case, where the attorney for the plaintiff and the plaintiff are seated); and the table at which the defense attorney is seated with the accused (or in a civil case, where the respondent is seated with counsel).

The jury box for the eleven jurors and the jury foreman or forewoman can be placed on either side of the courtroom between the bench and the attorneys' tables. A railing marks off that part of the courtroom where the case is heard and tried. Behind the railing are rows of spectators' benches; the number of benches set aside is determined by the size of the courtroom. Witnesses are usually seated in the viewers' section unless otherwise specified.

LAWYERS – TYPES

Criminal (Prosecuting, Defense)
Civil
Trial
Corporate
Bankruptcy
Marine
Probate
Patent
Real Estate
International
Insurance
Tax
Forensic
Divorce
Legal Aid or Public Defender

LAW ENFORCEMENT AGENCIES (NONFEDERAL) AND OFFICIALS

District Attorney's Office
County Prosecutor's Office
City Attorney's Office
State Attorney General's Office
Chief Magistrate's Office
Police Department (Local, City)
Sheriff's Department
State Police
Police Sciences
Transit Police
Highway Patrol
Police Commission
Chief of Police
Sheriff
Deputy Sheriffs
Marshal's Office
Deputy Marshals
Police Officers (male and female)
Chief of Detectives
Detectives
Justices of the Peace
Judges
Coroner
Magistrates
Medical Examiner

COURTS

U.S. Supreme Court
State Supreme Court
County Supreme Court
State Circuit Courts of Appeal
State Appellate Courts of Appeal
County Court
Night Court
Felony Court
Superior Court
Police Court
Court of Special Sessions

Maritime Court
Probate Court
Traffic Court
Surrogate's Court
Juvenile Court
Domestic Relations Court
Bankruptcy Court
Magistrate's Court
District Court
Small Debtors Court
Small Claims Court
Chancery Court
Courts of Common Pleas
Tax Court
Court of Claims
Court of Record
International Court

U.S. ARMED FORCES COURTS

General Court-Martial
Summary Court-Martial
Regimental Court-Martial
Special Court-Martial
Garrison Court-Martial
Court of Inquiry

CHURCH COURTS

Ecclesiastical and Disciplinary Courts

SPECIAL JURIES

Federal Grand Jury
Military Board of Inquiry
State Grand Jury
County Grand Jury
Coroner's Jury

8

Federal Bureau of Prisons

The Bureau of Prisons, which is part of the United States Department of Justice, has its headquarters, or Central Office, in Washington, D.C. (telephone (202) 724-3198). The staff of the Central Office are responsible for the control and coordination of all the activities of the agency. Major functions include planning, policy development, management of manpower and other resources, budget development, monitoring the quality of programs and services, and coordinating the activities of the regional offices and institutions.

In addition to these management functions, Central Office staff have primary responsibility for public information activities, legal and legislative affairs, and relations with the Congress and policy-making administrators in other government agencies, as well as in private organizations.

Central Office staff also carry out such functions as adjudicating appeals for inmates and employees, directing research and evaluation projects, designing automated information systems, managing environmental health and safety programs, and conducting management-employee relations with the sole bargaining agent for Bureau employees, the American Federation of Government Employees (AFL-CIO) Council of Prison Locals.

NEW FACILITIES

Marianna, FL—Federal Correctional Institution
Capacity—750 beds, including 150-bed satellite camp
Medium Security
Activation: Camp, March 1988
Main Institution, May 1988

Los Angeles, CA—Metropolitan Detention Center
Capacity—588 pretrial detainees
Activation: October 1988

Sheridan, OR—Federal Correctional Institution
Capacity—550 beds, with adjacent 250-bed satellite camp
Medium Security
Activation: May 1989

Bradford, PA—Federal Correctional Institution
Capacity—550 beds, with adjacent 150-bed satellite camp
Medium Security
Activation: June 1989

Fairton, NJ—Federal Correctional Institution
Capacity—550 beds
Medium Security
Activation: October 1989

Jesup, GA—Federal Correctional Institution
Capacity—666 beds
Activation: October 1989

Many other small construction or renovation projects are underway to increase the capacities of existing Bureau facilities.

Federal Bureau of Prisons

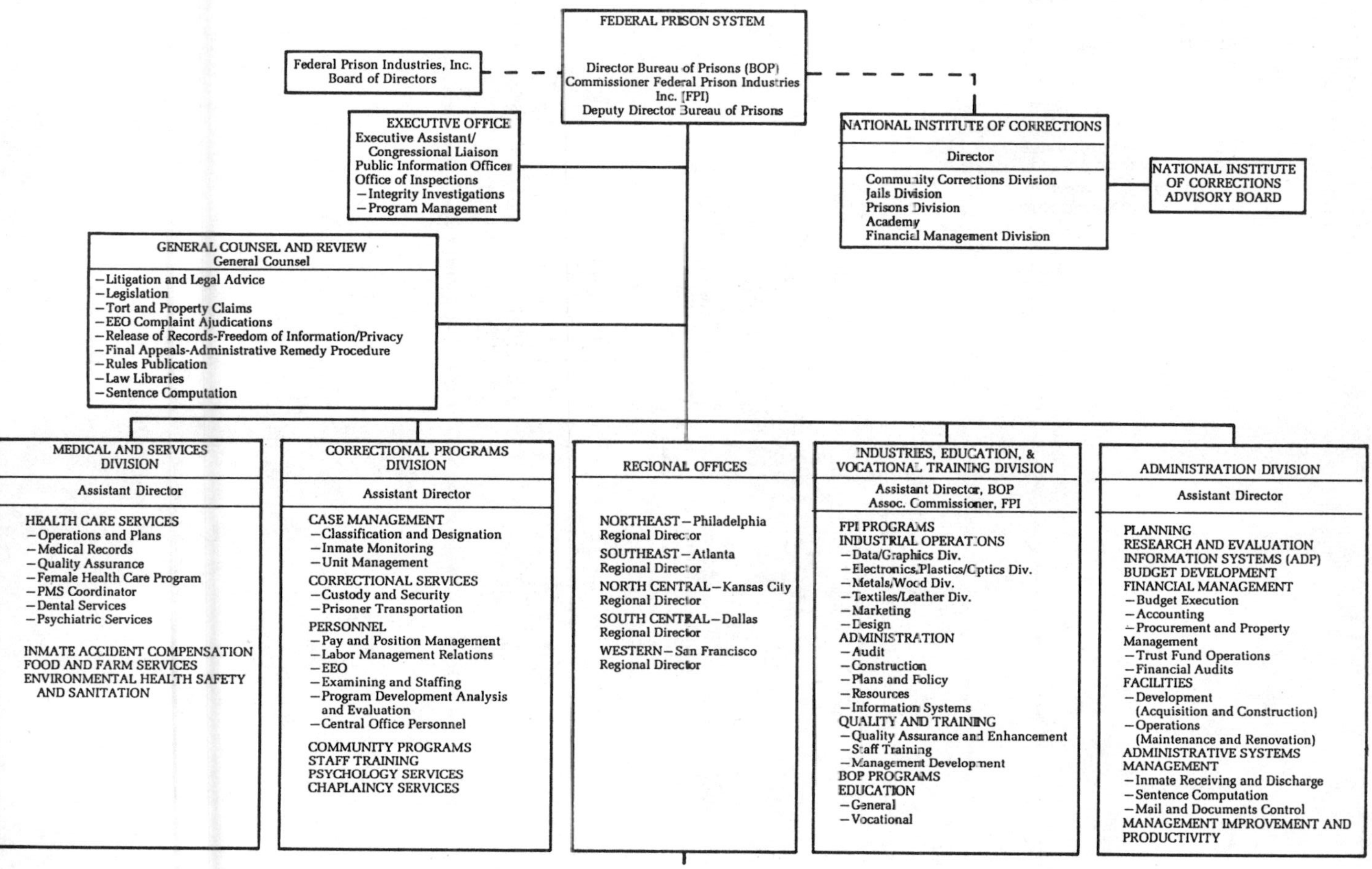

Federal Correctional System

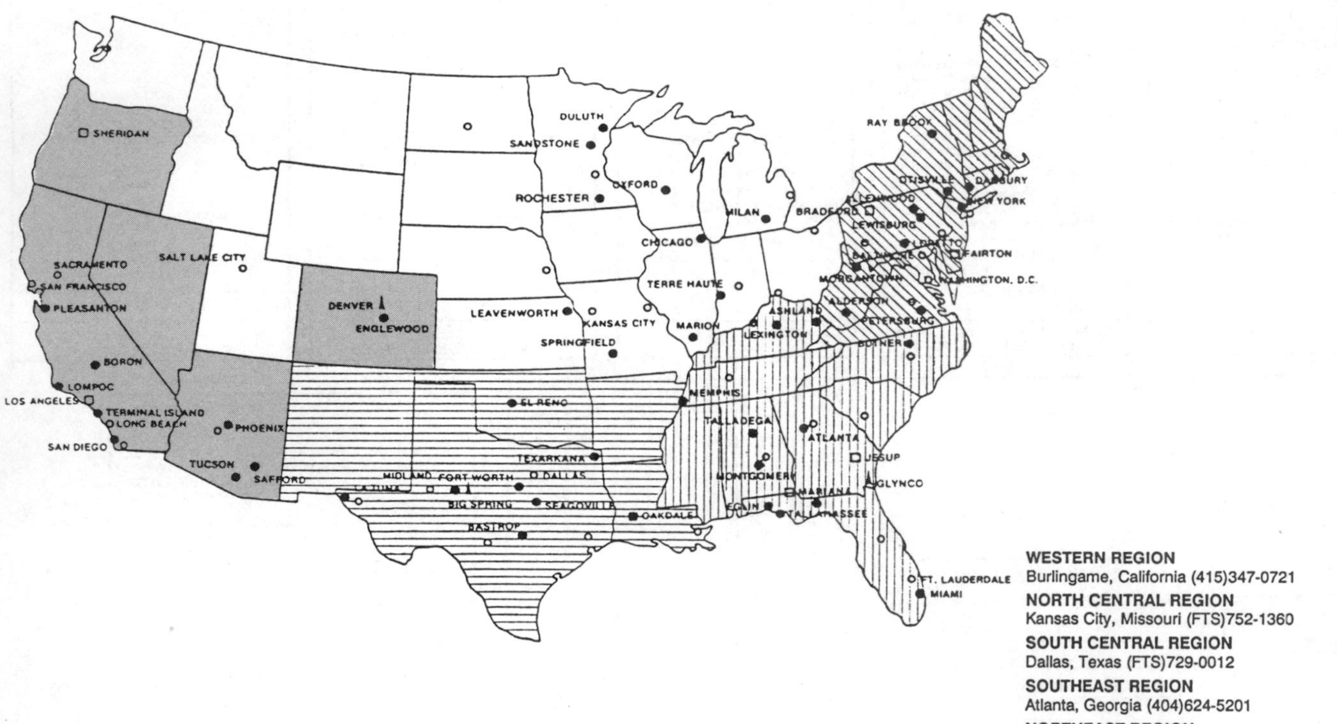

WESTERN REGION
Burlingame, California (415)347-0721

NORTH CENTRAL REGION
Kansas City, Missouri (FTS)752-1360

SOUTH CENTRAL REGION
Dallas, Texas (FTS)729-0012

SOUTHEAST REGION
Atlanta, Georgia (404)624-5201

NORTHEAST REGION
Philadelphia, Pennsylvania (FTS)597-6315

FEDERAL PRISON SYSTEM FACILITIES
COMMUNITY PROGRAMS OFFICES
FACILITIES UNDER CONSTRUCTION
STAFF TRAINING CENTERS

Federal Bureau of Prisons

Bureau of Prisons
Percentage of Population
Confined to Institutions by Offense

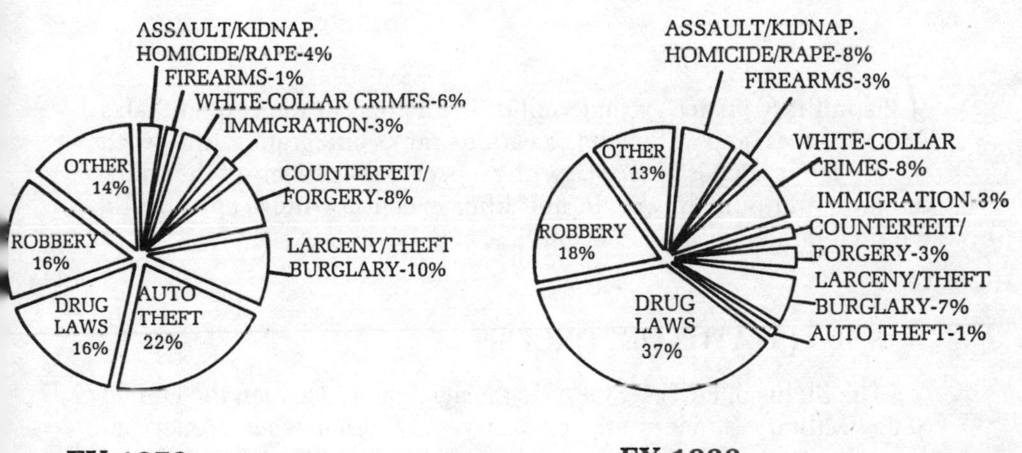

FY 1970 **FY 1986**

9

Military Justice System

The military justice system applies to all areas of the United States Armed Forces, and although the various ranks and grades differ with the various branches of service with respect to the officers of the court, the laws and punishment do not differ except for those specifically within a particular branch of service, e.g., naval law.

SOFA (STATUS OF FORCES)

The Status of Forces (SOFA) is the agreement between the United States Military Services and foreign governments where American forces are stationed. This agreement determines who retains jurisdiction when a U.S. serviceman or -woman is involved in a crime committed off the military base.

In most instances, when a member of the U.S. Armed Forces is serving overseas and commits a major crime off his or her military base, the serviceman or -woman is arrested and tried by a civilian criminal court of that nation, although that service personnel may be represented by military counsel or civilian counsel of his or her choice.

If the serviceman or -woman is convicted, he or she may, at the election of that foreign government, be imprisoned in that government's prison for the term of the sentence imposed.

In cases where a lesser crime has been committed, such as drunk driving, the perpetrator may be tried and sentenced by the court of that foreign government and subsequently, upon release from prison, be tried by his or her own military court for a military crime, such as absence without leave, improper conduct, unauthorized use of military property, etc. (See page 81, Uniform Code of Military Justice, Subchapter X, Punitive Articles.)

The following is excerpted from the *United States Army Command and General Staff College Student Text 27-1*, and is gratefully reprinted here with the permission of the U.S. Army:

CHAPTER 1
THE MILITARY JUSTICE SYSTEM

1.1 Introduction.

We often think of the law as being fixed and eternal, but in reality, the law is man-made, fallible, and ever-changing. Today's rules may become of historical interest only by tomorrow's court decision. Today's commanders and staff officers cannot rely on past knowledge of the military justice system. Today's officers must be aware of the current system and use it fairly and intelligently. Recent changes to the Uniform Code of Military Justice and the Manual for Courts-Martial have greatly improved the ability of commanders to effectively use disciplinary measures. This book will assist you to understand the current system and use it effectively.

This book is not intended to make you an expert in military justice. Rather, it is to provide an awareness of the major requirements of military justice. This book is not intended to replace the basic sources of military law. It is, however, an aid to effective decision making in the military justice arena. The most important thing to take away from this material is the ability to recognize a military justice problem so as to know when to contact your "expert" in the area—the staff judge advocate.

1.2 Background and Development.

An understanding of the legal basis for the military justice system must rest on an understanding of the history and tradition which shaped its development. Among the concepts that emerged from the American Revolution were the fear of excessive military power and the desire to keep the military strictly subservient to civilian control.

These notions were embodied in the Constitution. That document is the basic source for the military justice system.

Our system of military justice had its inception in the American Revolution. The Uniform Code of Military Justice that we currently use can be traced back through the Articles of War used during the American Revolution to the British Articles of War. The first Articles of War were adopted by the Second Continental Congress on 30 June 1775, just three days before George Washington, who was on the committee appointed to prepare the rules and regulations for the newly-created Continental Army, took command of it.

Our separate system of military justice differs from that of many other countries. A servicemember can be tried by court-martial for what is essentially a civilian offense as well as for uniquely military ones such as absence without leave, disobedience, disrespect, and misbehavior before the enemy. In many countries, civil courts handle all offenses committed by servicemembers which are not uniquely military. The reason for this expansive jurisdictional reach is the need to maintain discipline in order to have an effective fighting force. Because of force deployment, the military requires a justice system which is literally worldwide in its criminal prohibitions and its jurisdictional reach—unlike civilian criminal processes which are usually localized. Finally, it is doubtful that the civilian justice system could appreciate and meet all the varied concerns of military discipline.

1.3 The Purpose of Military Law.

The 1984 Manual for Courts-Martial probably states the purpose of Military Law best:

> The purpose of military law is to promote justice, to assist in maintaining good order and discipline in the armed forces, to promote efficiency and effectiveness in the military establishment, and thereby to strengthen the national security of the United States. Preamble, MCM, 1984, 3.

1.4 The Ever-Changing Military Law.

As is the case with most of our laws, military law has been reconsidered and revised in the light of new knowledge and experience. Among the major revisions were:

The Uniform Code of Military Justice, 1950. This Act of Congress combined the separate laws formerly governing the Army, Navy, and Air Force into one uniform code which governs all of the armed forces of the United States.

The Military Justice Act of 1968. A major revision of the Uniform Code occurred with this act. This act first gave servicemembers the right to a qualified lawyer at special courts-martial and established the military judiciary.

Since the 1968 Act, Congress has amended the Uniform Code several times in order to increase the efficiency of our military criminal law system:

In November 1979, Public Law 96-197 amended Article 2, UCMJ, to authorize court-martial jurisdiction over servicemembers entering the armed forces as a result of recruiter misconduct.

The Military Justice Amendments of 1981 eliminated the right of the accused to be represented by more than one military lawyer and permitted a commander or convening authority to direct excess leave for servicemembers who have been convicted by court-martial and are awaiting appellate review. Previously, the accused could only be placed on excess leave upon the approval of his or her request.

The Military Justice Act of 1983. On 6 December, 1983, the President signed this act, Public Law No. 98-209, 97 Stat. 1393. The effective date is 1 August, 1984. A new Manual for Courts-Martial has also been written. It includes provisions to implement the legislation. Its effective date is also 1 August, 1984. This revision is intended to streamline the military justice system and make it more responsive to commanders while retaining the fundamental rights of servicemembers. Among its provisions are a lessening of the commander's responsibilities to review courts-martial for legal sufficiency; streamlining procedures for detailing and excusing courts-martial personnel; and permitting appeal of final courts-martial to the U.S. Supreme Court.

1.5 Sources of Military Law.

Article I, section 8, of our Constitution provides that "The Congress shall have Power . . . To make Rules for the Government and Regulation of the land and naval Forces, . . ." This language is what gives the Congress the authority to enact the federal law called the Uniform Code of Military Justice.

Article II, section 2, states that "The President shall be Commander in Chief of the Army and Navy of the United States, . . ."

In Article 36 of the Uniform Code of Military Justice, the Congress authorized the President, as Commander in Chief, to issue procedural rules to implement the military justice system. This is the authority the President has used to issue the Presidential Proclamation called the Manual for Courts-Martial. It contains a detailed set of regulations supplementing and explaining the Uniform Code. It also contains maximum punishments. Article 36 of the UCMJ gave the President the power to establish punishments. This power was recently used to change the maximum sentences for drug offenses by Executive Order on 23 December, 1982. These Executive Orders have the force of law, although in the case of a conflict, the Constitution, then the UCMJ, have precedence.

The services can publish regulations to further implement the provisions of the above sources of military law. One example is Army Regulation 27-10, Military Justice. This regulation contains procedures that must be followed for such matters as administering nonjudicial punishment, reviewing the legality of pretrial confinement, etc.

Court decisions from military and civilian appellate courts must also be considered as sources of military law. For example, the United States Supreme Court's decision that counsel were not required at summary courts-martial is an example of court-made, as opposed to statutory or regulatory, law.

All of the foregoing, the Constitution, the UCMJ, the MCM, regulations, and the decisions of the appellate courts, are sources of military law. [Note: If your story turns on a precise point of military law or military judicial procedure, consult the appropriate regulation(s), as then amended, in the reference section of any large public library. The public information divisions of the various armed services may also be able to provide helpful materials for further research.]

1.6 Military Justice Personnel.

The Staff Judge Advocate is the legal adviser to the command. He will normally be a senior lieutenant colonel when assigned to a division, and a colonel for higher commanders and major installations. The UCMJ authorizes the SJA direct access to the convening authority. Besides supervising military justice, the SJA has functions in the administrative law, claims, and legal assistance areas.

Trial court personnel include military judges, trial counsel (prosecutor), and defense counsel.

Military judges belong to the U.S. Army Trial Judiciary. They are appointed by the Judge Advocate General from JAGC officers who have extensive trial experience and satisfactorily complete the judge's course. Special court-martial judges are usually majors. General court-martial judges are lieutenant colonels or colonels. Judges are assigned to the Trial Judiciary, which is independent of any local command, so they are rated by other judges, not commanders. This helps to preserve their independence and avoid command influence.

Defense counsel belong to a similar organization, the Trial Defense Service. It comes under the same parent organization as the trial judiciary, the U.S. Army Legal Services Agency. Thus, defense counsel are not assigned to local commands and owe their undivided loyalty to their clients. Defense counsel are rated by senior defense attorneys. A regional defense counsel supervises the defense counsel within a geographical region, and is who the commander can go to if he has a problem involving a defense counsel. The canons of ethics of the American Bar Association are applicable to all military lawyers. The canon that requires counsel to represent their clients zealously within the bounds of the law is especially important to defense counsel.

The trial counsel works for the command, and presents the case for the government (prosecution). His ethical duty is to see justice done. The trial counsel works for the Chief of Criminal Law (sometimes called Chief of Justice), under the Staff Judge Advocate.

1.7 Commander's Role.

One of the major differences between the military and the civilian justice systems is that the latter has no counterpart to the commander. Both systems have judges, prosecutors, and defense attorneys. The commander in our system has powers substantially equivalent to those of civilian judges and prosecutors. For example, a commander can issue a search authorization which is the military counterpart to the search warrants issued by civilian judges. Also, in the military, the commander decides who is to be prosecuted, a decision made by district attorneys or prosecutors in the civilian sector.

It should be noted that it is the commander in our system who makes many of these decisions—whether to prosecute or not, whether to approve a pretrial agreement (plea bargain)—not the military lawyers. Of course, the commander should seek the advice of his staff judge advocate before making these decisions.

Because the commander has so much power—unlike that of any civilians except judges—he or she must exercise that power wisely and fairly. The civilian sector has always watched carefully for abuses of the military justice system. In order that the people, acting through Congress, continue to permit commanders to exercise these broad powers, commanders' military justice actions must not only be fair, but be perceived to be fair.

It should also be remembered that the military justice system is a "tool" of discipline—and not the only one—not a substitute for good leadership. This is the reason that the commander has the ultimate decision-making power in the military justice system. The commander is in the best position to evaluate the effect of an offense on good order and discipline and to choose a "tool" to correct the situation. Many times military justice procedures will not be the best way to dispose of a disciplinary problem; courts-martial and nonjudicial punishment are often too severe, slow, or cumbersome, unsuited to the incident, the accused, or the commander's purpose. Often an administrative action such as counseling will suffice.

The complexity of the system and of the myriad factors that impact on good order and discipline requires that the commander exercise a Solomon-like judgment. As long as he or she obtains the facts and the advice of the staff judge advocate and dispassionately assesses them to make a reasoned, fair, and impartial decision, the military justice system will remain in the capable hands that have used it effectively for over 200 years—the hands of commanders.

10

Fundamentals of Investigation

An investigator's lot calls for much more than merely solving the crime. He must satisfy all of the needs of the local, state, or federal prosecutor and of the court. Discovering the identity of the criminal and apprehending that criminal is not sufficient in order to achieve a conviction. The investigator must provide the prosecutor with sufficient and conclusive evidence, opportunity, and motive; also, if possible, the investigator should present a witness or witnesses who can help substantiate any or all of the aforementioned items.

The three objectives of any investigator are:

Identifying the criminal.
Tracing and locating the criminal.
Proving the criminal's guilt in a court of law.

IDENTIFYING AND LOCATING THE CRIMINAL:

Naturally, before an investigator can trace, locate, and prove a criminal's guilt in court, he or she must first ascertain the identity of the criminal. This can be accomplished by:

Admission or confession by a suspect, although it is often necessary to support that admission or confession by corroborative evidence and/or an eyewitness, and, in the case of a homicide, a corpus delicti.* Otherwise the admission or confession may be denied in court, the defense counsel charging the prosecution with obtaining the admission or confession by duress or coercion.

In the event a crime has been committed and no one freely admits or confesses to the crime, the investigator must then attempt to ascertain a possible suspect or suspects. Identification of a suspect involves seeking:

Circumstantial evidence, such as *motive, opportunity,* and *associative evidence,* consisting of physical clues, personal property, a witness, and/or a pattern of the type of crime (modus operandi). A good investigator can often and easily determine if the crime was committed by a professional criminal or a novice.

Should the investigator elect to believe the suspect is a professional, he or she will then often turn to records of those possessing his or her M.O. (modus operandi) and the last known whereabouts of those with that M.O. in order to determine if any of those suspects had the opportunity to commit the crime. If both the M.O. and the opportunity exist, then that suspect or suspects will be brought in for questioning.

If the suspect or suspects are known to possess the M.O. of the crime, had opportunity, and subsequent to the commission of the crime have departed the city, then an All Points Bulletin (A.P.B.) would be issued to bring the suspect in for questioning.

In the event the investigator concludes that the perpetrator is an amateur, it is usually believed that the crime was committed because of opportunity, and sudden flight could quickly betray guilt. Here it would also behoove the investigator to look for a suspect who had motive, such as anger, profit, revenge, etc. (See section on motives.)

TIPOFFS, INFORMERS, ASSOCIATES OF A SUSPECT

Tipoffs, paid informers, and associates of a possible suspect can be of invaluable help to an investigator, and whenever possible, the investigator will seek out those who for one reason or another might

**Corpus delicti—Legal term for tangible evidence proving a crime has been committed.*

provide him or her with a lead or some piece of physical evidence that will eventually be used against the suspect should that suspect turn out to be the culprit.

Proving the Criminal's Guilt in a Court of Law:

Once a professional investigator has a possible suspect under investigation, it is up to the investigator to determine what physical means and what scientific means are available to use in seeking more evidence linking the suspect to the crime. The investigator might proceed by using stakeouts and various normal and electronic surveillance equipment.

The alleged act and the suspect accused, along with a positive connection to the crime, must be firmly established. This means that the investigator must be able to prove *motive, opportunity, associative evidence*, a corpus delicti (or evidence that a crime has been committed), *the elements of the offense, intent*, and evidence of the frame of mind of the accused. The investigator, and subsequently the prosecuting attorney, must prove that the accused knew what he or she was doing. In crimes where violence has taken place, the element of *malice* must be introduced, showing the intent to do injury to another. Legal malice is the state of mind of the person committing the crime and doesn't imply there was animosity or hate involved in the commission of the criminal act. Thus the motive for the crime and intent must be separately considered, as motive may be the underlying reason for committing the crime, while intent is the actual accomplishment.

THE FIRST TWENTY-FOUR HOURS

The first twenty-four hours are the most important hours following a crime, for it is within that period of time that clues and evidence have less chance to be disturbed and that witnesses' minds are still fresh and uncluttered with what they witnessed or overheard. In addition, should there be a description of a suspect given the investigator or clues found that implicate a possible suspect, the trail of the suspect is still fresh, and should a suspect intend to flee, it is still possible to pick up a trail before the suspect can completely vanish. Roadblocks can be set and airports, train stations, and bus depots can be watched for any sign of a possible suspect attempting to flee. The sooner a suspect has been described or identified, the sooner contacts can be made with any known associates, family members, or friends of the suspect; such contacts could lead to the whereabouts of the suspect or any plans to escape the suspect may have had.

THE SCENE OF THE CRIME

It is within the boundaries of the crime scene that the investigator finds the best opportunity to determine the means with which the crime was committed, clues and evidence that can point to a possible motive and to a possible suspect or suspects who may have perpetrated the crime. It is here that clues and much of the evidence and information pertaining to the crime can be found, protected, and interpreted.

The first officer arriving on the scene should note the time as well as observe and note as many of the elements pertaining to the crime scene as possible without physically touching, moving, or removing anything at the scene. In addition, the officer should note and record any sounds or odors present, the amount of light present, open or shut doors and windows, witnesses present; above all, he or she should make sure *nothing is changed or altered* when arriving on the scene. Efforts should be made immediately to cordon off the area and to keep family, friends, and curiosity seekers away from the scene. Depending on the crime, the first officer on the scene should make immediate radio contact with the section of the department (robbery, burglary, homicide, etc.). In the event of a homicide, he should not only inform Homicide immediately but also contact the coroner or the medical examiner.

If a suspect is discovered when the first officer arrives on the scene, the officer should attempt first and foremost to apprehend the suspect or take the suspect into custody, and then the other steps should be followed. While awaiting superiors or the investigator who will take charge of the case, the first officer on the scene must also get the names of any and all witnesses, keep witnesses separated until they are questioned, and protect the crime scene from any disturbance.

The six most important questions the officer in charge of the investigation must try to answer are: who, what, where, when, why, and how. The primary reason for visiting a crime scene is to: (1) attempt to reconstruct exactly what happened; (2) establish a motive for the crime; (3) attempt to discover a primary suspect; (4) discover clues that can lead to the identification of both the victim and the suspect; and (5) find evidence, legally obtained, that can be used in a court of law to substantiate the finding of the investigator and to aid the prosecution in obtaining a guilty verdict against the person or persons responsible for the crime. To help accomplish these goals, the investigator must always be concerned that the crime scene is as it was discovered.

Once something has been moved or touched, it can never be as it was again. The investigator should enter the crime scene with great caution, bearing in mind that there can be trace or impression evidence all around the scene. If the victim has been shot, knifed, or beaten to death, the investigator needs to pay attention to the mist or blood spatterings. Murder weapons as well as physical and trace evidence should never be bagged in plastic bags, as moisture gathering in the bag could have an effect on the evidence collected. Those on the scene should always bag evidence in a paper bag. Nothing at the scene, no matter how minute it is, should be overlooked, and the investigator should always take copious notes. In the event of a homicide or officer-involved shooting, no one should move the body until the medical examiner gives permission. Criminalists arriving on the scene are responsible for collecting and transporting trace evidence and imprint evidence to the police lab for further tests. Crime-scene photographs should be taken and sketches made of the victim and of the scene.

Witnesses must be questioned separately. Newspaper or TV reporters must not be given all information pertaining to the crime so as not to inform the responsible party or copycat criminals from knowing all that was discovered at the crime scene. Those important to the on-scene investigation, depending on the crime committed, might include any number of the following police, technicians, medical or special personnel:

Homicide investigators
Criminalist
Medical examiner
Crime-scene artist
Crime-scene still photographer
Videotaping specialist
Print people
District attorney
Forensic specialists
Arson investigators

Forensic psychologists or behavioral scientists

Measurements are essential in the processing of a crime-scene investigation, as is videotaping of the scene. Outdoor crime scenes require special care, as impression prints could easily be destroyed. Brush and twigs might contain blood samples, hair, and fibers. In the event of a homicide, it is essential to determine whether the remains have been touched by animals or insects. As at all crime scenes, the investigators should look carefully for any marks, scratches, traces, stains, possible lethal weapons, or objects that could have been used as such. Determining the time of death is very important as it can affect a suspect's alibi. The medical examiner can now more easily determine time of death by taking the victim's liver temperature. When the crime scene is a vehicle, both the inside and the outside of the vehicle must be carefully scrutinized, along with the surrounding area, for possible clues or evidence.

Checklist

The scene of the crime
Time of day
Condition of location where crime was committed
Signs of a fight
Documents, letters, notebooks, address books, will, insurance policy, photographs, mementos, reading material, news clips
Telephone calls made
Wounds on the victim
Position of victim
Condition of clothing of victim
Check of closets, drawers, furniture
Background on victim
Known family, associates, friends of victim
Blood spatterings
Weapon used in commission of crime
Physical, trace, and impression evidence gathered
Interrogation of witnesses
Possible suspects
Motive

INFORMATIONAL SOURCES TO INVESTIGATE

In writing a detective novel, screenplay, or teleplay, your investigator can't have clues just dropping into his or her lap out of the clear blue sky. Some clues or leads are usually discovered at the scene of the crime, but the writer must make his or her investigator work for more clues and leads in order to unseat the culprit and solve the crime. How does your investigator go about it? Well, there's always a possible witness or tipster, of course, but that's very convenient. Best to make the investigator work a little. Listed below are some of the people your investigator might talk to and some of the places and things he or she might sift through to pick up some valuable information needed to advance the plot and fill in some of the empty spaces.

People to Talk to About the Suspect, Victim, or Witness

Cab driver
Doorman
Switchboard operator
Secretary
Co-worker
Family members
Former spouse or lover
Street informants
Friends of victim or suspect
Banker
Bookie
Maid
Poolman
Gardener
Auto mechanic
Waiter or waitress
Former schoolmate
Teacher or college professor
Stock broker
Religious leader
Attorney
Travel agent
Country club, yacht club, private club
Bartender

Places to Check Out for Information About Suspect, Victim, or Witness

School class book
Newspaper morgue

Police records
Home
Office
Airlines
Hotels
Bank accounts
Bank vaults
Home safe
Mail
Old letters
Diary
Old shopping lists
Bills, paid and unpaid
Personal effects
Storage
Vehicle
Telephone and address book
Clothing, labels, cleaning marks
Appointment pad
Discarded papers in wastebasket
Files and records
Old and new photographs
Memoirs
Business cards collected
Awards, plaques
Legal papers (bankruptcy, divorce, change of name, etc.)
Stock certificates, bonds
Checkbook
I.O.U.'s
Unfinished correspondence
Unopened packages
Article that is apparently missing from normal place
Luggage stickers, tags
Passport (where traveled last)
Possible hiding places
Article moved from usual position
Garage
Lockers (gym, club)
Key ring for unusual key
Membership cards
Signet ring, medallions, religious medals
Strange markings, symbols

Medications
Mismatches (something that doesn't belong)
Threatening letters
Telephone answering service or recorder
Telephone bill (long-distance calls)
Receipts
Parking tickets (police, parking lots)
Cigarette butts, cigar butts, pipe tobacco
Signs of a visitor
Recent repair made

11

Surveillance

One of the most important elements of police work is *surveillance*, the act of shadowing, tailing, photographing, or listening in on a suspect, accomplice, or possible witness to observe and obtain information. Police officers and investigators conduct surveillance in order to:

Detect possible criminal activity.

Prevent or obtain evidence of a crime.

Discover or obtain information relating to possible accomplices, witnesses, location of evidence, to the crime.

TAILING OR SHADOWING

There are basically three types of shadowing or tailing techniques. One is employed generally to learn the habits, contacts, and associates of the suspect. Another is where the suspect must be followed despite the fact that the suspect may be aware of his "shadow," or where a witness is covered in order to protect the witness from harm.

Tailing or shadowing might be done by one individual or by teams alternating at various points so that the suspect does not become aware of one individual or one particular vehicle constantly present.

Tailing or shadowing is done on foot, by a vehicle or a number of different vehicles, airplane or helicopter, and by various forms of electronic surveillance.

TELEPHONE TAPS

Telephone tapping is probably the easiest form of electronic eavesdropping, as it takes no special skill and can be accomplished with common sense and a dime-store screwdriver. A court order is required to authorize a tap.

Following are the three means of telephone tapping:

A pick-up device that is not connected to the telephone.

A direct tap that is installed inside the instrument itself or between the instrument and the main telephone exchange.

A wireless FM or VHF radio receiver.

All of these means can be fed into a simple tape recorder.

The range of a tap that is wired into the instrument is naturally limited to the length of the connecting wires and can usually be detected by a physical search of the premises.

A **wireless tap** has an approximate range, depending on the transmitter, of one hundred yards to three miles. It is a simple device to install and can be detected by a radio-signal aid.

A **bug** wired into the room is also limited to the length of the wire; its microphone is connected to the recorder by wire. This method requires a bit more skill to put in place; however, the sound that is reproduced is of a much better quality.

A **wireless bug** is simple to conceal, and depending on the strength of the transmitter, has an excellent range of a hundred yards to a mile.

A **roaming wired bug** is quite sensitive and can easily be concealed upon one's person. It is usually difficult to detect. A **roaming wireless bug** is very similar to the aforementioned one.

The last type of device is a **combined telephone tap and room bug**. Its range is determined by the distance of the telephone service in use. What is unique about this setup is that the telephone number can be dialed from anywhere to pick up the conversation on the phone and in the room as well. Only a physical search can reveal it, and it must be switched on to be able to be detected.

Bugs vary in size, some being as small as a microchip.

ELECTRONIC SURVEILLANCE EQUIPMENT

Jammer
Scrambler
Decoder
Tap detectors
Recorder
Shotgun or rifle microphones
Receivers
Monitor
Transmitter
Phone tap
Attaché recorders
Bumper beepers
Pocket bug
Room bug
Wall listeners
Parabolic reflectors
Electronic stethoscope
Snake electronic keyhole listener

OTHER FORMS OF SURVEILLANCE

Stakeouts
Tailing
Photographic
Undercover
Telescopic
Nightscope
Videotaping

POLICE VEHICLES

Marked patrol cars
Unmarked patrol cars
Photographic unit
Patrol wagon
Motorcycles
Electronic surveillance vehicles

POLICE TECHNICAL AND SCIENTIFIC SERVICES

IDENTIFICATION SECTION
Fingerprint investigation
Plaster casting
Crime-scene photography
Evidence pickup and delivery
Identi-Kit
Crime-scene video recording
Crime-scene investigations

PHOTOGRAPHIC LABORATORY
Rush mug pictures
Technical photography
Evidence photography

CRIMINALISTICS LABORATORY
Trace evidence serology
Polygraph examinations
Firearm identification
Questioned-documents examinations
Breathalyzer calibration and repair service
Toxicology
Narcotics and dangerous drugs

12

The Police Crime Lab

Most police crime labs cover all areas of the scientific aspects of crime solving. These areas include fingerprints, ballistics, toxicology, examination of laundry and cleaning markings, hair and fibers, tracing materials and dyes, stains, traces and chemical analysis, casts and moldings, impressions, typewriter and handwriting analysis and identification, problems with documents, writing inks, examination of paper, comparisons, photographs, etc.

Police labs are designed for large police departments and are usually broken down into a number of sections. These represent a typical breakdown, which may vary from one city to another. In small cities or municipalities, many of these divisions may be combined or eliminated and the work sent out for processing.

Trace evidence
Serology
Crime-scene investigation section
Firearms section
Questioned documents
Photographic lab
Instrument section, covering design and construction of an apparatus
Toxicology
Narcotics and dangerous drugs

CHEMICAL EXAMINATIONS

Toxics
Explosives
Specimen comparisons
Unknown specimens
Narcotics
Incendiary and inflammables

BIOLOGICAL

Blood samples
Urine
Semen
Saliva
Hair and fiber
DNA typing

MARKINGS IDENTIFICATION

Tire impressions
Foot impressions
Fingerprints, handprints
Clothing markings
Personal effects
Trace evidence (glass, lenses, auto parts, paint)

FIREARMS IDENTIFICATION

Identification of cartridges, bullets, shells
Firearms
Distance and trajectory
Locks, keys, tool markings

DOCUMENTS SECTION

Handwriting analysis
Typewriters
Paper identification
Copiers

Indented writing (still relatively rare)
Writing instruments
Erasures

PHOTOGRAPHIC

Microphotography
Infrared photography
Ultraviolet photography
Radio photography
Contrast and filter

Science and technology move at such a rapid pace that it would be virtually impossible to list the most recent technological equipment being used in crime labs of law-enforcement agencies. It is therefore recommended that the writer contact the law-enforcement agency you are using in your story for an update on the equipment now available.

13

Identification Sources

- Albums (family, picture, class books)
- Auto licenses
- Bank books
- Biographies
- Birth certificates
- Birthmarks
- Bills and invoices
- Books
- Bracelets (I.D.)
- Business cards
- Charge accounts (stores, restaurants, purchases)
- Checks
- Church membership
- Club membership
- Clothing tags (manufacturers)
- College records
- Court records
- Credit cards
- Criminal records
- Dental records
- Eyeglasses and case
- Fingerprint records
- Family Bible

Hearing aid
Inscriptions
Laundry and dry-cleaning marks
Matchbooks
Medical records
Military records
Mortuary records
Office records
Passport records
Real-estate records
Repair receipts
Sales slips
School records
Social security records
Voting records
Welfare records

14

Arson Investigation

Arson is the malicious and willful burning of a private home, farm, or business structure. If it endangers the lives of persons as well as the property itself, most states provide for separate punishment under their laws pertaining to arson. The term *burning* need not imply the total destruction of the structure, but merely the ignition of the structure.

It is important to note that if the structure is used as a dwelling, it is classified as *inhabited*, although it is not necessary that a person be occupying the structure at the time the arson is committed. It is essential that *malice* or *criminal intent* be shown to conclude that arson has been committed.

In an investigation where arson is suspected, the investigator must establish evidence that the act of arson has been committed, physical evidence of a burning, criminal design such as an incendiary device, by the unexplained reason for the presence of inflammables or by an eyewitness. To this the investigator would attempt to add any other evidence to support the act of arson, such as any articles associated with arson and the suspect, linking the suspect to the scene, and evidence showing intent. Motives such as revenge, economic gain, and insurance fraud, as well as pyromania, would be investigated.

Pyromania types vary, but among those considered pyromaniacs are sexual deviants who derive sexual stimulation by starting a fire and abnormal or mentally disturbed people who seek some sort of hero status by setting the fire and alerting the fire department. Many of these individuals harbor secret desires to be firemen and then attempt a daring and dramatic rescue.

Following are *Liquid agents* with incendiary properties:

Alcohol
Benzol
Gasoline
Ether
Kerosene

Solids with incendiary properties include:

Coal dust
Grain

These substances burn quickly when mixed with air and ignited. Substances that burn upon contact with water are:

Sodium
Potassium
Calcium carbide

Oxidizing agents that when decomposing aid combustion include:

Nitric acid
Potassium permanganate in contact with glycerine
Quicklime mixed with water
Chlorates
Metallic peroxides

These are just a few among the many oxidizing agents that cause combustion. It is virtually impossible to list all contributors to a fire, for one would have to include electrical shorts of various kinds, causing a stove or flue to become a hazard, igniting oil-soaked rags, etc. This list could fill a book of its own.

MOTIVES FOR ARSON

To conceal a previous crime
To destroy company books or records
Revenge
To defraud an insurance company

Intimidation
Sabotage
Business rivalry
Thrill
Murder
Extortion

For additional information on arson, contact the arson squad of your local police or fire department.

15

Missing Persons

A *missing person* is not to be confused with a *wanted person*, although the police department is concerned with the location and identification of both. A *wanted person* is someone being sought by the police in connection with a crime, whereas a person considered *missing* is:

Someone missing for more than twenty-four hours

Someone missing less than twenty-four hours who is under the age of eighteen

Someone who has disappered without any apparent reason

Someone who is mentally deficient or not in full possession of all his or her faculties

An unidentified body

Although the police department's Missing Persons Bureau will attempt to do all in its power to locate a juvenile runaway who is reported as missing, their primary concern with a missing juvenile is whether or not the subject has involuntarily disappeared. The same applies to adults, except those who are reported missing and are not considered to be in full possession of their faculties. Determining the identity of a Jane Doe or a John Doe, which are the names given to unidentified female and male corpses, is also a responsibility of the Missing Persons Bureau.

Crimes usually associated with missing persons are:

Kidnapping
Homicide
Suicide

Those involved in attempting to locate a missing person should learn all they can about the following:

The physical description of the missing person
Hobbies, interests, personal habits
Educational background
Romantic involvements
Addictions
Sexual habits
Medical history
Family history
Personal relationships
Business and professional abilities or associations
Access to funds

STEPS IN ATTEMPTING TO IDENTIFY A JANE DOE OR A JOHN DOE

Check Missing Persons records.

Check fingerprints locally and send to state identification bureau and FBI.

Take photographs and distribute to TV and newspapers.

Identify clothing markings, labels, etc.

Examine remains for birthmarks, tattoos, scars caused by surgery or accident.

Make impressions of teeth for possible dental identification.

Take X-rays to determine presence of any illness or broken bones, or evidence of surgery.

Perform chemical analysis to determine whether drugs are present, to find information about last food ingested, and to check for evidence of poisons.

16

Investigation of a Burglary

Burglary is the entering of a premises for the purpose of committing a theft and is considered the most common form of theft. Remember that some jurisdictions distinguish between entering a dwelling at night and *housebreaking*, so the definition of *burglary* varies in different states. *Housebreaking* is simply the unlawful entering of a building with intent to commit a crime. To consider a housebreaking a burglary, the following elements must be established:

Breaking and entering occurred
The act took place at night
The dwelling belonged to another person
The offender's intent was to commit a crime therein

TYPES OF BURGLARIES

SAFE:

Rip Job: Using an electric drill and crowbar, a hole is made in upper- or lower-left corner. A bar is placed in the hole and the door is jimmied open.

Punch Job: Using a sledge and center punch, the dial is knocked off with a hammer, and the punch is held against the spindle and hit sharply. If the safe has tumblers at the end of the spindle, then the small sockets are broken when the spindle is forced back and the lock is released. Some safes are punchproof when the tumblers are off spindle.

Chopping: The safe is turned upside down to expose the bottom, the weakest section. A hole is made and a jimmy applied to permit access.

Carry Out: The safe is merely physically removed.

Click Job: Using a stethoscope and listening for the clicks as the combination falls into place.

Blow Job: Blowing the safe by using an explosive charge, usually a plastique.

Loft: Specialize in stealing from lofts.

Store: Late evening. Some, window smashers.

Residence and Private Dwelling: Day: Operates during daylight hours. Night: After dark.

Supper: As named, often while residents are having dinner.

Commuter: Usually from city, operates in suburbs.

Delivery Truck: Stealing from a van making a delivery.

Miscellaneous:
Bellhops
Maids
Elevator operators

17

Sex Offenses

Sex offenses include rape, molestation, child molestation, carnal knowledge, marital rape, sodomy, and other perverted sexual acts by either sex.

Rape is the act of having sexual intercourse without the consent and voluntary permission of the other party. The act of having sexual intercourse with a juvenile under circumstances wherein consent is implied is called *carnal knowledge* or *statutory rape.*

An individual may be found guilty of rape, assault with intent to commit rape, or attempt to commit rape if that individual aided, encouraged, or incited another to commit rape, or if that individual shared the intent, regardless of not having had intercourse with the victim.

ATTEMPT TO COMMIT RAPE

To charge the accused with an *attempt to commit rape,* one must prove the occurrence of an overt act wherein the offender proceeded far enough to demonstrate that the act of rape would have taken place if not for some intervention.

ASSAULT WITH INTENT TO COMMIT RAPE

Assault with intent to commit rape is a lesser charge than attempt, in that no overt act other than a threat took place. However, even if no physical force was employed but a weapon was present, the weapon could be considered to be a threat and/or a means of force.

CHECKLIST FOR THE INVESTIGATOR

Age of victim.
Marital status.
Employment.
Location of offense.
Places victim visited prior to rape.
Persons seen prior to offense.
Physical force used.
Weapon employed.
Resistance offered by victim.
Description of assailant(s).
Previous assaults on victim, if any.
Medical examination of victim and report on same.

18

Larceny

Anyone who steals, or wrongfully obtains by any means, any possession or article of value of another person, and who has no intention of ever returning same to that other person, is guilty of *larceny.*

The investigator must prove that the accused or suspect has wrongfully obtained and withheld the property specified by the party issuing the complaint, and that said property was indeed the property of the complainant. In addition, the alleged value of the property and the intent to permanently withhold it must be confirmed.

AUTO THEFT

When a vehicle is stolen, used, and then abandoned, the motive is temporary use, and the term for the charge is *temporary appropriation.* In most instances, temporary appropriation is caused by juveniles, joy riders, and professional criminals seeking to use a vehicle in the commission of a crime so that their own vehicle would not be identified in the getaway should there be a witness.

The real auto thief steals to profit from the vehicle he or she has stolen, either reselling the vehicle or stripping it and selling the parts. Although some thieves jump the ignition, most professionals resort to master keys, a punch device called a *code cutter* that makes blank keys based on the ignition code number. Another device used is referred to as a *slapper.* This device pulls out the ignition cylinder, allowing the thief to insert a replacement that is already equipped with the proper ignition key.

Included under larceny are:

Pickpockets
Lush workers (those who prey on drunks)
Bag stealers or muggers
Baggage thieves
Shoplifters
Hotel thieves
Credit-card thieves
Embezzlers
Those receiving stolen goods
Loan sharks
Computer theft and fraud
Confidence games
Art frauds
Securities frauds

CONFIDENCE GAMES

Con men have such a wide variety of swindles that it would be impossible to describe them all, particularly because new cons are being thought up every day. And since many cons might also easily fall under the category of fraud, stock manipulation, embezzlement, and other larcenous crimes, we will offer a small sampling of out-and-out cons that have been around for some time.

One of the oldest cons is known as the *money-making machine.* The con shows his victim a machine that has come into his possession, a machine that, as he demonstrates, actually produces dollar bills. The machine is sold to the victim, or the victim is asked to invest in the production of more machines like it.

The *inheritance* is a scam in which the victim is told he or she has come into an inheritance of some famous person or some extremely well-known millionaire, but that money is needed for litigation and proving the victim's right to his or her portion of the estate.

In a con involving *hot merchandise,* the victim is approached to buy something of great value: a fur, jewels, etc., the victim being led to believe that the merchandise has been stolen. In reality, the merchandise is inferior, and if the victim calls the police, all the perpetrator can be accused of is peddling without a license.

The *just-a-few-dollars-more* scam is usually performed by a scam artist who is content with picking up some small change, even though he or she can usually garner between a hundred and two hundred dollars a day. Appearing well groomed, friendly, and keenly intent on the merchandise he or she selects in a small but expensive retail shop, the perpetrator offers to pay for the merchandise by personal check and have it delivered to an address, after, of course, the check has cleared. As the salesperson happily writes up the order, the perp, about to write the check, suddenly realizes he left his cash at home and needs at least twenty or thirty dollars to get through the day. Could he write the check out for just a little more than the amount of the sale? Since the sale garners a sizable figure (as does the commission), and since the merchandise won't be shipped until the check clears, the customer is usually granted his or her wish. The perp leaves the store with the extra cash, never planning to receive the merchandise anyway, as the shipping address is a phony.

Phony airline tickets produce hundreds of millions of dollars in losses to many major carriers, and hundreds of millions in profits to the counterfeiters of airline tickets, who easily dispose of the bogus tickets to greedy travelers who think they're buying a discounted legitimate ticket.

The *pyramid* is one of those get-rich-quick scams that is motivated by greed by people who are promised big gains by investing in a short term investment. The scam artist develops a reputation for delivering when the first customer gets his or her money plus a substantial profit back, thus becoming a walking advertisement for the scam artist's plot. Once the chain begins, the new investors begin getting back less and less, as the scam artist pockets the difference from the investors without actually investing a dime, until the pyramid eventually comes tumbling down. The Pyramid scam was conceived by a master of the game, Charles Ponzi, in the 1920s and is sometimes referred to as the *Ponzi Scam.*

Computer scams are becoming more and more common. As computers become more sophisticated, so do computer crooks, who steal everything from invaluable software programs to billions of dollars in stocks and bonds to company and government secrets, and who alter credit-card billings, switch bank accounts, transfer funds illegally, alter records, produce false billings, and authorize false loans and payments.

Film piracy, record piracy, and *piracy of home videos* are also on the upswing, with major studios, independent producers, record companies, as home video tapes are being pirated and sold at huge discounts. Usually those involved in these piracies are employees who have access to the original print or master and see an opportunity to pick up some hefty extra cash by making deals with organized crime, who are capable of mass distribution of the pirated films and tapes.

Some of the largest money-producing scams are the many offers made through *mail-order ads* placed in the backs of magazines and those sent through the mail. Some of these mail-order scams offer products or services that are either not worth the money they're being offered for or are nonexistent. Among the most predominant and successful mail frauds are notifications that "you have been selected to appear in a new edition of 'Who's Who' in something- or someplace-or-other for a minimal insertion fee, or a notice that a subscription or service you had subscribed to (one you can't recall subscribing to) is now about to run out and you now have just thirty days to renew before the offer is withdrawn.

One of the slickest scams is to prey upon those who have just lost a wife, husband, son, or daughter by notifying the bereaved relative by mail or in person that the deceased party had, prior to his or her demise, ordered a Bible or some article that had been personalized or monogrammed and that it is now ready for delivery. Naturally, having no way of checking with the deceased about the order, and believing the obligation should be fulfilled, the bereaved accepts the article and usually pays a pretty sum for the merchandise, which had never been ordered.

Hundreds of scams, some old and some new, are perpetrated on the public every day. These are just a few samples of the work of con men and bunco artists. A telephone call or a visit to the Bunco Squad of your local police department or further selected research reading should provide you with a host of other larcenous scams.

19

Robbery

One of the leading forms of major crime is *robbery,* and many of the criminals involved in robberies specialize in robbing persons, stores, or premises. Although the following list offers some of the types of robberies committed, the list is by no means intended to be complete, as the variety of types are too vast to be encompassed in this chapter.

TYPES

Banks
Bank messengers
Stores (liquor, grocery, restaurants)
Gas stations
Gambling games
Casual strollers
Payroll clerks
Truck drivers
Cab drivers
Residences
Armored cars
Restaurants

TYPES OF WEAPONS USED IN ARMED ROBBERY

Revolver
Automatic
Machine gun
Shotgun
Blackjack
Knife

METHODS

Threats
Assault
Binding
Drugging
Beating

OBJECTS

Money
Jewelry
Merchandise
Credit cards
Articles of clothing (furs, etc.)

CRIMES COMMITTED IN ADDITION TO ROBBERY

Rape
Murder

20

Smuggling

The smuggling of illegal and dangerous drugs, weapons, aliens, works of art, currency, jewels, industrial products, antiques, national treasures, stolen or unauthorized documents, food, plants, animals, and unauthorized medications into or out of the United States is a serious criminal problem that threatens the health, economy, well-being, and safety of this nation and its citizens.

CONCEALMENT OF OBJECTS

In most cases, those involved in smuggling are extremely creative in their means of hiding and transporting whatever or whomever it is they are smuggling. The following list includes possible hiding places, depending, of course, on the size, shape, and the person or object being smuggled. Those involved in *the smuggling of objects* use false or concealed compartments in:

Luggage
Crates
Barrels
Books
Building materials
Film canisters
Cameras

Clothing
Kitchen equipment
Picture frames
Hearing aids
Industrial machinery
Musical instruments
Airplanes
Automobiles (doors, fenders, bumpers, truck, undercarriage, etc.)
Trucks, vans, campers (same as above)
Shipping containers
Merchandise such as TV sets, recorders, furniture, bottles, jars, vases, furniture, household appliances, etc.
Imported or exported art objects, vehicles, machine parts, canned or boxed food products
Coffins
Cremation urns
Religious artifacts or objects
Paintings (as part of same)
Dead bodies
Crevices of an individual's anatomy
Wheelchairs, canes, crutches, casts, bandaged areas
Small children, the elderly, or the disabled

CONCEALMENT OF INDIVIDUALS

The smuggling of individuals or groups of individuals is usually done with the aid of private airplanes, boats, ships, yachts, trucks, campers, vans, automobiles (trunks), in barrels, shipping containers, and by whatever other means individuals can be transported. Occasionally, more creative devices have been employed, such as flying aliens in with false passports and visas.

SUSPICIOUS PERSONS

Suspected smugglers, as creative and as professional as they may be, often give customs agents a reason to suspect their activities, such as:

Exhibiting a lifestyle inconsistent with a claimed occupation.
A passenger acting on behalf of someone who has paid cash for airfare supposedly being used for business.
An international carrier employee (ground crew, baggage handler,

cargo handler, freight forwarder) who seldom takes time off or insists on working the same shift coinciding with a particular flight.

Persons who constantly purchase small quantities of gasoline for vehicles as their vehicles might possibly have a modified gas tank used to transport contraband.

Persons depositing unusually large sums of cash in banks.

Persons requesting hotel or motel rooms with a view of the customs lane.

Persons who appear to be too much in a hurry.

Persons who have a difficult time looking an agent in the eye.

Individuals with children who tell their children to go on board ahead.

Persons paying cash for rental vehicles.

The purchasing of large amounts of masking (or similar) tape or plastic bags.

Suspicious vehicles visiting or frequenting a residence at all hours of day and night.

Persons doing excessive travel in and out of the United States when they have no visible means of support.

Persons doing business strictly on a cash basis requiring no receipts.

Persons having modifications or special compartments in their vehicles.

Private aircraft owners making frequent trips out of the country for recreational purposes or for no apparent reason.

Persons receiving large amounts of mail from outside the United States, especially from Colombia, Peru, Thailand, Brazil, and Pakistan.

Persons operating currency exchanges from private residences or personal vehicles.

AMONG AIRCRAFT AND AT AIRFIELDS

Passenger seats missing from plane.

Windows of aircraft curtained or covered.

Numerous boxes, duffle bags, plastic bags, other containers inside aircraft.

Aircraft flying or landing after dark without lights.

Trucks, campers, vans, often equipped with radios for use in contacting aircraft, waiting at or near area suitable for aircraft landings.

Landing at provisional runways in desolate area lit by vehicle headlights, signal fires, or lanterns.

Refueling from fifty-five-gallon drums or from back of pickup truck.

Paint chips, muddy wheels, dusty aircraft, or other evidence of operating from dirt strips.

Strong or unusual odors emanating from aircraft that might be used to cover scent of marijuana.

Aircraft with new paint, added doors, extra fuel tanks, or false or altered registration numbers.

Pilot or passengers reluctant to leave aircraft when being fueled or serviced.

Pilot or passengers displaying large amount of cash for making servicing payment.

AT MARINAS OR ON THE WATER

Boats purchased with large cash payments.

Demands for electronic equipment or repairs without regard to cost.

Purchase of heavy-duty trailers that have load capacities far in excess of weight of boat.

Boats specifically designed as sport fishers that have no sign of fishing gear.

Boats with changes in internal configuration such as raised deck, no access to bilges, added or modified fuel tanks, concealed compartments, or modified bulkheads.

Boats with false water line.

Improper or false registration.

Boats riding low in the water.

Boats running at night without lights.

Observing transfer of cargo from one boat to another at sea.

Communications between boat and short vehicle by unusual means, such as lights flashing, flags, etc.

AT CHECKPOINTS

Baggage with special or concealed compartments.

Bulky clothing.

Secreted somewhere on person (belt, undergarment, in anal passageway, in false teeth, inside pen, pencil, wristwatch, ring, hatband, radio, cassette player, pocket recorder).
On or in deceased person or in secreted coffin compartment.
Attached to pet.
Inside pet cage or pen.
Sewn into garment or in lining.
Carried by infant or minor.

21

Weapons Used in Commission of a Crime

Pistol
Automatic
Revolver
Rifle
Knife
Poison
Garrote
Bayonet
Bola
Bomb
Brass knuckles
Zip gun
Shotgun
Sawed-off shotgun
Six-shooter
Bow and arrow
Dart
Poison dart
Slingshot
Rock or hard object
Fire
Sword
Chain

Rope
Gas
Gasoline
Flame thrower
Grenade
Molotov cocktail
Machine gun
Acid
Drug o.d.
Billy club
Cutlass
Air gun
Ax
Tomahawk
Ice pick
Hammer
Gaff
Hook
Blackjack
Bazooka
Javelin
Broadsword
Vehicle

22

Explosives

Grenade
Nipple time bomb
Incendiary bomb
Magnifying-glass bomb
Alarm-clock bomb
Booby trap
Molotov cocktail
Bangalore torpedo
Nitroglycerin
T.N.T.
Plastique
Blasting gelatin
Dynamite

For detailed information regarding lethal weapons and the quantities constructed, read *The Anarchist Cookbook,* published by Lyle Stuart, New York, 1971.

23

Firearms and Manufacturers

Although there are literally thousands of types, calibers, and manufacturers of handguns and shoulder weapons available, in most instances, law-enforcement agencies and criminals rely primarily on handguns (nonautomatic) and automatic weapons, which include handguns, machine pistols, machine guns, and automatic rifles. The nonautomatic handgun can either be a *single-shot type,* which is manually loaded, fired, and reloaded, or a *revolver,* which has a rotating cylinder that could contain anywhere from four to twelve cartridges and can fire as many shots as the cylinder contains cartridges without having to reload. In revolver and single-shot handguns, the cartridge casing usually remains in the weapon after it has been fired, as opposed to the semi- or fully automatic weapons, in which case the cartridge casing is automatically ejected.

Automatic weapons, as implied, fire in succession for as long a time as the trigger is depressed and there are cartridges in the ammo clip. The semi-automatic (and many automatics can also be fired on semiautomatic) only fires one shot each time the trigger is pulled.

Almost all small arms, automatic, and semi-automatic firearms are rifled weapons, meaning that the rifling in the barrel of the weapon has spiraled grooves that are cut into the barrel, giving the bullet a stable trajectory when fired. Most shotguns are smooth bored, having no spiraled grooves in the barrel of the weapon.

Rimfire and centerfire ammunition. In rimfiring ammo, the primer is positioned in the rim of the base of the cartridge (in most cases in .22 calibers), while centerfire ammo has the primer positioned in the center of the base of the cartridge. Most small arms use centerfire ammunition.

Whereas most law-enforcement agencies use standard weapons issued to their department or agency, criminals use whatever type of weapon they personally prefer. Should the reader be planning to describe the weapons used by a particular law-enforcement agency, the author suggests the reader confer with that law-enforcement agency to see what weapons are issued to them and under what circumstances.

As stated earlier, there are literally thousands of types of firearms, models, and manufacturers, making it impossible to list each make and model. The following list is just a sampling of weapons available:

HANDGUNS-REVOLVERS

Ruger Bearcat .22
Ruger GP 100-.357
Smith & Wesson .44 Russian
Smith & Wesson .44 Magnum
Smith & Wesson .25
Colt 1917 GI
Smith & Wesson Brazillian
NAA (North American Arms) .22 LR
Springfield
Springfield (army)
Smith & Wesson N-Frame .44 Special
Smith & Wesson Police .686
Smith & Wesson .38/44
Dan Wesson .44 Magnum
Dan Wesson .22 Magnum
Dan Wesson .41 Magnum
Mathieu
Mauser
J. C. Higgins
Browning

HANDGUNS-AUTOMATIC AND SEMIAUTOMATIC

Charter—.38 undercover
Colt—Police .45
Lugar 7.65, 9mm Parabellum
357 Magnum (various)
Walther GSP

Webley (British)
Remington
Singer
U. S. General Officers M15—Rock Island Arsenal
Beretta Pistola Automatica—9mm
Beretta (short)—9mm
Beretta Pistola Automatica Brevetto—7.65mm
Walther .38
Walther PP
Walther PPK
Mauser-Werke HSc 7.65
Mauser C96
Heckler & Koch 9mm Parabellum and 7.65 Parabellum
Sauer P38
Browning 1910 Police 7.65mm auto, 9mm short
Makarov
Coonan
SIG-Sauer

MACHINE GUNS-AUTOMATIC AND SEMIAUTOMATIC
Calico 100
Plainfield
Universal
Uzi
AK 47
Colt AR-15
Ruger Mini 14
Barrett
British Lanchester
British Sterling
Sten
Pistola Mitragliatrice
OVP (Villa Perosa)
H & K .91, MPs, MPK5
Harrison & Richards
Thompson

RIFLES, CARBINES, AND SHOTGUNS
Browning rifle, auto-rifle
Calico
Enfield
F.A.L.N. (assault rifle)
Harrison & Richards (bolt action, carbine, ultra-auto)

J. C. Higgins
Martin
Mauser
Plainfield
Remington (rifle, carbine)
Universal (autoload carbine)
Winchester (rifle, carbine)
Kar 98k
Gewehr 98/40
Armlite (carbine)
Savage (shotgun, rifle)
Weatherby Fibermark (rifle)
Ruger
Sauer
Shiloh

TERMS USED IN FIREARMS IDENTIFICATION

Accuracy: The accuracy of firearms varies, depending on contributing conditions. The barrel must be as near perfect as possible. It must be of uniform size of bore its entire length, and the grooves of the rifling must be of uniform width and depth throughout without any defects. The fit of the bullet is of utmost importance. The bullet must be of correct size (diameter), hardness, density, and lubrication. The powder charge must be exactly the same for any cartridge. The primers also must have a uniform amount of priming composition.

Bluing: The colored finish of the metal parts of guns—in various parts of guns in various shades: black, blue, and brown.

Bolt: The part of the breech-loading rifle that pushes the cartridge into position and locks the mechanism to prevent its opening on discharge.

Breech: Rear part of a firearm, behind the bore.

Breech Block: The part of the breech-loading mechanism that closes the breech and receives the backward pressure of the explosion.

Buck and Ball: A cartridge with a round ball and three buckshot.

Buckshot: Lead shot, often used for riot control.

Bullet Shell: An explosive bullet with a bursting charge in a tube.

Bullets, Cannelured: An elongated bullet with grooves around it.

These grooves are used for holding the lubricant or for crimping purposes.

Bullet, Elongated: Longer than it is wide; the opposite of the round bullet.

Bullet, Flat-point: A bullet with a flat nose.

Bullet, Hollow-point: One with a hollow point for the purpose of increasing the mushrooming effect upon impact.

Bullet, Metal-case: A bullet with a jacket of metal that completely encases the nose.

Bullet, Metal-point: A bullet having lead-bearing and metal tip.

Bullet, Soft-point: A metal-cased bullet with a tip of lead, which enables it to mushroom on impact, thereby increasing the striking energy.

Bullet, Wad-cutter: A bullet that is almost cylindrical in shape with a flat top. Specially adapted to target shooting, as it cuts a clean-edged hole.

Bull's Eye: The center of the target or a shot that hits the center.

Butt: The rear portion of the gunstock, which is placed against the shoulder in firing.

Caliber: Diameter of the hole in the barrel, and in rifled arms, diameter of this hole before rifling, expressed in decimal fractions of an inch.

Cannon: Ordnance or artillery.

Carbine: A short-barreled rifle.

Cartridge: The container for an explosive charge, which may or may not include the bullet. The modern cartridge is placed in the gun, ready to fire. Early cartridges were broken, the contents emptied into the chamber or barrel.

Cartridge Case: A metal container for the explosive charge.

Catch: A part of the mechanism for holding another part in a desired position, as the bayonet catch, safety catch, locking catch, etc.

Center-Fire Cartridge: One in which the priming composition is in a cap in the center of the base of the case.

Centimeter: The 1/100 part of a meter, or 0.3937 of an inch. An inch is the equivalent of 2.540 centimeters.

Chamber: The rear end of the barrel; this end receives the shell or cartridge.

Clip: A device for holding several cartridges together so that they may be loaded simultaneously in the gun.

Cock: (1) The movable portions of the firing mechanism, corresponding to the hammer on modern guns. (2) To place the cock in position ready to fire.

Combustion: Burning of the powder in the barrel.

Corrosion: The deterioration of the inside of the barrel case by the chemical action of the products of combustion after firing, usually due to neglect.

Crimping: A mechanical operation used in loading metallic cartridges; done by compressing the mouth of the metallic shell or case to hold the bullet in place. Applied also to shot shells.

Cylinder: The chambered, breech part of a gun that revolves around an axis to expose the cartridges successively for firing.

Double-Action: A term that refers to a revolver that is cocked and fired when the trigger is pressed.

Drift: A term that denotes the lateral deviation of the flight of the bullet from its vertical plane with the axis of the bore from which the bullet is fired.

Ejector: A device that throws out the fixed cartridge case, or a firearm equipped with such a device.

Firearms Identification: Deals with the characteristic features of various arms and ammunition by which units may be identified. It is a branch of forensic science/criminalistics often employed in criminal cases involving the use of firearms. Every firearm has individual characteristics. These are transmitted to or imprinted on the bullets and shells. Characteristics can be definitely established by comparison with a test bullet or shell fired from the particular weapon using special instruments, such as the *comparison microscope.*

Firing Pin: That part of the firing mechanism that strikes the cap or primer to explode the powder charge.

Flare Pistol: A large pistol used to fire flares for illumination or signaling.

Fulminate: An explosive substance or compound that ignites when struck, such as fulminate of mercury.

Gauge: The diameter of the bore of a gun, expressed in the number of balls of that diameter required to make a pound. Thus, a "12 gauge" gun is one with a diameter of such size that twelve balls of lead, each fitting the bore, weigh one pound. This is sometimes called "12 bore." Usually used in regard to shotguns.

Grooves: The cavities inside a rifle barrel, usually spiral, by which a bullet, when expanded and forced forward, receives a spinning motion, giving it an accurate flight.

Hair Trigger: A trigger requiring only a light touch for firing.

Hammer: The part of the mechanism that strikes the primer directly, or strikes the firing pin. In flintlock days, the frizzen was sometimes called a hammer.

Handgun: A hand-held firearm such as a pistol, automatic, or revolver.

High-Power: Military and sporting rifles using small caliber bullets driven by a large charge of smokeless powder.

Ignition: The setting on fire of the powder.

Impact: A blow. The force of a bullet striking an object.

Jacket: A covering for a bullet.

Lock: (1) The firing mechanism. (2) To set the safety to prevent firing.

Machine Gun: An automatic gun firing small-arms ammunition. In the American military sense, it refers to weapons fired from a mount, such as a bipod or a tripod; but Europeans tend to include automatic rifles under this classification.

Magazine: That part of a repeating firearm that holds cartridges to be fed into the gun.

Millimeter: Measurement used to designate caliber.

Muzzle: The mouth, or forward end, of a gun.

Muzzle Velocity: The velocity of a bullet at the muzzle.

Oval-Bore Rifling: A bore that is oval shaped, the oval being twisted to give the bullet a spinning motion. This was developed to take the place of lands and grooves. Most rifles with this feature were made by Lancaster of London around 1850.

Patch: A metal jacket for the bullet, or a small cleaning cloth.

Penetration: That which a bullet will pass through when fired from a specified length of barrel. Often expressed in inches.

Percentage of Pattern: Number of pellet marks in a thirty-inch circle over a forty-yard range, divided by the number of pellets in the load.

Percussion Cap: A small metal cup holding fulminate placed on the tube or nipple of a percussion gun. When struck, the sparks enter the barrel through a hold and fire the charge.

Pins: Pieces of iron or steel used to hold the barrel and stock together.

Pistol: Of a single-shot type, where the cartridge is inserted in the chamber at the near end of the barrel; or of the automatic type, where the cartridges are inserted in a clip in the butt or handle, and fired from one hand.

Pistol Carbine: A pistol that has a detachable shoulder stock so that it can be fired either from the hand or from the shoulder.

Powders: The powders used in loading are: black, semismokeless, and smokeless. Smokeless powders are divided into two types: the first is known as *bulk,* meaning that its charge corresponds, or nearly so, in bulk to the charge of black powder; the second is the *dense* type, which means that it is denser and of much less bulk.

Pressure: The force exerted in the cartridge chamber and bore of the barrel by the powder gasses. Usually described in pounds per square inch.

Primer: The percussion "cap" used to ignite the powder charge.

Priming Powder: The gunpowder in the pan used to set off the main charge.

Pump Gun: A repeating rifle, especially one with a lever suggestive of a pump handle.

Range: The distance to the target; the maximum distance a bullet will travel.

Recoil: The backward motion of a gun when fired, commonly called *kick.*

Repeater: A gun that can be fired several times without reloading; usually applied to rifles and carbines.

Rest: Any support to steady the gun during aiming and firing.

Revolver: (1) A firearm, usually a pistol, with cylinder of several chambers arranged to revolve on an axis and discharge the shots in succession. (2) A firearm with several barrels revolving about a common axis.

Rifle: A shoulder firearm having spiral grooves cut in its bore to give the bullet a spinning motion and thus, greater accuracy. It differs from a carbine in having greater length and weight.

Self-Loading: Semi-automatic; the fired cartridge is extracted and ejected, and a live cartridge is placed in position ready to fire.

Shell: The case for holding the charge for breech-loaders.

Shocking Power: The force delivered to the projectile on impact, the result brought about through combination of striking energy and penetration.

Shot: (1) A projectile. (2) Small pellets. (3) The number of bullets that can be fired without reloading.

Shotgun: A firearm intended for the use of a number of small pellets rather than a single bullet.

Sight: An aiming device on a gun, such as *telescopic sight, open sight,* etc.

Slide Action: The mechanism of a repeating rifle, operated by the manual movement of a slide under and parallel to the barrel.

Spherical Bullet: One that is a round ball.

Spiral Rifling: Cutting spiral grooves in the surface of the bore of the barrel of a gun.

Stock: The wooden part of a firearm; that portion that fits against the shoulder in firing.

Striker: A hammer or firing pin.

Stud: A projection on a gun for holding another part, such as the *bayonet stud* or the *sight stud.*

Swivel Gun: One fired from a swivel mount.

Take-Down Rifle: A firearm, the barrel of which can be readily taken from the action; employed for securing compactness in carrying the gun.

Trajectory: As applied to a bullet, the path of the bullet through the air.

Trigger: The part of the lock pulled by the finger to release the cock or hammer and fire the piece.

Trigger Guard: A metal loop or rectangle protecting the trigger.

Trigger Plate: The portion of the mechanism through which the trigger enters.

Trigger Pull: The amount of pressure necessary to release the trigger. Riflemen refer to this as a *one-pound pull* or a *two-pound pull,* i.e., requiring a pressure of one pound or two pounds to release the trigger. A hair-trigger pull is a very light pull; other terms are *creeping pull, dragging pull, still pull, hard pull, smooth pull, fine pull.*

Velocity: The speed of a projectile in its flight, designated in feet per second. The velocity of bullets fired from pistol and revolver barrels varies. The velocity of a bullet has an important relation to its trajectory, energy, range, stopping power, etc.

Wad: A yielding substance, usually of felt, placed over the powder of a shot shell for the purpose of controlling the gas blast.

Windage: The allowance made for drift of a bullet.

Wobble: The unsteady rotation or spin of a bullet; usually caused by insufficient twist in the rifle barrel.

24

List of Crimes

Abduction
Adultery
Affray
Aiding and abetting
Armed robbery
Arson
Assault
Auto theft
Battery
Bigamy
Blackmail
Bookmaking
Bootlegging
Bribery
Burglary
Compounding a felony
Concealment of birth or death
Conspiracy
Counterfeiting
Disorderly conduct
Disturbing the peace
Drunk driving
Drunkenness

Dueling
Embezzlement
Escape from lawful imprisonment
Extortion
False impersonation
False imprisonment
Forgery
Gambling
Grand larceny
Hijacking
Homicide
Illegal sale of arms
Impersonating an officer
Incest
Indecent exposure
Industrial espionage
Kidnapping
Larceny
Libel and slander
Littering
Loan sharking
Loitering
Manslaughter
Manslaughter, voluntary
Manslaughter, involuntary
Misconduct in office
Murder
Narcotics (sale, possession, smuggling)
Obstruction of justice
Perjury
Piracy
Prostitution
Rape
Rape, statutory
Receiving stolen goods
Resisting arrest
Rioting
Robbery
Sabotage
Slavery
Smuggling
Suicide

Swindling
Tampering with evidence
Trespassing
Unlawful assembly
Vandalism
Weapons (selling, carrying concealed, firing in public)
White slavery

CRIMES ASSOCIATED WITH POLITICS

Assassination
Bribery
Blackmail
Compounding a felony
Conspiracy
Cover-up
Embezzlement of government funds
Falsifying records
Fraud
Graft
High treason
Libel and slander
Malfeasance in office
Misuse of government funds
Perjury
Treason
Unauthorized destruction of public records

CRIMES ASSOCIATED WITH BUSINESS AND PROFESSIONS

Arson
Compounding a felony
Copyright or patent infringement
Counterfeiting
False advertising
False records or books
Hijacking
Illegal stock transactions

Industrial espionage
Insider trading
Mail fraud
Possession of stolen merchandise
Record piracy
Revealing privileged information
Sale of illegal goods
Sexual harassment
Tax fraud
Theft

DOMESTIC CRIMES

Assault
Battery
Child abandonment
Child abuse
Child molestation
Harassment
Husband beating
Incest
Marital rape
Mercy killing
Nonpayment of child support
Parent abuse
Wife beating

CRIMES ASSOCIATED WITH RACKETEERING (nonorganized)

Blackmail
Illegal siding business
Illegal stock-and-bond trading
Insurance frauds
Mail-order fraud
Phony accident claims
Phony land promotions
Phony mediums
Phony money-producing schemes

Protection extortion
Quack doctors
Shell games
Skimming
Swindling

25

Crime Glossary

Abduction: Taking a man's wife, child, or ward without his consent or consent of the parent or guardian, by fraud and persuasion, or by open violence, for the purpose of marriage or prostitution.

Adultery: In some states, voluntary sexual intercourse between persons, one of whom is lawfully married to another, both parties being guilty. Intercourse by a married person with one who is not his or her spouse, the married person only being guilty.

Affray: The fighting of two or more persons in some public place to the terror of the people. Not premeditated.

Arson: Willful and malicious burning, or causing to be burned, of a building or dwelling. There must be some burning, however slight, and the burning must be caused maliciously. Arson is a felony at common law.

Assault: An unlawful attempt or application of force and violence, to do a hurt to another.

(1) Common or simple assault is where there are no aggravating circumstances, for example, a blow delivered within striking distance but which does not reach its mark.

(2) Aggravated assault is committed with the intention of committing some additional crime. This includes assault with a deadly weapon. There must, to constitute a criminal assault, be at least an apparent ability to commit battery.

Battery: Assault by any force, however slight, applied to another person directly or indirectly.

Bigamy or polygamy: Committed where one, being legally married, marries another person during the life of his or her spouse.

Bribery: Receiving or offering any undue reward by or to any public official in order to influence any act or behavior in office.

Burglary: Breaking and entering the house of another with intent to commit a felony, whether the felony be actually committed or not. To constitute the crime:

(1) There must be an actual or constructive breaking and an entry.
(2) The house or building broken into and entered must belong to another person.
(3) The breaking and the entry must be with the intent to commit a felony in the house.
Burglary is a felony.

Compounding a felony: An offense by a person who, having been directly injured by a felony, agrees with the criminal that he or she will not prosecute him, the criminal, on condition of receipt of a reward or bribe not to prosecute.

Conspiracy: A combination or agreement between two or more persons to do an unlawful act. This offense is usually divided into:

(1) The end to be attained is in itself a crime.
(2) The object is lawful, but the means by which it is to be attained are unlawful.
(3) The object is to do an injury to a third person, though if the wrong were inflicted by a single individual, it would be a civil wrong and not a crime.
Conspiracies are misdemeanors, unless made felonies by statute.

Counterfeiting: To copy or imitate without authority or right, and with a view to deceive or defraud by passing the copy or thing that has been forged for that which is original or genuine.

Disorderly conduct: A term of loose and indefinite meaning, generally signifying behavior that is contrary to law, and more particularly to disturbing the public peace or shock the public sense of morality.

Disturbance of the peace: Interruption of the peace and order of a neighborhood or community by unnecessary and distracting noises.

Drunkard: One whose habit is to get drunk, whose inebriety has become habitual. A *common drunkard* is defined by statute in some states as a person who has been convicted of public drunkenness a number of times within a limited period.

Dueling: The fighting of two persons, one against the other, at an appointed time and place, upon a precedent quarrel. To challenge another to duel, or to provoke another to send a challenge constitutes the crime, even though no actual fighting takes place. If the duel takes place and one of the parties is killed, the other is guilty of murder, and all who are present abetting the crime are guilty as principals in the second degree.

Embezzlement: A crime defined generally as the unlawful appropriation of property to his or her own use by a servant, clerk, trustee, public officer, or other person to whom the possession has been entrusted by the owner.

Escape: The departure out of custody of a person lawfully imprisoned, before he or she is entitled to liberty by the process of law. Escapes are either *voluntary* or *negligent.* The former is the case when the keeper voluntarily concedes to the prisoner any liberty not authorized by law. The latter is the case when the prisoner contrives to leave prison by force, or any other means, without the knowledge or against the will of the keeper. *Prison breaks* are the breaking and going out of confinement by one who is lawfully imprisoned. A *rescue* is the forcible delivery of a prisoner from lawful custody by one who knows that the prisoner is in custody.

Extortion: The unlawful taking by an officer of money or anything of value that is not due the officer. The distinction between *bribery* and *extortion* is that the former is the offering of a present, or receiving one if offered; and the latter is the demanding of a fee or present. Extortion in many jurisdictions is sometimes called *blackmail.*

False imprisonment: The unlawful arrest or detention of a person without warrant, or by an illegal warrant for that purpose by force and constraint without confinement.

False impersonation: The criminal offense of falsely representing some other person and acting in the character thus unlawfully assumed, in order to deceive, gain some profit or advantage, or enjoy some right or privilege.

Forgery: The falsely making of, or altering with intent to defraud, any writing which, if genuine, might apparently be of legal efficacy, or the foundation of a legal liability. To constitute the crime, the making or the alteration must be false, and it must be committed with the intent to defraud.

Homicide: The killing of any human creature; the act of a human being taking away the life of another human being. Homicides are ordinarily classified as *justifiable, excusable*, or *felonious. Justifiable homicide* is the taking of a human life under circumstances of justification, as a matter of right, such as self-defense or other causes set out in the statute. *Excusable homicide* is the killing of a human being by misadventure. *Felonious homicide* is the wrongful killing of a human being, of any age or either sex, without justification or excuse in law, of which offense there are generally two degrees.

Larceny: The felonious stealing, taking, and carrying away the personal goods of another from any place, with a felonious intent to convert the goods to the taker's use and make them his or her property without the consent of the owner. The goods must be personal and not real property, and the intent must exist at the time of the taking. In most jurisdictions, the taking need not be for the advantage of the thief, and it need never be for pecuniary advantage.

Larceny, grand and petty: Statutes now provide that lesser thefts are classified as *petty* larceny or thefts, while major thefts are classified as *grand* larceny or thefts.

Libel and slander: Both are malicious defamations—expressed either by writing, printing, sign, or pictures or the like—that tend to blacken the memory of one dead; or to impeach the honesty, integrity, virtue, or reputation; or to publish the natural or alleged defects of one who is alive and thereby expose that person to public contempt, ridicule, or hatred. *Libel* refers to written defamation, and *slander* refers to verbal defamation.

Manslaughter: The unlawful killing of a human creature without malice, either expressed or implied, without deliberation, upon a sudden heat of passion, or in the commission of an unlawful act or a lawful act without due caution and circumspection. The distinction between *manslaughter* and *murder* rests on malice. In manslaughter, though the act that occasioned the death was unlawful or likely to be attended with bodily mischief, malice, either expressed or implied, is presumed to be wanting. Malice is the very essence of murder. The statutes and decisions vary as to what constitutes manslaughter, and there are various degrees of manslaughter recognized in some states.

Manslaughter, voluntary: The taking of a human life committed voluntarily upon a sudden heat of passion.

Manslaughter, involuntary: The taking of a human life while committing an unlawful act—not felonious or tending to cause great bodily harm—or in committing a lawful act without using proper caution or requisite skill, and therefore unguardedly or undesignedly killing another.

Misconduct in office: This is considered malfeasance and a misdemeanor for any public officer in the exercise of the duties of office; to do any illegal act or abuse discretionary power with which that officer is invested by law, for an improper motive.

Murder: The unlawful killing with malice aforethought of one human being by another. By statute, the crime is divided into two or more degrees, according to the heinousness of the deed. Murder is a felony. Where malice aforethought exists, every homicide is murder. Most of the states divide the crime into two degrees, *first* and *second*; however, in a few states, there are as many as five degrees.

Obstructing justice: A misdemeanor by statute in many states. To obstruct public or private justice by resisting or obstructing an officer in the exercise of his or her duty, or by preventing attendance of witnesses.

Perjury: The willful assertion as to a matter of fact, opinion, belief, or knowledge made by a witness in a judicial proceeding as part of his or her evidence under oath, whether given in open court or in an affidavit.

Perjury, subornation of: The procuring of another to commit perjury; perjury must actually have been committed.

Piracy: A robbery or forcible depredation upon property on the high seas without lawful authority and with intention to steal. The term is also applied to the illicit reprinting or reproduction of a copyrighted book or print or recorded device, and to unlawfully plagiarizing from such materials.

Rape: Having unlawful, forcible, carnal knowledge, without consent, including instances where:

(1) resistance is overcome by actual force;
(2) no actual force is used, but because of person's condition, consent cannot be given;
(3) person is below the age of consent;
(4) consent is extorted by fear of immediate bodily harm; and
(5) submission is induced by fraud without intelligent consent.

Rape, statutory: Having sexual intercourse with one under statutory age.

Receiving stolen goods: The short term usually given to the offense of receiving any property with the knowledge that it has been feloniously or unlawfully stolen or embezzled. The receiver must know that it was stolen and must have felonious intent to withhold the property from the owner.

Rioting: Any use of force or violence that disturbs the public peace, or any threat to use such force or violence by two or more persons acting together and without authority of law.

Robbery: The felonious taking of personal property in the possession of another, from one's person or immediate presence and against his or her will, accomplished by means of force or fear.

Suicide: Self-destruction; the deliberate termination of one's existence.

Trespass: An unlawful act committed with violence, actual or implied, causing injury to the person, property, or relative rights of another.

Unlawful assembly: The meeting together of three or more persons to the disturbance of the public peace, and with the intention of cooperating in the forcible and violent execution of some unlawful private enterprise.

Weapons: Instruments used in fighting; instruments of offensive or defensive combat. The term is chiefly used in law in the statutes prohibiting the carrying of "concealed" or deadly weapons.

White slavery: A term used in the U.S. statutes to indicate a female, with reference to whom an offense is committed under the Mann White Slave Traffic Act of June 25, 1910, which prohibits the transportation of women and girls in the interstate and foreign commerce for immoral purposes.

26

Cons, Dupes, and Trickery

Many times, in order to gain a confidence, cause someone to confess, gain possession, or plan a crime, a character in the writer's story must resort to conning, duping, or tricking his or her opponent. The following list contains some suggested cons, dupes, and tricks that could be employed:

Feeding someone misinformation.
Convincing another party that he or she is innocent.
Causing another party to believe something has happened that really hasn't occurred.
Convincing another party that he or she has been double-crossed.
Convincing the other party that what he or she has is counterfeit.
Pretending to be an informer.
Causing the other party to believe an accomplice has talked or has turned against him or her.
Pretending that someone (a witness, an accomplice, etc.) is dead.
Pretending a victim or witness is still alive.
Convincing someone that something counterfeit is real.
Pretending to be someone else.
Pretending to know already another's plan.
Convincing another that he or she has already been defeated.
Causing someone to believe he or she has been betrayed.
Pretending to know another's secret.

Stalling for time.
Causing another to act before he or she had planned.
Pretending to have changed sides.

DEVICES TO AID IN CONNING, DUPING, AND TRICKERY

Use of another's voice by imitation, electronics, etc.
Use of false papers or identification.
Leaving false prints.
Use of doctored photographs.
Use of counterfeits.
Use of theatrical sets.
Use of illusionary or special effects.
Playing on another's fears.
Use of hypnosis.
Use of brainwashing.
Playing on another's emotions—guilt, etc.
Planting false evidence.
Use of the occult.
Playing dead.
Use of psychology.
Use of false reports (medical, accounting, police).

27

Narcotics and Drug Addiction

Narcotics (the selling, use, and addiction of drugs) is probably the number-one area of crime in the United States today. It is a multimillion-dollar business, international in scope and activity, and is unquestionably the most destructive element in society throughout this country and the entire globe. The production and sale of drugs has in actuality become, in some instances, the national product of some foreign countries who, believe it or not, are so reliant on the income it produces that they are considering the legalization of their number-one export. As the problems associated with drugs are now so well known, it requires no further elaboration as to their effect on society and crime.

DRUG ADDICTION

Addiction is the state of utter dependency on drugs, in which they are necessary in order to function physically and mentally. When deprived of the substance, the addict has a physical craving manifested by symptoms of withdrawal, which cause severe mental and physical distress.

NARCOTICS

Narcotics are drugs of addiction (see list).

SYNTHETIC ANALGESICS

Synthetics are drugs that carry the effect of a narcotic but that have been synthesized and are therefore less expensive. Many of these are listed as narcotics by federal and state regulatory agencies.

TOLERANCE AND DEPENDENCY

With habitual use of a drug, the tolerance to that drug is increased, and the user requires progressively increasing dosages in order to properly function. As tolerance takes place, the span of time usually decreases between the taking of the drug. If the addict becomes deprived of the drug, he or she becomes physically and mentally ill to the extent that the addict will resort to crime in order to service the habit.

USE AND EFFECT

Each drug has its own properties and effects, and the means of administering the drug varies with the type of drug the user is taking. Some narcotics can be taken in more than one way, e.g., ingestion, sniffing, or injecting, which may require the use of a hypodermic needle, medicine dropper, bent spoon, and some means of tying off the limb so as to make the veins more accesible.

DRUG TRAFFICKING

Trafficking in drugs means the transporting or smuggling of illegal narcotics for eventual sale. As most illegal narcotics are produced outside of the United States, those dealing in the trafficking of drugs employ many creative means of smuggling and moving their contraband into the United States. In most instances, the drugs are brought in already refined, and all that is necessary is for the drug to be cut before it is ready for sale on the street. Some of the means employed are boat, cargo vessels where the drugs can be hidden or disguised with the cargo, airplanes landing in remote, deserted areas, and body *carriers*, sometimes referred to as *mules*.

POINTS OF ORIGIN

Cocaine is a white, crystalline powder from the coca shrub, a plant that was cultivated by the Andean Indians prior to the Spanish occu-

Narcotics

Drug	Chemical or Trade Name	Description	How Taken	Typical Dose	Duration of Effect	Initial Signs	Risks of Abuse	Physical Dependence
NARCOTICS								
Opium	*Papaver somniferum*	Dried milk of opium-poppy pod	Smoked or swallowed	Varies	6 hrs.	Euphoria Drowsiness	Loss of appetite Painful withdrawal symptoms	Yes
Morphine	Morphine sulphate	Derivative of opium	Injected	15 mg	6 hrs.	Euphoria Drowsiness	Loss of appetite Painful withdrawal Impaired breathing	Yes
Heroin	Diacetylmorphine	Derivative of morphine	Injected	Varies	4 hrs.	Euphoria Drowsiness	Loss of appetite Painful withdrawal Constipation	Yes
Methadone	Dolophine Amidone	Synthetic analgesic	Swallowed or injected	10 mg	4-6 hrs.	Less acute than opiates	Loss of appetite Painful withdrawal Constipation	Yes
DEPRESSANTS								
Barbiturates	Phenobarbital Seconal Nembutal	Barbituric acid derivative	Swallowed	50-100 mg	4-12 hrs.	Drowsiness Muscle relaxation	Incoherence Depression Withdrawal difficulty	Possible
Meprobromate	Miltown Equanil	Non-barbiturate sedative	Swallowed	Varies	4 hrs.	Drowsiness Muscle relaxation	Incoherence Depression Withdrawal difficulty	No
Methaqualone	Sopor Quaalude	Non-barbiturate sedative	Swallowed	75-100 mg	4 hrs.	Drowsiness Muscle relaxation	Delirium Coma	No

STIMULANTS								
Cocaine	Methyl ester of benzoylecganine	Isolated alkaloid of coca leaf	Sniffed or injected	Varies	Varies	Excitation Talkativeness Tremors	Loss of appetite Irritability Insomnia	No
Amphetamines	Benzedrine Dexedrine Methedrine	Synthetic central-nervous system stimulant	Swallowed	2.5-5 mg	4 hrs.	Alertness Talkativeness Activity	Irritability Confusion Aggressiveness	No
HALLUCINOGENS								
Marijuana	*Cannabis sativa*	Flowering resinous top of female hemp plant	Smoked	1 or 2 cigarettes	4 hrs.	Relaxation Euphoria Vagueness	Altered perception Impaired judgment	No
Peyote	3, 4, 5-trimethoxy-phenethylamine	Dried cactus buttons containing mescaline	Swallowed	350 mcg	12 hrs.	Exhilaration Anxiety Gastric distress	Visual hallucinations Paranoia Possible psychosis	No
LSD	d-lysergic acid diethylamide	Synthetic compound 400 times more powerful than mescaline	Swallowed	100 mcg	10 hrs.	Excitation Exhilaration Vagueness	Visual and auditory hallucinations Possible psychosis	No
DMT	Dimethyltryptamine	Synthetic compound similar to mushroom alkaloid psilocybin	Injected	1 mg	4-6 hrs.	Excitation Exhilaration	Possible psychotic reaction	No

Some Substances Not Used For Medical Purposes

Substance	Common or Slang Names	Active Ingredient	Source	Pharmacologic Classification	Medical Use
Alcohol	Booze, Juice, Sauce, Brew, Vino	Ethanol, Ethyl Alcohol	Natural (from fruits, grains, vegetables)	CNS depressant	Solvent antiseptic, sedative
Marijuana	Pot, Grass, Dope, Weed, Homegrown, Sinsemilla Maui-wowie, Thaisticks, Joints, Roaches, Indica: Concentrated resin called Hash or Hashish	Tetrahydrocannabinols (THC)	Cannabis sativa	CNS depressant, hallucinogen	Experimental research only
Amphetamines	Ups, Uppers, Speed, Crank, RX Diet Pills	Amphetamine Dextroamphetamine Methamphetamine (Desoxyephedrine)	Synthetic	CNS stimulant	Control appetite. Narcolepsy—some childhood behavioral disorders; relieve depression
Amphetamine Look-alikes	Legal stimulants, Ups, Uppers, AMS, AKS, RJS	May contain caffeine, Ephedrine, Pseudoephedrine,Phenylpropanglamine	Synthetic/natural	CNS stimulant, decongestant, appetite depressant	None
Cocaine	Coke, Rock, Toot, Blow, Snow, Pearl Flake	Cocaine Hydrochloride Benzoylmethylecgonine	Natural (from coca leaves)	Local or topical anesthesia	Local or topical anesthesia
Cocaine Freebase	Base Freebase	Cocaine base	Natural (prepared from Cocaine Hydrochloride)	Local or topical anesthesia	Topical anesthetic ointments
Barbiturates	Barbs, Bluebirds, Blues, Tooies, Yellow Jackets	Phenobarbital Pentobarbital Secobarbital Amobarbital	Synthetic	Sedative Hypnotic	Sedation, Epilepsy
Methaqualone	Ludes, 714S, Sopor	Methaqualone	Synthetic	Sedative hypnotic	Sedation
Heroin	H, Horse, Junk, Smack, Stuff, Brown Sugar	Diacetyl morphine	Semi-synthetic (from morphine)	Narcotic analgesic	None legally
Morphine	White Stuff, M, More	Morphine Sulphate	Natural (from Opium)	Narcotic analgesic	Pain relief
Codeine	Schoolboy	Methylmorphine	Natural (from Opium) semi-synthetic (from morphine)	Narcotic analgesic	Ease pain & coughing

Oxycodone		14-Hydroxydihydro-Codeinone	Semi-synthetic (Morphine-like)	Narcotic analgesic	Pain relief
Meperidine		Meperidine Hydrochloride	Synthetic	Narcotic analgesic	Pain relief, prevent withdrawal, discomfort
Methadone	Dolly	Methadone Hydrochloride	Synthetic	Narcotic analgesic	Pain relief, prevent withdrawal, discomfort
Inhalants	Solvents, Glue, Transmission fluid, Toluene	Organic solvents	Synthetic	None	None
Nitrous Oxide	Laughing Gas, Gas, Whippitts, Nitrous, Blue Bottle	Nitrous Oxide	Synthetic	Inhalation anesthetic	Anesthesia
Butyl Nitrite	Liquid Incense, Room Deodorizer, Rush, Locker Room, Locker Popper	Butyl Nitrite	Synthetic	Vasodilator	None (Amyl nitrite used in Angina Pectoris)
LSD	Acid, LSD-25, Blotter Acid, Window-pane, named after pictures on paper, Mesc	D-Lysergic Acid Diethylamide	Semi-synthetic (from Ergot Alkaloids)	Hallucinogen	Experimental research only
Mescaline (Peyote Cactus)	Mesc, Peyote, Peyote Buttons	Mescaline	Natural (from Peyote Cactus)	Hallucinogen	None
MDA, MMDA, MDM	Love Drug, Ecstasy, XTC	34-Methylenedioxy-amphetamine Analogs of MDA	Synthetic	Amphetamine-based hallucinogen	None
DOM	Straserenity Tranquility, Peace	2.5-Dimethoxy-4-methyl-amphetamine	Synthetic	Amphetamine-based hallucinogen	None
Psilocybin	Magic Mushrooms, Shrooms	Psilocybin	Natural (from Psilocybe Fungus—a type of mushroom)	Hallucinogen	None
PCP	Crystal, Tea, THC, Angel Dust	Phencyclidine	Synthetic	Dissociative Anesthetic	Once used as a veterinary anesthetic
Coffee, Tea, Colas	Espresso, Cafe, Natural Stimulant, Guarana, Guaranine	Caffeine	Natural	CNS stimulant	Mild stimulant
Tobacco	Cigs, Smokes, Butts, Cancer Sticks, Coffin Nails	Nicotine	Natural (from Nicotina Tabacum)	CNS Toxin	Emetic

Some Substances Not Used For Medical Purposes (*Continued*)

Form	Abuse and How Used	Effects Sought	Long Term Possible Effects	Physical Dependence Potential	Psychological Dependence Potential
Liquid	Taken orally, applied topically (rubbing alcohol)	Intoxication, Sense Alteration, Anxiety reduction	Toxic Psychosis, addiction, neurologic damage	Yes	Yes
Plant Particles (dark green or brown)	Smoked or eaten	Euphoria, relaxation, increased perception	Bronchitis, Conjunctivitis, possible birth defects	Possible	Possible
Tablets, Capsules, Liquid, Powder (white)	Taken orally or injected	Alertness, activeness	Loss of appetite, delusions, hallucinations, toxic psychosis	Possible	Yes
Capsules or Tablets	Taken orally	Alertness, activeness, weight loss	Hypertension, stroke, heart problems	Possible	Yes
Powder (white) or Liquid	Snorted or injected	Stimulation, excitation, euphoria (subtle)	Loss of appetite, depression, convulsions, nasal passage injury	No	Yes
White Crystal	Smoked, injected	Intensified Cocaine effects	Weight loss, depression, hypertension, hallucinations, psychosis	Yes	Yes
Tablets or Capsules	Taken orally or injected	Anxiety reduction, euphoria	Severe withdrawal symptoms, possible convulsions, toxic psychosis	Yes	Yes
Tablets	Taken orally or snorted	Euphoria, aphrodisiac	Coma, convulsions	Yes	Yes
Powder (white, grey, brown)	Injected, snorted or smoked	Euphoria	Addiction, constipation, loss of appetite	Yes	Yes
Powder (white), Tablets or Liquid	Taken orally or injected	Euphoria	Addiction, constipation, loss of appetite	Yes	Yes
Tablets or liquid (in cough syrup)	Taken orally or injected	Euphoria	Addiction, constipation, loss of appetite	Yes	Yes
Tablets	Taken orally or injected	Euphoria	Addiction, constipation, loss of appetite	Yes	Yes
Tablets or Liquid	Taken orally or injected	Euphoria	Addiction, constipation, loss of appetite	Yes	Yes
Tablets or Liquid	Taken orally or injected	Euphoria	Addiction, constipation, loss of appetite	Yes	Yes
Various	Inhaled or huffed (poured on a rag or towel and inhaled by mouth)	Intoxication	Impaired perception, coordination, judgment; toxicity from solvent impurities	No	Yes

Gas in Pressurized Container	Inhaled	Euphoria, relaxation	Kidney or liver damage, peripheral neuropathy, spontaneous abortion	No	Possible
Liquid	Inhaled	Exhilaration	Damage to heart and blood vessels, may aggravate heart problems	No	Yes
Tablets, Capsules, Liquid, or Paper Squares	Taken orally	Insight, distortion of senses, exhilaration, mystical/religious experience	May intensify existing psychosis, panic reactions	No	Possible
Tablets, Capsules, Raw Drug (Buttons)	Taken orally	Same as LSD	Milder than LSD	No	Possible
Tablets or Capsules	Taken orally	Same as LSD	Milder than LSD	No	Possible
Tablets, Capsules or Liquid	Taken orally	Stronger than LSD effects	Same as LSD	No	Possible
Mushrooms, rarely as Tablets or Capsules	Taken orally	Same as LSD	Milder than LSD	No	Possible
Tablets, Powder in Smoking Mixtures	Smoked, snorted or taken orally	Distortion of senses	Psychotic behavior, violent acts, psychosis	No	Possible
Beverage	Taken orally	Alertness	May aggravate heart problems	Possible	Yes
Snuff, Pipe Cut Particles, Cigars or Cigarettes	Smoked, snorted or chewed	Relaxation	Loss of appetite, habituation, lung cancer	Possible	Yes

pation in the Southern Hemisphere. The major producing countries are Colombia, Chile, Peru, and Bolivia, although other countries are also producing the drug in increasing amounts.

Crack, also known as rock cocaine, is the result of changing the structure of cocaine hydrochloride from the salt to the free base. By this method (heating the salt form in the presence of alkali), the cocaine is changed into a form that can be smoked. Smoking allows the cocaine to go directly to the lungs, as opposed to being inhaled through the nose, as with ordinary cocaine. Inhalation does not provide the rush that crack users experience.

Opium is derived from the oriental poppy plant, grown mainly in Asia, although the poppy has now been cultivated in other countries such as Mexico, Cuba, and the Balkans. The major producers and suppliers of opium are India, Turkey, Thailand, Pakistan, Laos, Mexico, and Afghanistan. Although opium was once primarily smoked, it has produced such derivatives as morphine and heroin, which are injected.

Marijuana is one of the most widely used of the illicit drugs, and comes from the hemp plant, which grows wild or can be cultivated. Primary sources are Mexico, Cuba, Turkey, Greece, India, Syria, Africa, the United States, and Brazil.

Mescaline or Peyote can be found in northern Mexico and the southwestern part of the United States, and is derived from the peyote cactus.

Psilocybin is a hallucinogen extracted from a form of mushroom found in Mexico.

Barbiturates are probably the most abused type of drugs available to the addict. They are readily obtainable from a physician, hospital, or local pharmacist if the user has the right connections.

A list of most known drugs can be found on the following pages, along with a dictionary of drug "slanguage" used by those trafficking, selling, and addicted to narcotics.

POSSESSION

Possession of a narcotic or illicit drug is a crime, as it constitutes the probability of use or sale. It is very conceivable that a user might also be dealing in drugs in order to support his or her habit.

SELLING

Selling or dealing in drugs is a much more serious offense than possession. Criminal trafficking or dealing in drugs is, in most cases, the domain of the professional criminal, and in most instances, it is connected with a large ring and/or organized crime. Those at the top of the ladder in drug trafficking and dealing usually have expertise in evading the law and escaping detection and prosecution, despite the valiant attempts of law enforcement to discover and prosecute them to the fullest extent of the law.

Needless to say, drug traffickers and dealers are powerful people with a great many connections and an enormous financial empire with which to bribe and pay off those government officials and police who can be corrupted. Like most big businesses, those dealing and trafficking in drugs build and operate no differently than any other large business. Those at the very top are usually well insulated from those who work beneath them. Their business has many levels of sale and distribution, ranging from the grower or producer to wholesalers, mules, pushers, and peddlers. A mule, pusher, or peddler could be a member of organized crime, neighborhood street gangs, users, pimps, prostitutes, students or even an ordinary citizen who sees an opportunity to make a quick buck.

NARCOTICS–PACKAGING AND DISTRIBUTION

For the purpose of smuggling large quantities of cocaine (cocaine hydrochloride), and for distributing smaller amounts, the following methods are used to package the drugs:

MULTI-KILO

1. Duct tape
2. Heat-seal plastic
3. Fiberglas
4. Casting material
5. Brown tape
6. Trash bags

WHOLESALE–Multi-ounce

Large, plastic Ziploc bags

STREET DISTRIBUTION

1. Bindles (pharmaceutical fold)
2. 2″ × 2″ Ziploc bags
3. Sno-seals (basically same as bindles)

CRACK OR ROCK COCAINE DISTRIBUTION
Usually sold in 2″ × 2″ plastic bags.

TAR HEROIN—SMUGGLING Multi-kilo
1. Clear plastic wrap
2. Ziploc bags
3. Various tapes

POWDERED HEROIN SMUGGLING—Multi-kilo
1. Blocks (compressed)
2. Plastic wraps
3. Casting materials

TAR HEROIN—Wholesale distribution
1. Ounce balls wrapped in plastic wrap

POWDERED HEROIN—Wholesale distribution
1. Film canisters
2. Plastic

TAR AND POWDERED HEROIN—Street distribution
1. Balloons
2. Bindles
3. Candy twists (tar only)

PHENCYCLIDINE (PCP)—Wholesale distribution
Gallon bottles—apple juice, cider

DEALER QUANTITY—distribution (one pint or one liter)
Grape juice, root beer, Listerine bottles

STREET SALES—distribution
1. Vanilla extract bottles, one-ounce bottles
2. Cigarettes (tinfoil bindles)

MARIJUANA SMUGGLING—Multi-kilo
1. Trash bags
2. Bales, plastic encased

POUND QUANTITY DISTRIBUTION
1. Ziploc bags (storage size)
2. Kilos, tape wrapped

28

Crime Drugs

DRUGS OF ADDICTION AND INTELLECT-INFLUENCE – REPRESENTATIVE

Alcohol
Amanita muscaria
Amphetamines (pep pills)
Amyl nitrite
Atropine
Awa
Ayahuasca
Barbiturates (goof balls)
Belladonna
Benzedrine
Betel nut
Bufotenine
Caffeine (via coffee)
Cannabis indica
Charas
Chicropon natrium
Chloral hydrate
Cocaine
Codeine
Cough syrup
Crack (rock cocaine)
Dagga
Dexedrine

DMT
Epena
Ether
Fly agaric
Ganga
Glue
Goof balls (barbiturates)
Hallucinogens or psychedelics (LSD, DMT, mescaline, peyote, etc.)
Hanu
Hashish
Hemp
Heroin
Hydrangea
IT-290
Jimson weed
Kat (Khat)
Kava
Kief
Laudanum
Lotus flower (mythical odyssey)
LAD
LSD (acid)
Mandrake
Marijuana (pot)
Mescaline
Methamphetamine
Methedrine
Mexico's magic mushrooms
Morning glory seeds
Morphine
Nalline
Nembutal
Nicotine
Oblivion (happiness pill)
Opium
Paregoric
Parica
Pep pills (amphetamines)
Percodan
Peyote (mescaline)
Philopon/Secobarbital

Psilocybin
Reefers (marijuana cigarettes)
Rock cocaine (crack)
Sedatives
Sleeping tablets
Snuff
Speed (methedrine)
PCP
Tea
Tobacco

Also wine, whiskey, champagne, gin, cognac, brandy, absinthe, rum, sherry, tequila, mescal, vodka, etc.

29

Slanguage

"Slanguage" used by those involved in the criminal world and in the drug culture is seldom, if ever, chiseled in stone. It changes constantly.

The slanguage collected and listed on the following pages has been compiled over a period of years, and although the author has attempted to update the wordage, by the time this book has gone to press, much of the present wordage will have changed again.

It is respectfully suggested that you check with local authorities for the most recent slang term to determine if the one listed is still in use. Also, you may suggest that the writer coin your own slang term when you desire to, as there are no hard-and-fast rules when it comes to slanguage in the criminal and drug worlds.

UNDERWORLD SLANG WITH EMPHASIS ON DRUG CULTURE

This incomplete list represents jargon heard or used from 1970 to 1973 in California; an asterisk indicates rarely used terms or localized terms.

***Abbot:** Nembutal (barbiturate)

***Acapulco Gold:** High grade of marijuana from Mexico with a gold tint

***Ace:** Marijuana cigarette

Acid: LSD

***Acid freak:** Habitual user of LSD who displays bizarre behavior

***Acid head:** User of LSD

Acid rock: Psychedelic music

***Afro:** Natural hair style for blacks (naturally curly state)

***Agates:** Nembutal

Alice B. Toklas: Brownie with marijuana baked in it

Angel grass (dust): Parsley saturated with PCP

Antsy: Nervous, restless; typical feeling from using amphetamines

Ameba weed: Parsley saturated with PCP

Amped-out: Fatigue after being under the influence of methamphetamine

***Apples (red apples):** Secobarbital

***Artillery:** Injection paraphernalia

At ("where it's at"): Where everything is occurring

Bad: Tough, downer, wrong

***Bad scene:** Unpleasant experience

***Bad trip:** Panic reaction or unpleasant experience from hallucinogen

Bag: Quantity of drugs packaged in various containers, such as paper, balloons, plastic bags, etc.

Bale: 75 to 500 pounds of marijuana compressed into a bale similar to hay

Balloon: Quantity of drugs, usually heroin, packaged in toy balloons

Barbs: Barbiturates

Barrel: 100,000 pills or specific type of LSD based on shape of tablet

Base: Free basing or smoking cocaine

B.C.: Birth-control pills

Bean: Pill, commonly referring to benzedrine tablets or capsules

Beautiful: All purpose term of approval

Behind stuff: Using heroin

Bennies: Benzedrine tablets

***Bernice:** Cocaine

Bindle: Quantity of drugs packaged in various containers; same as *bag*

Black beauty: Bi-phetamine capsules (methedrine capsule)

Black stuff: Smoking opium

Blacktar: Distilled, concentrated heroin

Black wings: Symbol worn on white motorcycle gang jacket indicating having had sex relations with a black person

Blast: To smoke a marijuana cigarette; fun

***Block:** Quantity of compressed hashish

Blow: To smoke a marijuana cigarette; to inhale cocaine; cocaine; get lost

***Blue dot:** Type of LSD wherein a blue dot of LSD is placed on a small piece of paper

Blues: Sodium amytal

Body trip: To be under the influence of a drug that affects the physical condition of a person, such as heroin, as opposed to a *mind trip* (as with LSD)

Bomber: Unusually large marijuana cigarette

Bottle: 100 pills

Bowl: Pipe used for smoking hash

Boy: Heroin

Bread: Money

Brick: 2.2 pounds of a drug, commonly used for marijuana that is packaged in a brick shape

Broad: Female

Brother: Male Negro or members of the same group

Brown stuff: Heroin from Mexico with brown coloration

Brownie: Traffic cop

Bubble gum: Anything that appeals to young adolescents

Bubble gummer: A young adolescent

Bug: To annoy; itching sensation; sensation due to cocaine poisoning

Bullet: One-year sentence to county jail

Bummer: Bad, unpleasant

***Bum trip:** Bad experience

Bunk: Poor-quality drugs

Burn: Substance sold in lieu of narcotics; to cheat or steal

Burned: User has received bad or weak drugs

Burned out: Mentally incapable as a result of drug use

Bush: Marijuana

Butch: Female homosexual who plays male role

Buy: To purchase narcotics

Buzz: Immediate feeling after use of a drug

C: Cocaine

***C&H:** Cocaine and heroin

***C&M:** Cocaine and morphine

Can: Ounce of marijuana

Cap: Capsule

Cap up: Transfer drug in bulk form into capsules

Carga: Heroin (Spanish term)

Carry: To be in possession of a drug

***Cartwheel:** Benzedrine tablets

Case: To have a criminal complaint against one

Cavalry: Police reinforcements

***Cecil:** Cocaine

Changes: Adjustments

Chemicals: Synthetic drugs

Cherry: Novice

China white: Asian heroin, white in color

Chippy: Irregular habit; occasional user

Chiva: Heroin

Citizen: Outsider; nonuser; square

Clean: Not in possession of drugs; not engaged in illegal activities; refined marijuana

Clean up: To stop using drugs

***Coca-cola:** Cocaine

Cocaine blues: Depression from discontinuing the use of cocaine

Coin: Money

Coke: Cocaine

Coke out: Excessive use of cocaine to the point of incoherency

Coke spoon: Specially made, tiny spoon for inhaling cocaine

***Cokie:** Cocaine user

Cold turkey: Refers to stopping use of heroin suddenly with no assistance from other medicine

Come down: To begin to come off the influence of drugs

Connect: To make contact

Connection: Person who sells drugs; a source

Contact high: Being under the influence of a drug through contact and not actual use

Cooker: Any type of container used to hold the drug while it is being heated; a chemist in an illicit drug lab

Cook, cook up: To prepare a drug for injection by heating it in water to dissolve

Cool: O.K.; good

Cop: To purchase drugs; steal; to obtain

***Copilot:** Benzedrine

Cop out: To admit something or plead guilty

Cotton: Small piece of cotton with drug residue from using the cotton as a filter when preparing the drug for injection

Cotton mouth: Hard, dry feeling in the mouth after smoking marijuana

Crack: Crystallized cocaine

Crank: Methamphetamine

Crash: To sleep or come down from being under the influence of a stimulant; a stupor

Crash pad: Place to sleep

***Crate:** A large quantity of pills, usually 50,000

Crib: One's home or residence

***Crink:** Methamphetamine

Croaker: Doctor

Cross-tops: Benzedrine tablets

Cruise: Homosexual looking for a partner

Crutch: Device used to hold a marijuana cigarette

Crystal: Methamphetamine

***Cube:** Sugar cube containing LSD

Cut: To adulterate drugs to obtain a larger quantity

Cut loose: To release

D.E.A.: Drug Enforcement Agency

Deal: To sell drugs

Dealer: Anyone who sells drugs

***Deck:** Packet of heroin

Dexies: Amphetamine tablets (dexedrine)

***Diamonds:** Amphetamine tablets

Dig: To understand; to like (circa 1950s)

Dime: Ten; ten dollars

Dime bag: Ten dollars' worth of drugs

Dirty: To possess drugs or be under the influence

***Dolly:** Methadone

Dome: Form of LSD usually in capsule

Dope: Any narcotic or dangerous drugs, usually heroin

Do it: To go or leave

Do up: To inject

Down, get down: To inject a drug. Went down: oral copulation

Downer: Drug with a depressant effect; low mood

Drag: Something or someone who is boring; to smoke a marijuana cigarette; street

Dresser, full dresser: Stock motorcycle

Dried out: Detoxified, withdrawn from a drug

Dripper: Syringe

***Drivers:** Benzedrine

Dropped: Taking drugs through the mouth

Dropper: Syringe

Dude: Male

Duke in: To introduce

Dump on: To unload

Dust: Money

Dyke: Lesbian

Dynamite: Unusually strong or pure drug; terrific

Eat: To swallow drugs or narcotics; to engage in oral-genital sex

Eight ball: Method of packing ⅛ ounce, related to cocaine

Elbow: Method of packaging one pound of cocaine

Emma, Miss: Morphine

Engine: Outfit for smoking opium

Eye opener: First drug used during the day

Factory: Location where illicit drugs are manufactured

Fifty cents: Fifty dollars' worth of drugs

***Fin:** Five dollars

Finger lid: Measure amount of marijuana in plastic bag by using fingers, for example, three-fingered lid

Fit: Injection paraphernalia

Five cents: Five dollars' worth of a drug

Fix: To inject a drug

Flake: Cocaine

Flaky: Unstable

Flash: Euphoria following the taking of a drug; sudden thought; to vomit after taking drugs

Flash powder: Methamphetamine

Flashback: Recurring experience from effects of LSD

Flat: Table of LSD

Flipped out: Crazy

Fluff: To run a powdered drug through a sifter or nylon stocking to give it a soft, light texture

For sure: Exactly, right

Fox: Attractive female

Freak: Heavy user of a drug; scared

Freak out: Bad experience

Free base: To smoke cocaine

Freeze: The numbness caused by using cocaine

Fried: Nonfunctional mind due to drugs, often amphetamines

Front: To give in advance of receiving

Funky: Can mean *good* or *bad*, depending on how used, but most commonly meaning *bad*

Fuzz: Police

***Gage:** Marijuana

Garbage: Bad or poor-quality drugs

Gay: Homosexual

Gee: Gasket between needle and syringe

Geeze: To inject a drug

Get back: Stay calm

Get down: To use a drug

Get it on: To begin or start something

Get off: To use drugs

Get rocks off: Enjoying yourself or sexual climax

Gig: Job; means of obtaining money

***Gimmicks:** Injection paraphernalia

Girl: Cocaine; Negro female

Going down: Happening; process of oral copulation

***Gold:** Acapulco gold marijuana

Goods: Merchandise; drugs

Gopher: Errand boy

Goofball: Barbiturate

***Gow:** Narcotics; opium-pipe cleaner

Grass: Marijuana

***Greta:** Marijuana

***Griefo:** Marijuana

Grider: Motorcycle front end with single spring

Groove, groovie: Very good; to enjoy

Guide: Experienced LSD user who supervises another's LSD trip

***Gum:** Opium

***Gun:** Injection paraphernalia

H: Heroin

Habit: Need for a drug; addiction

Hang tough: Take it easy

Hang it up: To abstain from something or delay; mental block

Happening: Event; action (circa 1950s, 1960s)

Hard stuff: Heroin, cocaine, morphine

Harry: Heroin
Hash: Hashish
Hassle: Trouble with someone
***Hay:** Marijuana
Hear you: Understand
Head: Drug user
***Hearts:** Amphetamine (dexedrine)
Heavy: Bad or violent person; extreme
Heeled: Having money
***Hemp:** Marijuana
Hep or hip: To be aware of (circa 1950s)
***Her:** Cocaine
Hink: To make paranoid
***Him:** Heroin
Hit: To inject a drug; to borrow or attempt to borrow a drag of marijuana cigarette
High: Under the influence
Hog: Person who uses any drugs available; stock motorcycle
Hold or holding: To be in possession of drugs
***Holster:** Needle holder of any sort
Honky: Derogatory term for a white person
Hooked: Addicted
Hop: Opium
Horn: To inhale drugs through the nose
Hot shot: A fatal dose of narcotics, usually heroin
Hype: One who uses hypodermic needle to inject drug
In pocket: To possess drugs
Jam: Cocaine
Jelly: Cocaine
Job, Do a: Physically hurt someone
Joint: Marijuana cigarette; state prison; penis
Jolt: Injection of drug; feeling after injecting a drug
Joy pop: Irregular use of narcotics
Jug: 1,000 pills

Juice: Influence; methadone in orange juice; liquor
***Juju:** Marijuana
Junk: Heroin
Junkie: Heroin addict
Kee, kilo, key: 2.2 pounds of a drug, usually marijuana or heroin
***Keep the faith:** Expression said upon departure
Keg: 50,000 pills
Keister plant: Drugs hidden in rectum
Key: Method of packaging one kilo (2.2 pounds)
Kick: To stop; to stop taking a particular drug, especially heroin
King's habit: Use of cocaine
Kinky: Very strange, unusual
Kit: Injection paraphernalia
Knock off: To stop; to murder
Lab: Equipment used to manufacture drugs illegally
Later: To see or talk to a person at a later time
Lay: Sexual intercourse; to give something
Laying paper: Passing bad checks
L.B.: Pound
***Leaf:** Opium
Lid: One ounce of marijuana
Lieutenant: Right-hand man of a large drug dealer
Lighten up: To take it easy or stop
Lightweight: Something or somebody of no consequence
Like: Expression used for emphasis or to gain attention
Line: Cocaine poured out in a thin line on a table, book, album, etc., for inhaling into the nose with a straw
Lit up: Under the influence of a drug
Loaded: Under the influence of a drug
***Loaf:** 2.2 pounds of marijuana
Looking: Seeking to purchase drugs
Lose your cool: To lose control of oneself
Low rider: Down-and-out addict. Low riders: group distinguished by their vehicles built low to the ground

Ludes: Quaaludes
***M:** Morphine
M&Ms: Seconal tablets shaped like M&M's candy
Machine: Motorcycle
Machinery: Injection paraphernalia
Mainline: To inject a drug directly into the vein
Maintain: To remain calm
Make a buy, make a meet: To purchase drugs
Make it: To leave
Mamma: Negro female; girlfriend of all of one group who is willing to have sex with any member at request
Man: Police officer; dealer of drugs
Manicure: To clean stems and seeds from marijuana
Mark: Victim
***Mary Jane, Mary:** Marijuana
Matchbox: Old term for container of marijuana (penny matchbox)
Menita: Baby laxative used for cutting cocaine
Meth: Methamphetamine
Merchandise: Narcotics or drugs
Merck: Pharmaceutical cocaine
Mexican brown: Mexican heroin
Mic (Mike): Micrograms; average dose of LSD is 250 mics
Mickey Finn: Chloral hydrate in a drink used to knock out a victim
***Microdots:** Type of LSD
Mind game: Psychological game of wits
Mind trip: Drugs causing psychological changes
Minibeans: Small benzedrine tablets
Morning shot: First injection of the day
Mouth habit: Oral drug habit
***Mud:** Opium
Muggles: Marijuana
Mule: Go-between from the dealer to the buyer (transports dope)
Munchies: Sensation of hunger caused by smoking marijuana
***Nail:** Hypodermic needle; one marijuana cigarette

Narc, nark, narco: Narcotics officer

Natural: Natural hair style of blacks

Needle freak: One who injects drugs into the vein or skin

***Nemmies:** Nembutal

Nickel: Five dollars

Nigra: High-grade, dark-colored marijuana

Nineteen: Nineteenth letter of alphabet, *S* for *speed*

Nod: Dozing as a result of drugs, usually heroin (after injecting heroin, Hype "goes on the nod")

No way: No chance

Number: Marijuana

O.D.: Overdose of a drug, many times fatal

Off: To get rid of

Off the wall: Sudden change of mood

***Oil-burning habit:** A big habit

One and one: Two measured lines of cocaine, one per nostril

***Orange sunshine:** Type of LSD

***Orange wedges:** Type of LSD

Outfit: Injection paraphernalia

Out front: Open, honest (to put money out front: to advance money prior to delivery of drugs)

Out of it: Not in touch; removed

Overamped: Refers to someone who has injected too much methamphetamine

Overdose: Too much of a drug; to take too much of a drug

Overstock: Front-end extension on a motorcycle

***Owsley:** High-quality LSD

O.Z.: Ounce

Ozer: Packaging one ounce

Pad: User's residence

Panama red: High-grade marijuana grown in Panama

Panic: Scarcity of drugs

Paper: Quantity of narcotics contained in a small, folded piece of paper; cigarette paper

Paper acid: LSD on a small piece of paper

Paper hanger: Forger

Paquete: Packaging for twelve balloons of heroin

Peace pill: PCP

Peaking: Reaching the highest point of being under the influence

Peddler: One who sells (illicit) drugs

People: Mixture of a drug and another substance; family, relatives

Pep pill: amphetamine

Piece: One ounce of a narcotic, usually heroin; gun; sexual intercourse

Pill freak: User of any type of pill

Pillow: 25,000 amphetamine tablets, usually packaged in a black plastic bag

Pinch: Small sample of a drug

***Pink lady:** Secobarbital capsule

Plant: To set someone up by placing drugs in his or her possession without the person's knowledge

Plunger: Syringe

Point: Needle

Pop: To take a drug by injection or orally

Popped: Arrested

Pot: Marijuana

***Power sign:** Fist salute (bikers use left hand)

Prop: Phenyl-2-propanone (chemical used to manufacture methamphetamine)

Psychedelic: Mind changing

P-2-P: Phenyl-2-propanone (chemical used to manufacture methamphetamine)

Punk out: To pass out

Push: To sell drugs

Pusher: Person who sells drugs

Quarter: Twenty-five dollars; twenty-five-dollar balloon of heroin

Quarter piece: One-fourth ounce of a certain drug (usually heroin)

Rabbit: To run away; person buyer uses to test dope

Rack: Numerous (three to ten) capsules taped together

***Rainbows:** Tuinal

Rank: Crude; impolite

R.D.'s: Secobarbital

Reds: Secobarbital

Redneck: Ultraconservative individual; sometimes referred to as "Oakie"

***Reefer:** Marijuana cigarette

Register: Show of blood in syringe during an injection to indicate that the vein was punctured

Ride: Car

Rig: Injection paraphernalia

Roach: Partially smoked marijuana cigarette

Roach Clip: Holder for a marijuana cigarette

Rock: Crystallized cocaine (same as *crack*)

Rock house: Residence to sell drugs, usually crystallized cocaine

Roll: Ten pills in a roll (usually tinfoil)

Run-it-down: Go-between from dealer to buyer; someone who does all the leg work for another

Rush: First exciting euphoria from taking a drug

Scab: Abscess caused by injection of a drug; ugly female

***Scag:** Heroin

Scam: Occurrence of interest; con game

Scarf: To swallow a drug

Scene: Place or environment

***Schmeck:** Heroin

Score: To purchase drugs; to have sexual intercourse

Script: Drug prescription

Shit: Heroin

Shoot (up): To inject a drug

Shooting gallery: Place used by users to inject drugs

Short: Vehicle; smaller-than-expected amount of a certain drug

Shot: House or room

Shot (up): Having injected drugs

Sick: Withdrawal experienced by a user; condition of needing a drug to remain normal

Sissy bar: Chrome upward extension for the back of a motorcyle seat

***Skag:** Heroin

Skid lid: Motorcycle helmet

Skin pop: To inject a drug under the skin rather than into the vein

Smack: Heroin

Snort: To sniff a drug through the nose

Snow: Cocaine

Snowbird: Cocaine user

Spaced (out): In a daze

Speed: Methamphetamine

***Speedball:** Mixture of heroin and a stimulant drug such as cocaine or amphetamine

Spike: Needle

Spoon: Quantity of a drug, approximately one-half gram of heroin

***Sporting:** Using cocaine

Square: Nonuser

Squirrely: Refers to a strange person

Stash: Total amount of a drug one possesses, often hidden

Step on: To adulterate drugs to obtain a larger quantity

Stick: Marijuana cigarette

Stone: To emphasize something, e.g., stone fox (sexy female)

Stoned: Under the influence

Straight: Square; not a drug user

Street people: Persons who use drugs or are related to drug users in the underground culture; homeless persons

Strung out: Addicted

Stuff: Heroin

Sugar (milk) habit: Addict's desire for sweets caused by a large amount of milk sugar mixed with everyday heroin

Super: Really good

Swing man: Supplier; connection

Tabs: Tablets

Taco: A Mexican

***Tar:** Opium

Taste: Small ration of a drug

***Tea:** Marijuana

Ten-cent bag: Ten-dollar bag

Tie off: To prepare for injection by placing a tourniquet around the limb to be used

Tie rag: Homemade or makeshift tourniquet used during the injection of drugs

***Tin:** One ounce of marijuana

T.J.: Tijuana, Mexico

Toke up: To light a marijuana cigarette

Tools: Injection paraphernalia

Too much: Utmost

Tough, tuff: Good

Tracks: Supravenous scars from injection of drugs

Trick: Date or customer of a prostitute; victim; foolish person

Troll: To be looking to sell

Trip: To be under the influence of a drug; to travel to score

Trucking: Moving

Turkey: Bad narcotics or substance in lieu of narcotics

Turn on: To take drugs. Turn someone on; to give someone drugs

Turtle: LSD or PCP tablet shaped like a turtle shell

Uncut: Pure form of a drug

Upper: Amphetamine

Up-tight: Upset

User: Drug addict

U.S.P.: Pharmaceutical methamphetamine

Water: Methamphetamine

Wasted: Unconscious or almost unconscious from being under the influence of a drug

Way out: Extreme

Weed: Marijuana

Weekend habit: Small, irregular habit

Wedge: Type of LSD, usually a tablet

Whites: Benzedrine

White stuff: Heroin, usually Chinese

Windowpane: Type of LSD

Wired: Under the influence

Withdraw: To stop using narcotics

Works: Injection paraphernalia

Wrong: Bad or untrustworthy

Yellows: Nembutal

Zee: One ounce of a drug; sleep

Zig-Zag man: The man shown on Zig-Zag brand cigarette papers, which are commonly used to roll marijuana cigarettes

Zonked, zonked out: Loaded or O.D.'d on drugs

STREET-GANG SLANGUAGE

The following list contains terms and phrases that are, as of this writing, used by street gangs, primarily the Los Angeles Blood and Crip gangs. As these terms and phrases change frequently, it is best, for writing purposes, to contact your local law-enforcement agency for recent updates and changes.

Ace kool: Best friend, back-up

Base head: Person hooked on cocaine

Beemer: BMW vehicle

Benzo: Mercedes Benz

Blob: Crips' nickname for Crip gang member

Blood: Piru, non-Crip

Bo: Marijuana

Boned out: Quit, chickened out, left

Book: Run, get away, leave

Break: Run, get away

Break-down: Shotgun

Bucket: Old, raggedy car

Bud: Marijuana
Bullet: One year in custody
Bumping titties: Fighting
Busted: Shot at someone
Buster: Young guy trying to be a gang member; fake gang member
Check it out: Listen to what I have to say
Chill out: Stop it, don't do that
Colum: Colombian marijuana
Crab: Bloods' nickname for Crip gang member
Cragared down: Low-rider-type car
Cuzz: Crip
Do a ghost: To leave, leave the scene
Double-deuce: .22-caliber gun
Down for mine: Ability to protect self
Drag: Ability to sweet-talk girls
Draped: Wearing a lot of gold jewelry
Drop a dime: Snitch on someone
Deuce and a quarter: Buick 225 vehicle
Durag: Handkerchief wrapped around head
Dusted: Under the influence of PCP
Eastly: Very ugly person
Eight-track: Two-and-a-half grams of cocaine
Esseys: Mexicans
Everything is everything: It's all right
Four-five: .45-caliber gun
Freak: Good-looking girl
Fresh: Good looking, clean
G-ride: Gangster ride; stolen car
Gang-banging: Involved in gang activity
Get down: Fight
Gig: Gathering
Glass house: '77 or '78 Chevy
Head hunter: Female who does sexual acts for cocaine

High roller: Successful drug dealer
Holding down: Controlling turf or area
Homey: Fellow gang member
Home boy: Fellow gang member
Hood: Neighborhood
Hook: Phony, imitation
Hoopty: Car
Hustler: Not into gangs, strictly out to make money
Illing: Making mental mistake
Jacked-up: Beat up or assaulted
Jammed: Confronted
Jim Jones: Marijuana joint laced with cocaine and dipped in PCP
Juiced: Vehicle with hydraulics to raise and lower car
Kibbles & Bits: Crumbs of cocaine
Kicking back: Relaxing, killing time
Kool: It's all right
Laces: Chrome, spoke rims
Lady: Girlfriend
Let's bail: Let's leave
Lifts: Hydraulics to raise and lower car
Liquid juice: PCP
Lit up: Shot at
Lizard butt: Ugly girl
Mack: Ability to sweet-talk girls
Main man: Best friend, back-up
Making bank: Making money, usually illegally
Man: Cop, policeman
Mark: Want-to-be gang member
Mobile: Proper, nice looking
Molded: Embarrassed
Monte C: Monte Carlo vehicle
Mud duck: Ugly girl
O/G: Original gangster

On the pipe: Free basing cocaine
Packing: Gang member has gun in his possession
Player: Not into gangs, strictly out to make money
Popped a cap: Shot at someone
Primo: Marijuana joint laced with cocaine
Rag: Color of gang; handkerchief
Raise: Leave
Recruiting: Looking for good-looking girls
Red eye: Hard stare
Ride: Car
Ride on, rode on: To go to a rival neighborhood in vehicles to attack other gangs
Righteous: True or affirmative answer
Rock: Crystallized cocaine
Roo-rah: Loud talking
Ru: Piru
Rush: To sweet-talk girls
Scandalous: Deadbeat person, bad person
Scratch: Embarrassed
Set: Neighborhood
Sherm: PCP
Slob: Crips' nickname for Blood gang member
Snaps: Money
Sprung: Addicted to cocaine
Squab: Fight, argue
Stall it out: Stop doing what you're doing
Strawberry: Female who does sexual acts for cocaine
Talking head: Argue; wanting to fight
Talking smack: Aggressive talking
Trey-eight: .38-caliber gun
Trick: Phony sissy
Trip: Too much, something else
Turkish: Heavy, ornamental gold necklace, earrings
Up on it: Have knowledge of drug scene; successful in dealing drugs

Wack: PCP

Wave: Short, close-cropped haircut

What it "b" like: Blood greeting

What it "c" like: Crip greeting

What's up: What's going on

Questions or information (about the Bloods and Crips Los Angeles gangs) should be directed to the Los Angeles County District Attorney's Office, (213) 725-5081, or California Department of Justice-BOCCI, P.O. Box 903357, Sacramento, CA 94203-3570; (916) 739-5715.

PRISON SLANGUAGE

Better people: High-grade or more intelligent prisoners

Blues: Regular prisoners

Block: Cell-block area

B.O.P.: Bureau of Prisons

Booty bandit: Bully who rapes young convicts under guise of protecting them from other cons

Bull: Prison guard

Bull ring: Exercise yard

Bus therapy: Punishment wherein convict is taken from cell during the night, given cigarettes and jacket, and put aboard a bus to another facility. Can continue for months from joint to joint with no commissary money and no other clothes or personal effects. Only immediate family can be made aware of whereabouts. Guise is to protect prisoner from other cons.

Bad time: In trouble; quarrelsome; depressed

Crib: Prison cell

Country club: Minimum security facility

Dime: Ten-year sentence

Fag (she): Effeminate prisoner

Feather bed: Padded cell

Fish: New prisoner

Good time: Getting along well

Hard time: Maximum security; tough work assignment

Hole: Solitary confinement

Joint: Prison

Joint handles: Nicknames given to cons by other cons, usually connected to or related to crime new con committed. If no joint handle is given, new con is generally not trusted by others.

Khakis: Newly arrived cons

Lockdown: When prisoners are placed back in cells

Mainline: Dining room

Nickel: Five-year sentence

Piano: Prison workbench

Population: Inmates of prison

Prune juice: Homemade wine

Rat: Informer, to inform

Screw: Prison guard

Shadow box: Visitors' room

Street: Outside world

Standup guy: Respected by other inmates

Stinger: Special wire plugged into light socket to melt chocolate bar for cocoa or instant coffee. Illegal but done.

Stash: Any illegal substance that is hidden

"Stranger in the Night": Tune whistled by inmates to alert other cons that guard is within hearing distance

Yard: Exercise yard

Yard bull: Guard in exercise yard

Warden's office: Toilet

Waste: To kill another prisoner

Working for Jesus: Religious prisoner with ulterior motive

Works: Prison laundry

POLICE SLANGUAGE

A.C.U.: Anti-Crime Unit

A.D.A.: Assistant district attorney

Apache: Signal given that Internal Affairs is around

A.T.F.: Alcohol, Tobacco & Firearms Agency

Bag 'em: Have corpse placed in body bag; insert clue for weapon in plastic bag for prints, evidence

Banker: Street term for person receiving or holding cash paid out for drugs

Blade man: Criminal known to consistently use a knife as a weapon

Book, The: Official rules and regulations

Book: Bookmaking operation

Busboy: Prisoner or suspect being shifted around

By the book: To go by the rules and regulations

C of D: Chief of Detectives

C of O: Chief of Operations

Caper: Crime

Caseload: Active cases pending

Catching: Officer on duty or assignment

Chicken hawk: Child molester

Choke: Choke hold on victim; also *fiend*

Chop shop: Place where stolen cars are stripped down by car thieves to be sold later

Collar: Arrest

Crew: Youngsters who come together to engage in crime

C.S.U.: Crime Scene Unit

Cuff: Handcuff

D.B.: Dead body

D.D.: Dying declaration

Dirty: Officer who is corrupt

D.O.A.: Dead on Arrival

Do-rag: Street term for tight head scarf

Drop gun: Nonofficial weapon carried by officer

Floater: Dead body recovered from water

Frisk: Examine for weapon or contraband

Garden room: The morgue

Heist: Robbery

Hit man: Contracted killer

Holding pen: Cell where prisoner awaits booking

Hose job: Street slang for oral sex

Hot: Refers to stolen merchandise

I.A.D.: Internal Affairs Division

In-and-out book: Record of officers transferred from place to place

Jakes: Uniformed police officers

Jane Doe: Unidentified female (usually a corpse)

John: Male customer for a prostitute

John Doe: Unidentified male (usually a corpse)

Job: The job; being on the police force

Jumper: Bail jumper; someone who leaps from a building, bridge, etc.

Keeper: Prisoner held on formal charges

Latent: Refers to an invisible (finger- or hand-) print created by natural oils, found on polished surfaces

Lead: Clue, direction to be followed

Leg irons: Sometimes used while transporting prisoner

Major crimes: Police section handling only major crimes

Make: Identity

Mark: Victim

M.E.: Medical Examiner

M.O.: Modus operandi, or method of operating

Mouthpiece: Criminal's attorney

Narc: Narcotics officer

No further: No other units need respond

On the take: Officer accepting illegal goods or money

Outside too long: Working the street for too long a period

Pat down: Frisk

P.B.A.: Police Benevolent Association

P.C.: Police Commissioner

P.D.: Public Defender

Pen: Holding pen for prisoners

Perp: Perpetrator of a crime

Pervert: Distorted, debased, as in sexual perversion

Piece: Gun

Pimp: Procurer for prostitutes

Plant: A stakeout; to place a misleading piece of evidence

Pocket man: Same as banker

Prossie: Prostitute

Rabbi: A protector, usually someone in higher office

Rap sheet: Record of arrests, convictions of a suspect

Rights: Miranda Law, requiring that anyone arrested must be informed of his or her legal rights

R.K.C.: Resident Known Criminal file

R.M.P.: Rapid Mobilization Plan

R.P.C.: Released Prisoner Cases

Shadow: To follow a suspect

Shitcan: Homicide unlikely to be solved

Shoofly: Officer working for Internal Affairs Division

Snitch: Informer

S.O.P.: Standard Operating Procedure

Spike: Drug user's needle

Stakeout: Observation of a suspect or location where a suspect is to appear or a crime is to take place

Suit: Young, educated officer likely to advance to headquarters

Tap: Wire or telephone tap

Ten card: Officer's force record card

Throwaway: Gun or clothes worn and discarded by mugger to avoid pursuit

Tin: Officer's badge

T.O.: Table of Organization, a chart that illustrates the chain of command

T/P/O: Time, place, and occurrence

Two-way radio: Informer

Watering hole: Officers' hangout

Whip: Officer in charge

Wired: Carrying recording device; location having a recording device
Zapped: Shot

ON-THE-ROAD SLANGUAGE

This list constitutes a partial reference to the slang used by truckers and other radio-equipped vehicles with respect to law-enforcement agencies.

Badge on a beaver: Female officer
Batman and Robin: Two officers in a patrol car
Big hats: State police only
Black-and-white: Police patrol car
Blueboy: Local or state police
Charlie's Angel: Female officer
D.C.'s: Federal officers
Eye in the sky: Police chopper
Hound dog: Local or state police
Mama bear: Female officer
Mister Do-right: Local or state police
Mounty: Local or state police
Pig on a wheel: Motorcycle officer
Pink Panther: Local or state police
Prez-Fuzz: Federal officers
Rent-a-cop: Private security
Smoke for rent: Private security
Smoke in the sky: Police chopper
Smokey: Local or state police
Spy in the sky: Police chopper
Two-wheel smokey: Motorcycle officer
White knight: Local or state police

GENERAL CRIME SLANGUAGE

Ammo: Ammunition
A.R.: Armed robbery

Bad mouth: Derogatory statement

Bag man: One who moves or transports for organized crime

Bag lady: Same as above

Ball: Sexual intercourse

Bananas: Insane

Beat: To cheat or steal

Beat the rap: To get acquitted

Be down on: Be angry at, disapproving of

Belcher: An informer

Betty: Skeleton key

Bike: Motorcycle

Biker: Member of a motorcycle gang

Bitch: Homosexual who is effeminate

Bite: To solicit for a loan, as in "to put the bite on"

Blade: Knife

Bleeder: Extortionist

Blow: To leave

Boiler: Auto

Boogie: To leave

Book: Bookmaker's betting organization; to leave

Bookends: To go as a pair; "two peas in a pod"

Bookie: One who takes bets; one who "makes book"

Boost: To shoplift or steal

Booster: Shoplifter or thief

Bopper: One who shoots firearms; a hit man

Brain bucket: Motorcycle helmet

Brother: One of ours, usually associated with blacks

Bug: Burglar alarm; listening device, wire

Bugs: Crazy, insane

Bull: Policeman

Bum rap: False, unjustified accusation

Bummer: Rotten; bad luck; a depressing situation

Burn: Shoot; electrocute

Bust: A police raid; to be arrested ("busted")

Buster: Blackjack

Butterfly man: Forger

Button man: Someone who selects or points out the job

Buzzer: Policeman's shield

Call girl: High-priced prostitute

Candle and blood: Initiation into Mafia

Candy: Jewelry

Case: Reconnoiter

Chatterbox: Machine gun

Chiv: Knife

Chopper: Machine gun; modified motorcycle

Christmas bundles: Large sums of money

Colors: Emblem or identifying colors on outlaw motorcycle riders' jackets or street gangs

Comer: Person on the way up

Con: To dupe someone out of money by gaining their confidence; confidence man; convict

Contract: Hired to kill

Cool: At ease, no problems, content

Cop out: To quit

Cop a plea: Plea bargain; to accept with explanation

Cracker: Southerner

Crash: To break into; to come down after a drug-induced high

Croak: To kill

Cush: Money

Cut: To share; a substance used to increase the amount of a drug (and thereby dilute its toxicity), as in adding baby powder or laxative to cocaine for greater profit

Diamond season: Warm weather

Dig: Understand

Dip: Pickpocket

Do him, her: To kill him or her

Down on: To dislike a person; oral sex

Drop: Receiver of stolen goods; to kill

Drying out: Abstaining from alcohol; getting over being drunk

Dude: Male

Enforcer: Someone who carries out or enforces instructions of a criminal boss, usually through physical intimidation

Faggot (fag): Homosexual

Fall: To be arrested, "taking a fall"

Far out: Favorable, good; extreme

Feds, Feebs: Federal law officers

Fence: Someone who buys and sells stolen goods

Finger: To point out or identify

Finger: As to "he gave me the finger"

Fink: Detective; an informer; "to fink," as in to betray or inform on a cohort

Fix: Bribe

Flag: Warning

Freebee: Free, at no cost or consideration

Frisk: Pocket picking

Fry: To electrocute

Fuzz: Police

Gash: White woman raped

Gat: Firearm

Get fresh: To buy new clothes

Going down: About to happen

Gone: Leaving now, as in "I'm gone"

Grease: To bribe, as in "grease" someone's palm with money

Grease ball: Italian or Latin extraction

Grifter: Swindler

Guinea: Italian

Hack it: Do it

Handle: Understanding; getting a good grip

Hanger banger: Stealer of pocketbook hanging on a woman's arm

Hanging paper: Passing bad checks

Hang it on him: To frame someone
Hardtail: Motorcycle with a rigid frame (no suspension in back)
Hard time: Jail time in state prison
Harmon: Motorcycle front end with no springs
Harness: Uniform
Harness bull: Police
Head: As in oral copulation
Head screw: Prison warden
Heat: Police chase; police pressure; police officer
Heater: Gun
Heavy: Serious, of great importance
Hebe: Jew
Heister: Highway robber, as in truck hold-up
High: On drugs; happy
Hit: Kill
Hit on: To approach someone sexually; to borrow
Hock: To pawn; to annoy someone
Home boy: Neighborhood kid; gang member
Hooker: Prostitute
Hots, The: To like, especially to like a person sexually
Hustle: To steal; confidence racket
Hype: Short-change; make a big deal of something
Jimmy: To pry open
John: Rich guy; prostitute's customer
Joint: Marijuana; prison
Jugs: Woman's breasts
Jumper: One who jumps bail; one who leaps from window
Junk: Drugs, usually heroin
Kook: Strange person
Kinky: Weird, strange, abnormal
Lam: Escape
Legit: Legal
Liz: Police patrol

Looker: Attractive woman

Limey: English motorcycle

Main man: Close associate; boss; partner

Make: To obtain something; to detect

Man, The: Police

Mark: Proposed victim, usually of a swindle or scam

Marker: Gambling I.O.U.

McCoy, The Real: Genuine

Mickey Mouse: A piece of junk

Moll: Woman, usually a gangster's girlfriend

Moll buzzer: Picker of women's pockets

Mouthpiece: Lawyer

Mug: To rob a person by physical manhandling

Mule: One who transports drugs

Nailed: Arrested

Nippers: Handcuffs

One large: One hundred dollar bill

One-percenter: Outlaw motorcycle group (1 percent of motorcycle riders)

Oreo: "Uncle Tom"-type black, i.e., white on the inside, black on the outside

Out of sight: Great

Owe me one: To owe an outstanding favor

Packin': Possession of a weapon; to take a rider on the back of a motorcycle

Pad: Living quarters

Paddie, paddy, patty: White person. In Boston, Irish

Paperhanger: Counterfeit money passer

Peter: Bank vault or safe

Peterman: Safecracker; someone who illegally enters a bank vault to steal money

Pig: Police officer; woman who is a slut or ugly

Pin: Identify an individual by his lifestyle

Pinch: Arrest

Pineapple: Bomb

Plant: Place selected for robbery; place of concealment; a spy placed in a trusted situation

Plastic: Fake, not real

P.O.: Parole or probation officer

Pokey: Jail

Post time: Time to start

Pushed out of shape: Angry

Put it down: To stop; to degrade

Put on: To tease or deceive; to confuse

Putt: Modified motorcycle

Putten: To go for a motorcycle ride

Queen: Male homosexual

Queer: Counterfeit money; homosexual

Quiff: Prostitute

Rabbi: Protector

Raffles: Burglar

Rags: Clothes

Raked: Car raised in back; extended front end of motorcycle without raising ground level

Raincheck: Parole

Ranch: Residence

Rap: To talk; arrest or conviction; time in prison; to assume blame

Rat: To inform or betray

Rattler: Freight train

Read: To analyze or understand

Righteous: Good; honest, the truth

Right on: Good, perfect

Ripoff: A scam; stolen ("ripped off"); to be arrested; sexual intercourse

Rock: Diamonds or precious gems; crystallized cocaine

Rock house: Heavily fortified and protected house dealing in drugs, usually rock or crack

Rod: Firearm; penis

Roust: To be hassled by police

Run: Group of motorcycle riders going somewhere, usually at least fifty miles away

Sap: Fool; blackjack

Scam: Ploy; plot; confidence racket

Scene: A location, usually of a crime; a social event; to draw attention to

Schmuck: Fool

Scoot: Modified motorcycle

Scooter tramp: Outlaw-motorcycle-gang member

Score: To have sexual intercourse; the loot; to obtain drugs

Scratch: Money; bad check

Screw: Police; to have sexual intercourse

Shades: Sunglasses

Shafted: Taken advantage of

Shank: Knife

Shill: Decoy

Shine (on): To ignore a person or plans; to tease

Shit: Dope

Sing: To confess; to inform on others

Sister: Female associate, usually black

Skim: Taking money from profits before delivery

Skip: To leave town; to jump bail

Slammer: Prison

Sled: Car

Sleepers: Wallets

Snatcher: Kidnapper

Snitch: Police informer

Solid: O.K., all right

Soul: Black-styled quality

Sounds: Music

Squeeze: Put pressure on

Split: To leave

Springer: Motorcycle front end that has dual springs

Stall: Confederate who obscures thief or hinders pursuit
Standup guy: Someone who can be depended upon
Stiff: Convict
Stir: Prison
Stoolie: informant
Stretch: Prison- or jail-sentence term
Sucker: A dupe; victim
Sucker pockets: Pockets on outside of garments
Suede: Black
Take: The money a corrupt policeman takes, as in "on the take"; the spoils of a racket or a robbery
Take a cab: To leave
Take for a ride: Death trip of a hoodlum, or of a hoodlum's enemy
Take out: To murder
Tell it like it is: To tell the truth
Threads: Clothes
Tight: To be close to someone; friend
Till: Cash register; any place money is stashed
Tin man: Police
Together: State of self-understanding
Torch: To start a fire, usually arson; to pine over the loss of someone, usually romantically
Torch job: Arson
Torpedo: Gunman; killer
Trike: Three-wheeled motorcycle
Trumpet: Triumph motorcycle
Turn: To inform to the police
Turn a trick: To prostitute
Twist: To inform to the police
Uncool: Unknowledgeable; not acting in a suave or socially accepted manner
Up front: Straightforward
Uptown: Big time
User: Drug addict

Vibes: Feelings

Vig: Loan shark's interest on loan

Vine: Clothes

Wagon: Car; coroner's van; police van

Washed: Refers to money that has been channeled through an intermediary to conceal its source

W.A.S.P.: White Anglo-Saxon Protestant

Waste: To murder

Wheel: Boss; to bet one horse with all others in the race

Wheels: Car; woman's breasts

Wheelman: Driver of a getaway car

Wheeler-dealer: Big man; con artist

Whiskers: Police

Wiped out: Tired, exhausted

Wired: Strung out; carrying a recording device

Wire room: Bookie's place

Wop: Italian

Yaleman: Expert with locks

Yancy: Nervous

Yard: One hundred dollars

Yid: Jew

Zap: To shoot

Zip gun: Homemade gun

30

Crime

METHODS OF ESCAPE

Tunneling
Shooting way out
Taking hostage
Commandeering vehicle
Distraction
Use of ladder
Use of rope
Hiding or stowing away
Scaling
Underwater
Leaping
Driving
Running
Using explosives
Sawing
Kicking down
Fighting
Airshaft and sewer crawling
Forged papers
Helicopter drop—rope or ladder
Impersonation

Key theft
Overland hiking and hiding
Sudden dash
Suspension from height
Swimming

MEANS OF EXECUTION

Axing
Suffocation
Beating
Burying alive
Arson
Drowning
Cremation
Throwing from height
Shooting
Garroting
Electrocuting
Overdosing drug
Hit and run
Poisoning
Gassing
Hanging
Impaling
Exposing to wild animal
Exposing to extreme cold or heat
Stoning
Starving
Throwing acid
Frightening
Bombing
Stabbing
Exposing to disease
Crashing (auto)

UNUSUAL MEANS OF DISPOSING OF BODY

Incinerator—cremated
At sea

Fed to animal or fish
Compactor
Auto crusher
Down well
Sealed in wall
Buried under floor
Acid
Cut into small pieces and disposed of in different places
Placed in existing, marked grave
Dropped in quicksand
Disposed of in trash (bagged)
Buried in woods
Dropped from plane

ACTS OF VIOLENCE, TORTURE, CRUELTY

Bone breaking
Bone crushing
Acid throwing
Binding
Kicking
Beating
Blackjacking
Branding
Burning
Chaining
Arm twisting
Bleeding
Burying alive
Cigarette burning
Disfiguring
Dragging
Pressing with weights
Impaling alive
Mutilating
Needles under fingernails
Pistol whipping
Hair extraction
Hook hanging
Electric shock
Freezing

Flogging
Blinding
Decapitating
Boiling oil
Flesh-eating ants
Exposing to wild animal
Snakebite
Powerful light in eyes
Dripping water on head
Bread-and-water diet
Genital crushing
Genital electrical shocking
Head twisting
Leg twisting
Stretching
Forced marching
Forced perversion
Castration
Amputation
Crucifixion
Depriving of sleep
Fingernail pulling
Whipping
Frightening
Incarcerating in tight quarters
Skull crushing
Suspending by thumbs
On the rack
Incarcerated in room with rats
Rubber-hose beating
Salting wound
Starving
Thumb twisting
Teeth pulling
Eye gouging
Stoning
Tar-and-feathering
Chain beating
Hanging upside down
Standing in confinement
Rib cracking
Lead-pipe beating

Spreading apart
Shattering kneecap
Running over by auto
Shooting
Strangling
Garroting
Knifing
Slow poisoning
Drowning
Slow drowning
Immersion in hot water
Setting afire
Scalping
Gang-banging
Forcible rape
Sodomy
Forcing to view an atrocity
Thrown to man-eating fish
Thrown to man-eating animal
Thrown from high place
Hanging
Axing
Deafening by sound (high decibel)
Tearing of flesh
Burning by steam
Bombing
Gassing
Mugging
Poison darts
Cat o'nine-tail lashing
Burning at stake
Thumbscrew
Hot wax
Kidnapping
Sandbagging
Slave labor

31

Police Codes

The role of police communications as the backbone of police tactics has never been more essential than today, when radio and television are being used so effectively in crime prevention and detection. To facilitate more rapid communication, codes have been devised by which one or two words can tell the whole story. It is worth noting that the codes are used principally for saving air time and not for security reasons.

Two basic codes are used with many variations. They are usually called the *Nine Code* and the *Ten Code.* In recent years, the latter code has been gaining favor. The Association of Police Communications Officers has for some time been urging the universal adoption of the Ten Code in order to standardize the code system.

Note that codes differ from one area to another. Consult the police department of the locale where your story is set to determine the equivalents of these LAPD codes.

TEN CODE

Code 1: Your convenience
Code 2: Urgent, no red light and siren
Code 3: Emergency, use red light and siren
Code 4: No further assistance needed

Code 5: Stakeout
Code 6M: Misdeameanor want
Code 6F: Felony want
Code 6AD: Felony want, armed and dangerous
Code 7: Mealtime
Code 8: Box alarm
Code 10: Bomb threat
Code 20: Assist officer, urgent
Code 30: Officer needs help, emergency
Code 33: Emergency in progress, do not transmit
187: Murder
207: Kidnapping
211: Robbery
245: ADW (assault with deadly weapon)
261: Rape
288: L & L conduct (lewd & lascivious)
311: Indecent exposure
415: Disturbance
415F: Family disturbance
460: Burglary
480: Felony hit-and-run
481: Misdemeanor hit-and-run
487: Grand theft
488: Petty theft
502: Drunk driver
503: Stolen vehicle
505: Reckless driving
510: Vehicle speeding
647: Vagrant
647A: Child molest
10-1: Receiving poorly
10-2: Receiving O.K.
10-4: Message received O.K.
10-5: Relay to ______________
10-7: Out of service at ______________
10-7B: Out of service, personal
10-70D: Off duty
10-8: In service
10-8X: In service with female. Mileage:
10-9: Repeat
10-10: Out of service at home
10-12: Visitors or officials present

10-13: Weather and road conditions
10-14: Escort
10-14F Funeral detail
10-15: Have prisoner in custody
10-16: Pick up
10-19: Return to/enroute station
10-20: Location
10-21: Phone your office, or:
10-21A: Phone home my ETA is ____________
10-21B: Phone your home
10-21R: Phone radio
10-22: Cancel
10-23: Standby
10-25: Do you have contact with ____________
10-28: Registration
10-29: Check for wanted
10-32: Drowning
10-33: Alarm sounding
10-34: Open door
10-35: Open window
10-39: Status of ____________
10-40: Is ____________ available for phone call
10-45: Ambulance, injured
10-46: Ambulance, sick
10-49: Proceed to ____________
10-50: Obtain a report
10-51: Drunk
10-52: Resuscitator
10-53: Man down
10-54: Possible dead body
10-55: Coroner's case
10-56: Suicide
10-56A: Attempted suicide
10-57: Firearms discharged
10-58: Garbage complaint
10-59: Malicious mischief
10-62: Meet the citizen
10-65: Missing person
10-66: Suspicious person
10-67: Person calling for help
10-70: Prowler
10-71: Shooting

10-72: Knifing
10-73: How do you receive
10-80: Explosion
10-86: Any traffic for ______________
10-87: Meet officer
10-91: Stray animal
10-91A: Vicious animal
10-91B: Noisy animal
10-91C: Injured animal
10-91D: Dead animal
10-91F: Animal bite
10-91H: Stray horse
10-97: Arrived at the scene
10-98: Finished with last assignment
11-24: Abandoned vehicle
11-26: Abandoned bicycle
11-54: Suspicious vehicle
11-79: Accident, ambulance enroute
11-80: Accident, major injury
11-81: Accident, minor injury
11-82: Accident, property damage
11-83: Accident, no detail
11-84: Traffic control
11-96: Leaving the vehicle to investigate an auto. If not heard from in ten minutes, dispatch cover. (Give license and location.)

POLICE CODES AND TRAFFIC VIOLATIONS

001: Operating after permit refused, canceled, or suspended
002: Driving under the influence of liquor or drugs
003: Minor law
004: Failure to stop; accident resulting in death or personal injury
005: Perjury, false affidavit or statement under oath
006: Turning off lights to avoid identification
007: Manslaughter or negligent homicide
008: Any felony in the commission of which a motor vehicle is used
009: Legally adjudicated insane
010: Minor
012: Violation while transporting explosives
201: Loaning or altering a permit

202: Operating after permit revoked
203: Displaying canceled, revoked, suspended, fictitious, or fraudulently altered license
204: Smoke screen
301: Leaving after colliding, no personal injury
302: Failure to give information and render aid, personal injury
401: Failure to report an accident
501: Permitting unlicensed operator to drive
601: Reckless driving
602: Speeding (exceeding posted speed limits by ten miles or more)
603: Violation contributing to an accident
604: Failure to grant right of way
605: Failure to grant pedestrians right of way
606: Failure to grant blind pedestrian right of way
701: Speeding
702: Improper passing
703: Automatic signal
704: Stop sign
705: Failure to keep right of center
706: Crossing center line
707: School bus
708: Following too closely
709: Operating without a license
710: Operating on expired license
711: Failure to dim headlights
712: Improper license
713: Driving too slowly
714: Racing or speed contest
715: Wrong way, one-way street
716: Improper turn
717: Failure to give hand signal
718: Failure to stop for emergency vehicle
719: Operating unregistered motor vehicle
720: Failure to obtain special chauffeur's license
721: License restriction
722: Operating on instruction license unaccompanied
723: Inadequate brakes
724: Failing to obey officer's signal
725: Operating emergency vehicle unsafely
726: Failing to obey traffic-control device
727: Failing to obey flashing signal lights

728: Failure to make required stop
729: Failure to leave car tracks
730: Coasting down grade
731: Operating motorcycle or motor bicycle contrary to law
732: Driver of emergency vehicle failing to exercise care
733: Failure to stop at R/R crossing
734: Driver's view obstructed
735: Following fire apparatus too closely
736: Operating unfit vehicle
737: Displaying license of another
738: Failing to stop at through highway
739: Unlawful taking of motor vehicle
740: No headlights
741: Crossing over fire hose
742: Improper truck loading
743: Improper lights
744: Restricted use of television
745: Improper equipment
746: Motor vehicle height, weight, width, and length requirements
747: Improper loading
748: Failure to obtain chauffeur's license
801: No license in possession
802: No registration card in possession
803: Failing to change address
804: Inadequate muffler
805: False evidence of title or registration
806: Improper registration
807: Failing to obtain license and/or license tags within thirty days
808: Tampering with motor vehicle
809: Damage to highways
810: Unlawful use of license
811: Failure to display warning device on disabled vehicle
812: Failure to deliver certificate of title
813: Unnecessary use of horn

32

Correctional Institutions

Cities, states, and the Federal government each have their own penal systems that are clearly defined by law as to their operation. However, it is the type of crime and jurisdiction in which the crime was committed that determines whether the criminal shall be tried by a city court, a state court, or a federal court. Criminals convicted in a city court, state court, or federal court will be sentenced and committed to one of that city's, state's, or federal penal institutions.

As it would practically require a book in itself to include all the city, state, and federal penal institutions, I have selected the penal institutions in the state of California to serve as a broad example of the various types of penal institutions across the nation. I have also reprinted the document "Visiting Instructions" used at the U.S. Penitentiary at Lampoc, California, as an example of what is required when visiting an inmate at a federal institution. I heartily recommend that you research the particular penal institution you may wish to write about for further information on location, type of facility, inmate population, operation, etc.

CALIFORNIA'S CORRECTIONAL INSTITUTIONS

The Program

The California Department of Corrections administers 16 major institutions, 34 secure conservation camps, two community correctional centers and more than 66 local parole offices.

The department is responsible for the control and programming of more than 67,000 persons in institutions and about 38,000 in the community under supervision of parole agents.

Institutions are classified as Security Levels I-IV. Level I is minimum, Level IV is maximum, and Levels II and III are medium security confinement.

The following information is designed to give a capsule summary of the institutions and camps which the department operates. For additional information, write to:

Department of Corrections
Communications Office
630 "K" Street, Room 211
P.O. Box 942883
Sacramento, CA 94283-0001

October, 1987

The Institutions

SAN QUENTIN STATE PRISON (SQ)

Address: San Quentin State Prison, San Quentin, CA 94964
Warden: Dan Vasquez
Population: 3,000
Opened 1852

San Quentin, California's first and best known penal institution, is located on the north shore of San Francisco Bay in Marin County. San Quentin dates its origin to the prison ship "Wabau," which was anchored off Point Quentin in 1852 with 92 prisoners aboard. Construction of the prison on 20 acres of nearby land began in the same year.

Today, the prison occupies 432 acres and houses 3,000 inmates, a third of whom require the department's highest level of security. The prison complex includes four large old-style cell blocks, a modern maximum security unit, minimum security work crew quarters, a medium security compound with modular dormitories, an industries complex, maintenance and vocational shops, and a medical facility. The state's only gas chamber is located in San Quentin and all male inmates under sentence of death are housed at San Quentin.

San Quentin has traditionally housed the state's most notorious prisoners. During the last decade, San Quentin has shared duty with

Folsom Prison and Tehachapi (Southern Max) as Level IV or Maximum Security. Level IV is the security designation for the most disruptive, or violent inmates, or those who present the greatest risk of escape. San Quentin also houses Level I (Minimum Custody), and Level II (Medium Custody). After 135 years of providing maximum security housing for the state's roughest inmates, San Quentin is undergoing a transition to a Level II facility.

An aggressive prison construction program is providing California with state-of-the-art, high-tech Maximum Security prisons that will carry the mission so long fulfilled by San Quentin. The new construction and extensive renovation of San Quentin will allow a shift from a Level IV mission to a Level II mission. San Quentin will continue to house Levels I, II and IV, but Level II will be predominant.

CORRECTIONAL TRAINING FACILITY (CTF)

Address: P.O. Box 686, Soledad, CA 93960-0686
Superintendent: Eddie Myers
Population: 5,511
Opened 1947

The Correctional Training Facility is actually a complex which consists of three separate facilities. The oldest part of CTF dates from 1946 when a camp center administered by San Quentin was opened on the site. In 1947, this became an institution in its own right. When the Central Facility was opened in 1951 as a medium security institution, the former camp center became known as South Facility. In 1958, the North Facility opened and the three-facility complex was officially christened the "Correctional Training Facility."

The CTF complex is located on a 965-acre site in the Salinas Valley about 20 miles south of Salinas.

CTF-Central is an armed perimeter, cell-type institution for medium security inmates. It also contains two high security protective housing units.

North Facility is also an armed perimeter, cell-type facility for medium security inmates, most of whom are involved in some type of educational/vocational program.

CTF-South is a Level I facility and houses most of the inmates who perform work outside the security perimeter.

A comprehensive program of industrial and educational activities is available to CTF inmates. Emphasis is on basic training for employment in a recognized trade. The CTF's educational program meets the needs of inmates by offering classes on elementary and secondary levels as well as a two-year and four-year college degree program. Various vocational programs are also available.

CALIFORNIA INSTITUTION FOR WOMEN (CIW)

Address: P.O. Box 6000, Corona, CA 91718
Superintendent: Annie M. Alexander
Population: 2,243
Opened 1952

Until 1933, women prisoners in California were housed in a segregated building on the grounds at San Quentin. In 1929, legislation established an independent facility for women at Tehachapi which became operational in 1933. The present 120-acre site in San Bernardino County was acquired and a new women's institution was established in 1952.

CIW is one of two facilities designated by the Penal Code exclusively for female felons. All female felons committed to the Department of Corrections are received at CIW. Buildings at CIW provide double-bunked rooms and dormitories, in addition to general population housing units and the reception center.

CIW is rated as a Level III/IV institution and houses inmates integrated by custody Level I through IV in its general population.

Approximately 35 percent of the inmate population is involved in an education program.

CIW is designated as the camp training center for female inmates who are administratively assigned to Sierra Conservation Center and transferred to Camos Rainbow, Mailbu, Puerta La Cruz, or McCain Valley. CIW provides two inmate crews, under the direction of CalTrans, to work on state highway roadside beautification.

The Prison Industry Authority (PIA) work program at CIW consists of a textile factory involved in the manufacturing of shirts, jackets, and men's underwear. PIA is also training inmates in a joint venture with vocational education in furniture upholstery and is contracting with local state agencies to reupholster worn furniture.

FOLSOM STATE PRISON (FOL)

Address: P.O. Box W, Represa, CA 95671
Warden: R.G. Borg
Population: 6,944
Opened 1880

California State Prison at Folsom, first opened in 1880, is the state's second oldest correctional facility. Folsom is considered a high maximum security institution. Among its inmates are those serving long sentences, habitual criminals, hard-to-manage persons, and individuals who present a risk to the safety of others.

At Folsom, a walled perimeter encompasses three general population cell blocks and two maximum security housing units. Outside the main facility, Folsom's minimum facility serves as a 410-bed dormitory unit. Program features for minimum security inmates include outside work crew assignments and community re-entry resources for inmates nearing release.

Recently, three maximum security housing units with a design capacity of 1,536 and minimum security housing for 200 were completed. These are now fully occupied.

One of the state's best-known prison industries, the metal stamping and fabricating program which produces the license plates for California motor vehicles, is located at Folsom.

Academic classes from first grade through the college level are offered at Folsom, as are a variety of vocational training programs. Group counseling, organized recreation, and a number of inmate activity groups are also available to inmates.

The handicraft program at Folsom includes the operation of a hobbycraft shop located at the prison's main gate which is open daily to the public. Through this shop and an art show held each year, many inmates are able to display and sell art and craft products. The Folsom Art Show receives considerable local news media attention and is widely attended.

CALIFORNIA INSTITUTION FOR MEN (CIM)

Address: P.O. Box 128, Chino, CA 91710
Superintendent: Otis Thurman
Population: 6,676
Opened 1941

The California Institution for Men is situated on more than 2,500 acres in the city of Chino. CIM consists of four physically separate facilities.

When it was opened as California's third correctional institution in 1941, CIM was unique in the field of penology because it was known as the "prison without walls." CIM-Minimum is the minimum security facility and houses the largest number of inmates.

In 1951, an addition to the original facility was completed. This unit is now known as Reception Center-Central. It is one of two reception centers for newly sentenced male felons from Southern California counties. The reception centers are delegated the arduous task of ensuring the inmate is transferred to the appropriate prison.

The second reception center, Reception Center-West, a dormitory facility, processes pre-sentenced diagnostic cases for the courts, and houses overflow from the central reception center.

The fourth addition to CIM was in 1974 with the acquisition of a former state facility orginally built for the Youth Authority. Currently, this facility, CIM-East, serves as a parole violator processing unit.

All custody levels from minimum through maximum security are provided at CIM.

Vocational training provided at CIM ranges from animal grooming and television repair to commercial deep-sea diving. A full array of academic programs is also available. Work ethic values are taught in all vocational educational and work incentive programs. CIM provides a viable setting for those wishing to redirect their lives while emphasizing security and commitment to public safety.

DEUEL VOCATIONAL INSTITUTION (DVI)

Address: P.O. Box 400, Tracy, CA 95378-0004
Superintendent: Midge Carroll (Acting)
Population: 2,626
Opened 1953

Deuel Vocational Institution is a medium security institution located near Tracy in the San Joaquin Valley.

The institution proper is encircled by two chain link fences forming a security perimeter with eight gun towers. The design capacity is 1,506. Within the general population area of the prison, there are ten cell blocks and two inmate-worker dormitories. There is also one specialized administrative segregation unit. In addition to these units located within the armed perimeter, a 278-bed dormitory style facility, located on institution property, houses minimum custody inmates assigned to critical work projects outside the armed perimeter, including community work crews.

The institution's primary emphasis is on work/training incentive, whereby inmates who work or who are involved in the academic vocational programs can earn time off their sentences.

Academic courses are provided for inmates from basic nonreaders through college. Twenty-two vocational training programs are available to inmates. An extensive on-the-job training program involving vocational education, maintenance, and industries allows inmates to apply skills learned in vocational education to real work situations.

Prison Industries operates a furniture factory, mattress factory, textile assembly factory, trucking distribution center, farm and dairy where inmates are paid on the basis of skills, production, and hours worked.

Part of Deuel Vocational Institution will serve as a Reception Center in the future.

CALIFORNIA MEN'S COLONY (CMC)

Address: P.O. Box 8101, San Luis Obispo, CA 93409
Warden: Wayne Estelle
Population: 6,898
Opened 1954

The East Facility, completed in 1961, was originally designed to house 2,400 inmates but has been modified to house 4,300. The security perimeter consists of two chain link fences controlled by security wire and eight armed-guard towers.

The facility is divided into four units or quadrangles with a gate control tower located in the center. Each quad has its own dining room, elementary classrooms, athletic fields and contains two three-story buildings to house inmates. A well-equipped 65-bed hospital and clinic staffed by physicians, dentists, and other medical personnel is also available to serve the CMC population.

The primary mission of the California Men's Colony is to implement the department's goals of providing psychiatric treatment and evaluation for the CMC population who require such treatment. A team of psychiatrists, psychologists, and neurological consultants offers a comprehensive program of psychiatric evaluation and treatment. In addition, the East Facility offers both academic and vocational education classes through the college level. Prison Industries also operates several industrial programs at the institution which offers paid work experience.

The minimum-security West Facility was established in 1954 to house 1,400 inmates, but has recently been modified and renovated to house 2,400.

The West Facility offers academic education and vocational training classes.

Unit III, which is enclosed by a single non-towered fence line, includes inmate maintenance crews assigned to the National Guard Unit at Camp San Luis and inmates working outside the security perimeter fence at both CMC facilities. A work/fire camp (Camp Cuesta), operated jointly by the Department of Corrections and the Department of Forestry, is located on Unit III's grounds.

CALIFORNIA CORRECTIONAL INSTITUTION (CCI)

Address: P.O. Box 1031, Tehachapi, CA 93561
Superintendent: B.J. Bunnell
Population: 4,551
Opened 1955

The California Correctional Institution is located approximately 50 miles east of Bakersfield in a valley among the Tehachapi Mountains.

Legislation passed in 1929 authorizing the construction of the Tehachapi facility to provide living quarters for women felons. Previously, all female felons had been housed at San Quentin Prison. The institution was completed in 1932 and occupied by women beginning in 1933. In 1952, an earthquake forced evacuation of the buildings. The women were moved to a new facility which had been under construction near Corona.

The Tehachapi facility was reopened as a branch of the California Institution for Men in 1955, and it was declared a separate facility in 1964. Construction of a medium security addition was completed in 1967. Construction of two 500-man maximum security units was completed and the units were occupied in October, 1985. Construction of a 500-cell Level III unit was recently completed.

CCI acts as a program institution for the confinement of Level I through IV inmates who are willing to work and participate fully in available programs. Academic education from nonreader through high school is available with special programs for non-English speaking inmates. Vocational programs have 15 trade sections, and the Prison Industries program produces inmate apparel, flags, drapes, decals and office furniture. The religious program is one of the most active in CDC.

CALIFORNIA MEDICAL FACILITY (CMF)

Address: P.O. Box 2000, Vacaville, CA 95696-2000
Superintendent: Eddie Ylst
Population: 7,920
Opened 1955

The California Medical Facility was established by the Legislature in 1948 and originally opened at Terminal Island in 1950. The facility moved to its present location in 1955.

Originally designed to house 1,487 inmates, the capacity of CMF has been increased to house 1,854 with the addition of an outside dormitory. In 1956, the Northern Reception Center complex was added to process adult male felons from the Northern California counties, with a capacity of 472. The reception center also prepares presentence diagnostic evaluations for northern counties.

The main complex serves as a medical and psychiatric treatment facility for adult male felons. Programs include the treatment of chronic psychotics, group therapy, a 90-day observation program for evaluation of management cases, and medical treatment for inmates requiring surgery or long-term medical care. CMF also houses a work force of medium security inmates to support institutional operations.

CMF-South is the newest addition to the CMF complex. It stands within a separate fenced perimeter and is designed to provide housing for 2,404 Level II and III inmates, bringing the total capacity of the institution to 4,730. Although the name, CMF-South, implies a medical function, the specific focus of CMF-South is vocational training and prison industries production.

Inmates at CMF may participate in a variety of vocational and educational courses at the elementary, high school, and college level. CMF has a large selection of self-help and religious programs which are available. The institution also has an extensive arts and crafts program which includes public exhibitions and sales of inmate handicrafts.

CALIFORNIA REHABILITATION CENTER (CRC)

Address: P.O. Box 1841, Norco, CA 91760
Superintendent: Len Chastain
Population: 4,712
Opened 1962

Originally a private resort, then a hotel and later a U.S. Naval hospital, the property on which the California Rehabilitation Center is located was acquired in 1962 for the purpose of establishing a program for the treatment and control of narcotic addicts.

The institution now functions as a Level II facility for both male and female felons, as well as civil commitments with a history of drug abuse. CRC is located in Norco in Riverside County about 50 miles east of Los Angeles.

Buildings within the 93-acre complex include the original resort facility. Once occupied by Navy nurses and hospital wards, the buildings have been converted to dormitories.

The facility houses a population of approximately 1,000 women and 3,700 men in separate areas of the institution.

Program opportunities include academic education (elementary through high school and some college), vocational training classes (some co-ed), various work programs including a conservation camp (Camp Norco), a pre-release program to assist individuals with their re-entry needs, prison industries, and outside work crews. These crews work in the local community and under contract for CalTrans.

Inmates are also encouraged to participate in a variety of religious programs and self-help groups. Some groups are heavily involved in community programs concerning problems of alcohol or drug abuse, while others learn participatory management through councils established to meet with staff and help solve problems which arise within the institution. All physically capable inmates must participate in work or education programs.

CALIFORNIA CORRECTIONAL CENTER (CCC)

Address: P.O. Box 790, Susanville, CA 96130
Superintendent: William Merkle
Population: 5,098 (Including Camps)
Opened 1963

The California Correctional Center is located 80 miles north of Reno, Nevada, near the Lassen County city of Susanville.

The institution was originally opened as California Conservation Center in 1963 and served as the hub facility for Nothern California conservation camps. However, the mission of the facility was changed in 1975 from a camp center to a facility to house medium security inmates. The name of the facility was changed at that time to its present title, California Correctional Center, to reflect its new mission.

In July, 1982, the center was once more designated as the hub facility for the northern conservation camps. These ten camps have the capacity to house more than one thousand inmates. Five additional camps are being planned with a capacity to house an additional 500 inmates.

Although the primary mission is to service the camp system, there are several hundred inmates housed within the center who are not eligible to go to camp. Academic and vocational programs available to these inmates include repairs and modifications of wood, metal, automotive, clothing products, and shoes for state agencies. Cleaning and repair of clothing for schools and fire departments, local road cleanup and minor repair, park maintenance, and canvas modification and repair for the Department of Forestry are among other programs offered. The inmates housed inside the center are also assigned to support services. Support assignments include culinary, clerical, maintenance, and other duties needed to run the institution.

A new 500-bed unit was recently finished for medium security inmates. This consists of five buildings, each containing 100 cells.

SIERRA CONSERVATION CENTER (SCC)

Address: P.O. Box 497, Jamestown, CA 95327
Superintendent: R.E.Doran
Population: 5,592 (including camps)
Opened 1965

Opened in 1965, the Sierra Conservation Center's primary purpose is to train inmates for placement in the state's central and southern camps, which are jointly operated by the Department of Corrections, Department of Forestry, and the Los Angeles County Fire Department. The camps are located throughout Central and Southern California, from Sacramento County to San Diego County.

SCC is located near Jamestown in the state's historic gold rush country. The facility is divided into two housing units—one providing light security controls, the other medium. Both units utilize dormitory living.

Inmates are selected for SCC either directly from the department's reception centers or from other institutions.

Staff under contract from the Department of Forestry instruct inmates in fire fighting, reforestation, cutting fuel breaks, and flood control. In addition, a special program of physical conditioning prepares inmates for hard work in rugged terrain and on forest firelines prior to their camp assignment.

Vocational training programs include mill and cabinet work, masonry, welding, auto mechanics, body and fender work, and upholstery. While they are undergoing forestry and physical fitness training at SCC, inmates may take part in recreation, religious, self-help, and work programs.

The SCC main facility is designated as a Level I and II institution. A 5-building, 500-inmate Level III addition to the existing facility was recently occupied.

CALIFORNIA STATE PRISON, AVENAL

Address: P.O. Box 8, Avenal, CA 93204
Superintendent: Al Gomez

Design Capacity: 3,034
Opened 1987

The CSP-Kings County at Avenal is located roughly one and one-half miles southeast of Avenal, about 75 miles southwest of Fresno, on a 640-acre site.

The groundbreaking ceremony was conducted on December 18, 1985, and the first busload of inmates was received on January 28, 1987.

CSP Avenal is a program institution for the confinement of Level II inmates who are willing to work and participate fully in available programs. Academic education as well as a variety of vocational training programs will be available upon completion of construction. The Prison Industries Board has also approved a variety of industries for this facility.

MULE CREEK STATE PRISON

Address: P.O. Box 409099, Ione, CA 95640
Superintendent: Roger C. Schaufel
Design Capacity: 1,700
Opened 1987

Mule Creek State Prison is located just west of the town of Ione and about forty miles south of Sacramento.

Upon completion of construction, each of three facilities will contain five housing units for a total of fifteen. One housing unit is a 100-cell short-term Administrative Segregation unit, and the remaining housing units are 100 cells each, suited for general population.

On June 10, 1987, Facility C was activated and received inmates.

Mule Creek State Prison is a program institution for the confinement of Level I and III inmates who are willing to work and fully participate in available programs. Academic and vocational programs will be available upon completion of construction. The Prison Industry Authority has developed and approved a variety of industries for this facility.

RICHARD J. DONOVAN CORRECTIONAL FACILITY (RJD)

Address: P.O. Box 73200, San Ysidro, CA 92073-9200
Superintendent: J.M. Ratollo
Design Capacity: 2,200
Opened 1987

The Richard J. Donovan Correctional Facility at Rock Mountain is on a 774-acre site, southeast of the city of San Diego, approximately

12 miles inland from the Pacific Ocean and two miles north of the Mexican Border. The "Rock," as it is affectionately known, opened July 27, 1987. The facility will add 2,000 medium security (Level III) and 200 minimum security (Level I) beds to the California state prison system.

The prison has four 55-bed medium security facilities and one 200-bed minimum security facility.

The primary mission of the Richard J. Donovan Correctional Facility, Level III, is to provide housing and supervision for inmates requiring medium security. This Level III facility is primarily designed as a training and work-oriented facility which will provide comprehensive vocational, academic, and industrial programs. The facility provides work opportunities for 100 percent of the inmates.

The Prison Industry Authority Enterprises, approved for this prison, include a textile mill, key data entry service, vehicle refurbishing and repair, regional bakery, license plate factory, optical laboratory, and regional laundry. Vocational programs include, baking, meatcutting, landscape gardening, lens grinding, airframe mechanics, aircraft power plant mechanics, mill and cabinetry work, small engine repair, office machine repair, graphic arts and printing, machine shop practices, autobody painting, auto mechanics, dry cleaning, and building and janitorial maintenance.

The Richard J. Donovan Correctional Facility is designated as the department's Southern Deportation Unit and provides 200 beds for the utilization of this program.

The facility also is a Southern Processing Unit for parole violators, returned to custody (PV-RTC) for San Diego and Imperial counties. This unit will provide 200 beds for the processing of these cases.

The Richard J. Donovan Correctional Facility assists in fulfilling the department's goal to distribute inmates to geographic areas from which they were committed.

NORTHERN CALIFORNIA WOMEN'S FACILITY (NCWF)

Address: P.O. Box 213006, Stockton, CA 95213-9006
Superintendent: Teena Farmon
Design Capacity: 400
Opened 1987

The Northern California Women's Facility is located in San Joaquin County, just south of Stockton, adjacent to the Northern California Youth Center.

The first women's prison located in northern California, NCWF is a medium security facility, consisting of four 100-cell housing units.

The first inmates were received July 27, 1987, and design capacity was reached on August 12, 1987.

NCWF is a program institution for the confinement of inmates who are willing to work and participate fully in available programs. Basic adult education and vocational programs (electronics and data processing) are available for those inmates who are interested.

Prison Industries programs include Key Data Entry and Laundry Operations.

Conservation Camps

The conservation camp program has evolved from the system of road camps which was inaugurated in 1915. Known successively as Highway Camps, Harvest Camps, and Honor Camps, the camps were devised to relieve overcrowded prison conditions and create useful employment for inmates who could achieve minimum security status.

Today, the Department of Corrections, the Department of Forestry and other cooperating agencies jointly administer 34 conservation camps. Corrections is responsible for camp management, housekeeping and the supervision of inmates. Cooperating agency staff supervise the work of inmate crews and are responsible for custody of inmates on daily project duties.

The typical camp has from 80 to 120 inmates. Eight to ten correctional personnel and seven to eleven cooperating agency staff are assigned to each camp.

Inmates are assigned to camps after completion of training at SCC or CCC. Most inmates spend an average of one year in a camp assignment and are paid a small daily wage while assigned.

During an average fiscal year, camp crews spend more than one-half million man hours in fire suppression. Crews may be dispatched from camps hundreds of miles away from the scene of a major fire and sometimes spend a week or more at a fire camp location.

In addition to fire fighting, inmate crews undertake fire hazard reduction, fire and truck trail construction, reforestation, work related to the preservation and conservation of natural resources, and other projects for state, county, or local agencies.

While assigned to a camp program, inmates may enroll in academic classes and, at some camps, vocational training courses are also available. Most camps now have family visiting units for inmate use.

33

United States Penitentiary

VISITING INSTRUCTIONS

Families and friends of the men at USP, Lompoc (3901 Klein Blvd., Lompoc, CA 93436), are their primary contact with the community. Visiting, therefore, becomes much more important during the time a man is confined. Because of the special nature of the institution and our concern for the security and well being of the men here, we have developed the following instructions and regulations, which we ask you to follow.

Normally members of the immediate family (parents, brothers, sisters, wife, and children) are automatically placed on the inmate's approved visiting list. Persons who are not immediate family members and yet would like to be on the approved list should request so to the inmate's assigned unit management staff. After a person's name is placed on the approved list, it is not necessary to obtain permission in advance of a visit. All other persons must obtain permission in advance to visit. This may be done by writing to the inmate's assigned unit staff, USP, Lompoc, California 93436, at least four weeks before the visit is planned. If the visit is granted, the requesting party will be notified by letter of authorization, which must be presented to the institution at the time of the visit.

Visiting will be permitted from 8:30 a.m. to 3:30 p.m., weekdays and weekends, except on Tuesday and Wednesday, when the visiting room will be closed. Consideration will be given to opening the visiting room on federal holidays that occur on Tuesday or Wednesday. Legal holidays are New Year's Day, Washington's Birthday, Memorial Day, Independence Day, Labor Day, Columbus Day, Veteran's Day, Thanksgiving, and Christmas.

Each inmate will be allotted 40 points permitting 20 to 40 hours of visiting per month. On weekends and holidays, the inmate will be charged two points for each hour of visiting. On weekdays, the inmate will be charged one point for each hour of visiting. These limitations are necessary to avoid overcrowding in the visiting area and excessive loss of time from the inmate's program. Reasonable requests for additional visits due to unusual circumstances will be made in advance to the unit management staff.

Normally only four (4) persons are permitted to visit an inmate at any one time, including children. Visitors under sixteen years of age must be accompanied by a legal guardian, who must also be on an approved visiting list. Children must be the son, daughter, brother, or sister of the inmate. Visitors will be responsible for keeping the children in their company and under control within the bounds of the visiting area.

Female visitors are expected to use good taste in their dress. Persons who come immodestly or provocatively dressed will be denied the privilege of visiting.

Appropriate embracing, kissing, and handshaking by immediate family members will be permitted within the bounds of good taste at the beginning and termination of the visiting period.

All visitors must have some valid proof of their identification with them. I.D.s must have appropriate *picture* identification. Signature identification by itself will not be acceptable. Visitors may present a state driver's license, federal or state I.D. cards, welfare cards, or passports as picture identification.

Visitors may purchase candy, cigarettes, and beverages from the machines located in the visiting area. These items must be consumed by the inmate and his visitor during the visit. The inmate may take nothing back to his quarters. The visitor may bring only the following items into the visiting area: change purse, money, cigarettes, lighter or matches, comb, heart medication, jewelry normally worn, diaper bag to include baby bottle, food, clothes, diapers, powder, or lotion. Unauthorized items will be stored in security lockers provided in the front lobby or may remain in the visitor's vehicle. The visitor may retain the key to the locker during the storage period and return the key at the end of the visiting period.

To introduce contraband of any kind into this institution is a violation of Federal Law (Title 18, Section 1791, US Code).

Inmates are furnished all necessities, and visitors should refrain from bringing articles or gifts of any kind. Cameras and tape recorders are not permitted in the visiting area. Inmates will not be permitted to sign or exchange any papers during the visit. The visiting room officer may request a search of the visitor's personal property. Those visitors found with contraband items will be escorted from the institution and normally removed from the visiting privileges for an extended period or permanently.

The institution is located approximately five miles northwest of Lompoc. Drive west through the city on Ocean Avenue (Route 246), turn right on Floradale Avenue, proceed approximately three miles (through the traffic light, across the bridge, and around the bend) to the main entrance road. Signs will direct you to the main entrance. Taxi and bus service are available from Lompoc to the institution.

No parking is allowed on the roadway leading to the institution or in the circle drive immediately in front of the main gate. Visitors will be directed to the left side parking lot, where visiting parking is clearly marked. No occupants may remain in parked cars. Nonvisitors must leave the institution reservation and may return to pick up the visitors at a prearranged time.

We suggest you arrive no earlier than fifteen minutes before visiting begins, as we do not have adequate waiting room facilities, and you might be inconvenienced. Usually you will be permitted to visit as long as possible, but it may be necessary on occasion to limit the amount of visiting time to relieve overcrowding. Also, a failure to comply with these instructions may result in termination of the visit or suspension or cancellation of the visiting privilege.

34

Parole

WHAT IS PAROLE?

Parole is a period of supervision in the community beginning after an inmate's prison term reaches the legal maximum. This conditional release provides supervision and control over offenders after they return to society.

Parole is a critical period. Through the application of controls and provision of services, the parole agent creates favorable conditions for the parolee's successful adjustment. A law-enforcement professional, the agent has broad discretion over the life and street-level experience of a parolee. Both community protection and the parolees' transition are of paramount concern.

HOW LONG DOES PAROLE LAST?

The duration of parole is based on law.

Most convicted criminals are sentenced under the Determinate Sentencing Law, which defines the prison terms for all but life sentences. Nonlife inmates are subject to three years on parole but can be discharged from parole supervision after one year when no parole violations have been detected.

Offenders convicted of life sentences who have been released on parole are subject to five years under supervision; however, they can be discharged after three years if no parole violations have been detected during that time.

WHEN ARE INMATES RELEASED TO PAROLE?

Nonlifers: Under determinate sentencing, inmates are released when they serve the term imposed by the court. An inmate can reduce this sentence by satisfactory performance in prison work, training, or education programs. By law, an inmate will be awarded a six-month reduction in his or her sentence for every six months of full-time performance in a qualifying program.

Corrections is required to provide all eligible inmates an opportunity to participate in the work/training program. It is believed that participation in this program will instill good work habits, teach some skills, and improve reintegration into society.

Being involved in the work/training program is a privilege, not a right. An inmate can lose work-time credit by inappropriate behavior. However, a percentage of these lost work credits can be restored by subsequent good behavior.

Lifers: The Board of Prison Terms (BPT), an independent agency that works with Corrections, is responsible for setting parole dates for inmates serving life sentences. The BPT determines if and when these inmates are suitable for reentry into society.

Life sentences are for crimes of murder, attempted murder, kidnapping for robbery or ransom, aggravated assault by a life prisoner, train wrecking, sabotage, and exploding destructive devices causing mayhem. Inmates who have been convicted of an offense that involved the infliction of great bodily injury (including habitual sex offenders) and who have two or more prior terms for specified offenses also receive life sentences as habitual offenders.

All life sentences, except life without possibility of parole, have minimum-eligible-parole dates. The first parole-consideration hearing for a life prisoner is held approximately one year before the inmate's first parole eligibility date.

For lifers, release to parole is not automatic. The BPT annually denies parole to about 93 percent of those who have hearings. No single factor indicates an inmate's suitability or unsuitability for parole. The BPT reviews all facts of the case at the hearing, then, using its discretion and experience, makes the determination whether to grant or deny parole.

WHAT HAPPENS ON PAROLE?

Each parolee is supervised by a parole agent, who follows the parolee's activities. To determine the appropriate level of supervision, the agent conducts a *needs-and-risks assessment* for each parolee. Predictive indicators, such as latest commitment offense, criminal behavior patterns, and undesirable associations, are considered when assessing the possible risk to the community.

Based on the assessment, a parolee falls into one of four major categories:

High control—Has the potential for assaultive behavior or a history as a large-scale drug dealer.

High services—Requires support to meet psychological, physical, or employment needs.

Control/Services—Medium-risk; requires moderate amounts of both control and services.

Minimum—Low-risk with minimal support needs.

Parolees are provided services according to their identified needs. The parole agent is expected to make sure that each parolee's identified needs are met. In attempting to assist the parolee to make a successful parole adjustment, the agent uses various community programs, employment referrals, and emergency food and shelter.

Most parole-unit offices have a services specialist responsible for obtaining services for parolees. Paroles provide direct, cash assistance for indigent parolees and operates two psychiatric outpatient clinics for treatment of parolees with serious mental problems. Service agents and individual parole agents often work with other agencies to obtain services for parolees in need.

WHAT ARE CONDITIONS OF PAROLE?

Each parolee agrees in writing to abide by the following four conditions:

Parole Agent Instructions. Must obey all instructions given by the parole agent.

Release, Reporting, and Travel. Must report immediately upon release; notify change in residences; report when instructed.

No Criminal Conduct.

Weapons. Cannot own, use, have access to, or have under control, any type of weapon or ammunition.

In addition, special conditions of parole may be imposed individually for cause, including antinarcotic testing, treatment at a parole-outpatient clinic (for psychiatric monitoring), abstinence from alcohol, or prohibition against residing in a given location or associating with specific individuals.

Parolees are subject to search without a warrant by parole agents and law-enforcement officers.

WHERE IS THE PAROLEE PLACED?

Current law requires that parolees shall be returned to the county from which they were committed. CDC may release a parolee in a county other than the county of commitment if the placement would be in the best interests of the public and of the parolee. Placement to another county may be based upon the following factors:

The need to protect the life or safety of a victim, a witness, or any other person.

The verified existence of a unique work offer or an educational or vocational training program.

The last legal residence of the inmate.

The existence of family with whom the inmate has maintained strong ties and whose support would increase the chance of a successful parole.

The lack of necessary mental-health-treatment programs for outpatients in the county of commitment.

Public concern that would reduce the chance that the inmate's parole would be successfully completed.

Local chiefs of police or sheriffs are notified regarding persons paroled within their jurisdiction. Each month, detailed information on parolees and reentry inmates is provided to more than 200 California law-enforcement agencies. About 80 percent of all parolees are returned to the county of commitment.

CAN PAROLE BE REVOKED?

If a parolee violates the law or the conditions of parole, the agent in most cases will place the parolee in custody. The BPT then conducts a revocation hearing to determine if, in fact, a parole violation has occurred. If good cause is found, the BPT examines the facts of the case, the type of offense, and the parolee's adjustment on parole and determines if the parolee must return to prison. Violators may be returned to custody for up to twelve months. The BPT returns more than 90 percent of parole violators to prison.

If a parolee engages in misconduct while in custody, the revocation may be extended for up to twelve months.

REENTRY PROGRAMS

As a result of the dramatic increase in prison population, the use of community programs is expanding. Community reentry programs provide the opportunity for transition from close confinement to less restrictive living for selected inmates within 180 days of parole.

Work Furlough

Work furlough centers are operated by the Department of Corrections, private profit and nonprofit organizations, and county Sheriff's Departments. This program provides housing, food, and supervision to selected male and female inmates 90-120 days prior to their release. Inmates leave the facility during the day to work at a variety of jobs.

Prisoner Mother

Community prisoner-mother programs are operated by private profit and nonprofit organizations. By reuniting mothers with their children, the program hopes to alleviate the harm caused to children by the separation from their mothers during incarceration.

Also available to participants are drug- and alcohol-abuse counseling, parenting classes, vocational and educational training, and the opportunity to reintegrate into society.

Return to Custody

Return-to-custody facilities (RTCs) are operated by private organizations and by city and county law-enforcement agencies. RTCs offer carefully selected, low-risk male and female parole violators the opportunity to remain closer to their families during their parole-revocation period. These facilities also reduce the impact of the high-parole-violator population on prison overcrowding.

All inmates must meet the RTC screening criteria to be eligible for this reentry program. Violent offenders and those with sex crimes are ineligible.

Substance-Abuse Treatment

The Department of Corrections, in conjunction with the return-to-custody program, is developing a specialized program for substance-abuse treatment centers. For violators with drug- and/or alcohol-dependency problems, the program provides intensive substance-abuse counseling. It will consist of three thirty-day phases: phase one includes intake, program orientation, and treatment; phase two focuses on program participation and job development; and phase three is devoted to job placement and work furlough.

Restitution

Correction's first community restitution center was opened in early 1988. Its purpose is to provide a means for felons to repay their victims' financial losses. Restitution fees are ordered by the sentencing court or agreed upon by the defendant and victims.

The offender will be incarcerated at a community-based facility. He or she will be allowed to leave the center during specific hours for work only. At all other times, he or she must remain at the center.

When the offender receives a paycheck, work expenses will be deducted. The balance of the check will be divided into thirds: one-third paid to the department for operating expenses, one-third paid to the victim, and the final third given to the inmate.

This facility also serves as an alternative to imprisonment and will help lessen prison overcrowding.

House Arrest—An Innovation

Paroles runs a pilot "house arrest" system in Ontario and Indio. Low-risk parolees who normally would be returned to custody for drug use while on parole instead will be detained under arrest within their own homes.

Each parolee assigned to the project will wear an electronic monitoring device. The parolee in the Ontario portion of the project leaves the house for certain purposes, such as work, during specified time periods but must be at his or her residence all other times. When the telephone rings at undisclosed times of the day and night, he or she must be there to answer the call. The Indio area project does not permit the parolee to leave home. The electronic device transmits an alarm to a computer that will notify the parole agent if the parolee attempts to leave the home area.

Parole officials estimate that keeping 150 parolees on house arrest will save the state more than $2.5 million per year.

Parolees under house arrest must meet the following screening criteria: no serious crimes; no sex offenses; and no history of violence, large-scale drug dealing, or involvement with weapons.

PAROLE OFFICERS

The California Department of Corrections has authorized more than 1,000 parole agents. Located at seventy-one field offices throughout the state, these agents currently supervise more than 38,000 parolees. This translates to an average case load of about fifty-three parolees per agent. Supervision for each parolee costs about $1,200 per year.

For more information concerning parole, please contact one of the following offices:

State Headquarters:

Parole & Community Services Division
Corporate Center
501 J Street, Room 330
Sacramento, CA 95814
(916) 445-6200

Region I—Covers the entire Central Valley from Bakersfield to the Oregon border:

1631 Alhambra Boulevard
Sacramento, CA 95816
(916) 739-2860

Region II—Covers the San Francisco Bay Area:

Ferry Building, Room 2040
San Francisco, CA 94111
(415) 557-2861

Region III—Covers Los Angeles and the San Fernando Valley:

107 South Broadway, Room 3003
Los Angeles, CA 90012
(213) 620-2404

Region IV—Covers San Diego area, extending into Orange County:

1840 East 17th Street, Room 240
Santa Ana, CA 92701
(714) 558-4131

35

Criminal Law

The following pages offer some definition of criminal law; however, as a writer, you must be aware that the law varies in its complexities and from city to city and state to state, as do the circumstances of the crimes and the criminals involved, along with the way in which investigations of crimes are handled. When writing, it is always best to consult a legal expert.

Simplistically, a police officer discovers or receives information that there has been an infraction of the law committed, and in turn attempts to discover the identity of the crime and the criminal. The officer then seeks to capture, and help prove the guilt of the criminal by providing the prosecution with witnesses, evidence, opportunity, and motive after having read the accused his or her rights.

When the offense committed is a minor infraction of the law, the magistrate, before whom the accused is brought, disposes of the case at that time. In the event the crime committed is of a more serious nature, the defendant is held for further action by the court and is admitted to bail, should bail be warranted. The court then turns the case over to the district attorney or prosecuting attorney, who then charges the defendant, and a time for a preliminary hearing is set. At the hearing, the case is reviewed, with evidence presented at that time. Should that charge be a felony, the accused can be indicted and ordered to stand trial by a grand jury, or the grand jury can dismiss the charges should they agree that the evidence presented does not warrant a trial.

A defendant has the right to admit to the charge or plead "not guilty." Should he or she confess guilt and plead so, he will come before the court for sentencing. Should the defendant plead not guilty, a trial is ordered, the defendant to be represented by the defendant's own counsel, or if the defendant cannot afford counsel, one appointed by the court. At the trial, both the defense and the prosecution present their cases, including witnesses and evidence to substantiate their side of the case. If the jury finds for the state and against the defendant, the defendant is then sentenced (many times at a trial set merely to determine the sentence) and committed to prison or given a term of probation. Depending upon the accused and the circumstances, the judge may grant a reduction of the sentence or the possibility of parole.

SENTENCING

It is impossible to list the sentences fitting certain crimes, as both circumstances and the laws of each state vary. Consult the criminal-justice system of the city or state in which the crime you are writing about takes place.

CRIMINAL LAW DEFINED

Definition of crime: A *crime* is an act that is injurious to the public, punishable by the state by fine, imprisonment, or both, through a judicial proceeding. The elements of crime are so variable that it is impossible to give any specific definition that would be correct both inclusively and exclusively. As each state is independent in making and enforcing criminal law, the laws of each state must be examined to determine the criminal character of any act, its judgment and sentence.

The purpose of criminal law: Crimes are prohibited and punished to prevent injury to the public, which may include destruction or interference with government, human life, private property, or other valued institutions. Desire for vengeance or uncompensability of injury may also be included.

Reasons and purposes of punishment: One of the prime objectives is the protection of society. The object is to prevent the offender from committing future wrongs while providing opportunity to reform the offender, to make public punishment an example to others, and to bring about retribution for the wrong committed.

Distinctions between *crime and tort*: A *crime* is a wrong that affects the community in its aggregate capacity. A *tort* is a wrong apart from contract, which affects persons in their individual capacity. One is a public wrong, whereas the other is a private wrong. In the case of a crime, the wrongdoer is liable to criminal prosecution, whereas in the case of a tort, the offender is liable only to a civil action by the person injured.

Acts that may be both a crime *and a tort*: In such cases, the wrongdoer faces both criminal action by the state and civil action by the party he or she has injured. These two actions are separate and distinct. The object of the former is to punish as an example; the object of the latter is to compensate the injured party. Either action may precede the other, depending on the laws of the individual states.

The five sources of law: (1) The United States Constitution; (2) Acts of Congress; (3) State constitutions; (4) Acts of state and territorial legislatures (known as statutes); and (5) The common law. If a provision of the United States Constitution conflicts with an act of Congress, the latter is void. If a valid act of Congress conflicts with a provision of a state constitution, the latter is void. If a provision of a state constitution conflicts with a statute of the same state, the latter is void. And if an act of a state or territorial legislature conflicts with a provision of the common law, the latter is void.

The United States Constitution: Together with the treaties made in pursuance thereof, the Constitution of the United States constitutes the supreme law of the land.

Rights guaranteed to each individual under the Constitution of the United States: (1) Right of the writ of habeas corpus. (2) Protection against the passage of bills of attainder or ex post facto laws. (3) Equality before the law by forbidding the creation of a titled class by prohibiting the federal government from granting titles of nobility. (4) Right to a speedy trial in the case of accusation of a crime before an impartial jury at the place of the commission of the crime. (5) Freedom of religion, press, speech, assembly, and petition. (6) Right to keep and bear arms for national defense. (7) Protection against the unlawful quartering of troops. (8) Right to a grand jury indictment before trial for a crime, and to be confronted by witnesses, and to have the compulsory process to obtain witnesses and the assistance of counsel to establish innocence. (9) Protection against unreasonable search and seizure. (10) Protection against self-incrimination in any trial or in the giving of testimony. (11) Protection against being twice placed in jeopardy of life or limb for a crime. (12) Protection against cruel and unusual punishment and excessive bail. (13) Right to just compensation for any property taken for public use. (14) Right to a trial by jury in civil cases. (15) Protection against being deprived of life, liberty, or property without due process of law. (16) Protection against the impairment of the obligations of contracts by the states. (17) Equal protection of the law. (18) Guarantee of a republican form of government in the state in which the citizen resides. (19) Protection from abridgment by the states of the privileges and immunities of citizens of the United States. (20) Protection from slavery and involuntary servitude except as punishment for a crime. (21) Right to hold public office under the United States if the citizen meets the statutory and constitutional qualifications. (22) Rights to freedom of ingress and egress from a state. (23) Protection from domestic violence and foreign invasion. (24) Protection from the abridgment of the right to vote by a state on account of race or sex.

State constitutions: Each differs materially from the United States Constitution. The former constitutes the restrictions or limitations of powers, whereas the latter constitutes, for the most part, grants of power.

Acts of state legislatures: Unlike the Congress, state legislatures have inherent power to declare acts criminal and to impose penalties for their violation. State power, however, in these respects, is not absolute. Enactments of the state legislatures must not conflict with any provision of the U.S. Constitution, or of the state constitution, or with any valid act of Congress.

The English common law: The basis of the English common law, sometimes called the *unwritten law,* is immemorial usage and custom, and not legislative enactment. The generic term *common law* has been well defined as "those maxims, principles, and forms of judicial proceedings, which have no written law to prescribe or warrant them, but which, founded on the laws of nature and the dictates of reason, have, by usage and custom, become interwoven with the written laws; and, by such incorporation, form a part of the municipal code of each state or nation."

The American common law: Similar in most respects to the English common law, insofar as the Supreme Court of the United States has decided that English statutes that were enacted before the emigration of our ancestors, and that were in force at that time, and that are applicable to our conditions and surroundings, constitute a part of our common law.

Statutes: A statute provides that the state legislatures can punish any act unless restricted by the state or federal Constitution. The United States Congress has no power to declare and punish crimes except those derived from the federal Constitution.

Construction of statutes: Penal statutes are to be construed strictly against the state and in favor of the accused. Words must be given their full meaning. The courts will not strain and look for a meaning that may have the effect of declaring the statute of no effect. In construing statutes, the intention of the legislature is to be sought, and for this purpose the court will consider not only the act itself but its preamble, and will also look into similar statutes on the same subject, particularly the old law and the mischief to be remedied. All statutes are to be construed with reference to the provisions of the common law. In other jurisdictions, statutes are construed according to natural meaning.

Penal codes: Many of the states have adopted *penal* or *criminal codes*, which define what acts shall be punished as crimes. The code is intended to cover the whole law, and no act is a crime unless it is expressly declared so. Even in those states that have penal codes and do not recognize common-law crimes, the common law is in force to the extent that it may be resorted to for the definition of crimes that are not defined in the statutes prohibiting them.

Substantive criminal law: Relates to the definition and classification of crimes generally, the criminal act, the criminal intent, the capacity to commit crime and exemptions from criminal liability, the parties to crime, and a consideration of the important elements or characteristics of particular offenses.

The administration of criminal justice: Includes the following subjects: criminal procedure, police organization and administration, prosecution, accusation, the defense of accused persons, the organization of courts, pleadings, arraignment and trial, evidence, judgment and sentence, appeals, probation, parole, pardon, penology and prison administration, juvenile courts, special procedures for crime prevention, and laws designed to change social and industrial conditions in order to prevent crime. The federal government also has an elaborate system of administration of criminal justice.

Criminal procedure: Consists of the rules according to which the substantive law is administered. It includes whatever is embraced by the three terms *pleading*, *evidence*, and *practice*, and means those rules that direct the course of proceedings to bring defendants into court, and the proceedings followed in court after they are brought in.

Prosecution: Prosecutions in criminal cases are controlled by a group of officers called U.S. attorneys, prosecuting attorneys, county attorneys, district attorneys, city attorneys, and states attorneys. Consult your city, state, and federal law for the laws governing the qualifications and selections of these officers and prescribing their powers and duties.

Accusation: Accusations of guilty conduct may be made by complaints or affidavits, sworn to by injured persons or by police officers. This is true especially in the case of minor offenses. Accusations of felonies are made by indictments found by grand juries or by information filed by prosecuting attorneys, generally following preliminary examinations in magistrates' courts.

Defense of accused person: It is a universal principle of criminal law in the United States that a person accused of a crime is entitled to the advice of a lawyer and to be represented by him or her at his or her trial. In felony cases, this principle is carried further, and in many states, counsel is provided without cost for a defendant who is too poor to employ a lawyer. In most of the states, such counsel is appointed by the judge in the court where the defendant is standing trial. Some jurisdictions have an officer, known as a *public defender*, who represents defendants who are unable to provide counsel for themselves.

Pleadings: Pleadings in criminal cases are comparatively simple. Contrary to popular opinion, reversals of criminal cases on appeal are very infrequent. The pleadings used by the state in felony and some misdemeanor cases are the indictment and the information; affidavits and complaints in misdemeanor cases; and by the defendant, usually an oral plea of "guilty" or "not guilty." Other pleas, such as "former jeopardy," "insanity," or "alibi," are available or required in some states. Pleas in abatement, demurrers, motions to quash the indictment, and arrest of judgment are also available under some circumstances.

Arraignment and trial: The law regulates the procedure according to which the defendant is brought into court, is informed of his or her rights, and is placed on trial; it also controls the routine of selecting a jury, making the opening statements, introducing evidence, arguing the case to the jury, instructing the jury, and receiving the verdict.

Probation: Following a plea of guilty or a verdict of guilty, the defendant may be placed on probation by the trial judge, on such conditions as he or she may impose. In some states, the conditions of probation may be imprisonment in a county jail, reimbursement to the injured person, and payment of costs. In most states, conditions of probation include: keeping employed, avoiding bad companions, refraining from committing other crimes, and reporting to a probation officer. Violation of the conditions of probation makes the defendant liable to sentence as provided by law.

Parole: After the prisoner has served a portion of the term of imprisonment determined by the sentence, he or she may be released on parole, on conditions similar to those imposed in the case of probation. The power to grant parole, however, is vested in a state parole board or officer. (See chapter on parole.)

Pardon: The power to pardon generally belongs to the governors of the states. Pardon differs in theory from both probation and parole in that it assumes the innocence of the defendant, or circumstances mitigating responsibility for the crime, and returns the defendant to society free of ignominy and acquitted of all penalties related to the offense for which he or she has been pardoned.

Commutation of sentence: A change from the original punishment to which a person has been condemned to a less severe one.

Federal administration of criminal justice: For the administration of criminal justice as it relates to crimes against the United States, appropriate laws have been passed by Congress, and a complete parallel organization exists of police, prosecution, and courts. The United States commissioner has similar jurisdiction as the committing magistrate previously described, with power to accept bail and hold preliminary hearings. The United States District Courts, which have one or more divisions in each state, in the District of Columbia and in the territories, are the courts of general trial jurisdiction in criminal cases; they hold power also to grant probation. The United States Circuit Court of Appeals, organized in ten circuits and in the District of Columbia, have appellate jurisdiction in criminal cases. And the United States Supreme Court is the final court of appeals, both for cases arising in federal trial courts and in criminal cases arising in state courts that involve federal constitutional questions. Rules of procedure and evidence and forms of pleadings used in the federal courts are similar to those prevailing in the state courts, and probation, parole, and pardon are similarly used. The federal government maintains an extensive prison system under the direction of a bureau of prisons, an elaborate organization for the detention of criminals and for their release and supervision on parole.

Juvenile courts: One of the developments of law relating to the administration of criminal justice is that which has created the juvenile court and a new procedure for dealing with juvenile delinquents. The theory of these laws is that a child who commits an act that if committed by an adult would constitute a crime, is not criminal, and requires not punishment, but the training and direction that should have been given by the parent. In the juvenile court, the usual rules of procedure, pleading, and evidence are dispensed with and instead an informal administrative procedure is used. Under some circumstances, despite the existence of juvenile-court machinery, a child may be tried as an adult. In such cases, the writer is encouraged to enlist the aid of someone familiar with current juvenile law in the state in which the crime has been committed.

Special procedures for crime prevention: A number of special procedures have been created by law for checking crime. These include the abatement of nuisances, such as houses of prostitution, gambling resorts, and buildings used for the manufacture or sale of intoxicating liquor unless so legally provided for by the laws of that state. The confiscation of stills, automobiles, and ships used for the manufacture and transportation of illegal liquor and other agencies used to commit crimes is accomplished by similar procedures.

Classification of crimes: Crimes at common law are divided into *treason*, *felonies*, and *misdemeanors*. Some jurisdictions have a fourth classification, *minor* or *petty offenses*.

Merger of offenses: As a rule, where a person by the same act commits two crimes, one a felony and the other a misdemeanor, the misdemeanor merges into the felony; but if the crimes are of the same degree, both felonies or both misdemeanors, there is no merger. In some states, this doctrine has not been recognized, while in most states, it has been abolished by statutes allowing conviction of a lesser offense than is charged in the indictment if it is included in the offense charged.

Mental element in crime: Criminal intent. Every common-law consists of two elements: the criminal act or omission, and the mental element, commonly called *criminal intent.*

Motive is not intent: Motive is not an essential element of crime. A bad motive will not make an act a crime, nor will a good motive prevent an act from being a crime. Motive may, however, tend to show that an act was willful and done with criminal intent.

General intent—intent presumed from act: Where an act is prohibited on pain of punishment, intention on the part of one capable of intent and acting without justification or excuse constitutes *criminal intent.* In such a case, the existence of the intent is presumed from commission of the act, on the grounds that a person is presumed to intend his voluntary act and its probable consequences. Criminal intent exists when a person intends to do that which the law says is a crime.

Specific intent: When a crime consists not merely of commission but in an act accompanied by a specific intent, the existence of that intent is an essential element. In such cases the existence of criminal intent is not presumed from the commission of the act, but the specific intent must be proved.

Constructive intent: Where a person engages in the commission of a crime that is unintended by him or her, then the intent to commit the crime is carried over to the act committed and supplies the intent necessary to make the act a crime. The intent in such a case is called *constructive intent.*

Intent in cases of negligence: In crimes that consist of neglect to observe proper care in performing an act, or in culpable failure to peform a duty, criminal intent consists in the state of mind that necessarily accompanies the negligent act or culpable omission, e.g., slaughter, nuisance, escape.

Concurrence of act and intent: To constitute a crime, act and intent must concur. Not only must there be both an act and an intent to constitute a crime, but the act and intent must concur in point of time. An intent to do a prohibited act, abandoned before the act is done, is not punishable.

Conditions of criminality: To render a person criminally responsible for the commission of a common-law crime, four conditions of criminality must exist. The person must: (1) be of sufficient age; (2) have sufficient mental capacity; (3) act voluntarily; and (4) have criminal intent.

Criminal capacity: Since every crime consists of two elements, the act itself and the mental element (commonly called *criminal intent*), no person can be guilty of a crime unless he or she has a certain degree of mental capacity. Mental incapacity, which criminal law recognizes, exists to a greater or lesser extent in four classes of persons: infants, lunatics or insane persons, drunken persons, and corporations.

Infancy: At common law, a child under the age of seven years is conclusively presumed incapable of entertaining criminal intent and cannot commit a crime. Between the ages of seven and fourteen, a child is presumed to be incapable, but the presumption may be rebutted. After the age of fourteen, he or she is presumed to have sufficient capacity. In some states, the age of incapacity has been raised by statute, and in others, the age at which presumption of capacity begins has been lowered.

Insanity: In its legal sense, *insanity* is any defect or disease of the mind that renders a person incapable of entertaining a criminal intent. Since criminal intent is an essential element of every crime, no person who is so insane that he or she cannot entertain it is criminally responsible for his acts. Defect of the mind, as in the case of idiocy, or disease of the mind, as in the case of lunacy, may have the following effects: (1) It may render a person incapable of determining between right and wrong, and in such cases no criminal responsibility attaches. (2) It may render a person partially insane, or subject to insane delusions as to existing facts, but not in other respects insane, in which case the individual would be in the same situation as to responsibility as if the facts in respect to which the insane delusion exists were real. (3) It may deprive a person of freedom of will, as in a case of irresistible impulse, in which case some courts hold that the person is not responsible, while other courts hold the contrary.

Moral and emotional insanity, as distinguished from mental, does not exempt one from responsibility. Insanity is in no case an excuse, unless the act was the direct result of the insanity. Even if a person was sane when committing an act, that person cannot be tried if he or she is insane, as he or she is deemed incapable of conducting a defense; nor can an insane person be sentenced and punished, even after conviction.

Drunkenness: Voluntary drunkenness furnishes no ground of exemption from criminal responsibility, except: (1) Where the act is committed while laboring under settled insanity, or delirium tremens, resulting from intoxication; (2) Where a specific intent is essential to constitute the crime, the fact of intoxication may negate its existence; (3) The fact of intoxication may be material, where provocation for the act is shown; (4) No criminal responsibility attaches for acts committed while in a state of involuntary drunkenness, destroying the reason and will.

Ignorance of law: Ignorance on the part of the wrongdoer of the law that makes an act criminal is no excuse. If a specific intent is essential to a crime, and ignorance of the law negates such intent, such ignorance prevents the crime from being consummated.

Accident or misfortune: A person is not criminally liable for an accident happening in the performance of a lawful act with due care.

Justification: The law, on the ground of public policy, imposes the duty or allows the doing of certain acts, under certain circumstances, although individuals are injured thereby. In such cases, the acts are not criminal, but are justifiable. Such are certain acts done: (1) Under public authority; (2) Under parental authority; (3) In prevention of a crime; (4) In suppressing a riot, or (5) In making an arrest or preventing an escape.

Justification—duress: The concurrence of the will is, in general, necessary to make an act criminal. Therefore, when one is forced to do an act against his or her will, that person is, in general, not responsible for it, and therefore, on prosecution for any crime except murder, if the accused committed the act only because compelled to do so by threats of immediate death or serious bodily harm, he or she is excused.

Coercion—married women: If a married woman, in the presence of her husband, commits an act that would be a crime under other circumstances, she is presumed to have acted under her husband's coercion, and such coercion excuses her act. But this presumption may be rebutted if the circumstances show that in fact she was not coerced.

Provocation: Provocation is no ground for exempting one absolutely from criminal responsibility for his or her acts. However, grounds for mitigating circumstances may reduce the degree of the crime and the punishment.

Effect of joining in criminal purpose: When one or more persons join in the execution of a common, criminal purpose, each is criminally liable for every act done in the execution of that criminal act, whether done by oneself or by one's confederate.

Principal and accessories: Those involved in the commission of felonies are either *principals* or *accessories*, depending upon whether they are present or absent when the crime is committed. Principals are either: (1) Principals in the first degree, or (2) Principals in the second degree.

Accessories are either: (1) Before the fact, or (2) After the fact.

Principal in the first degree: The person who actually perpetrates the deed, either by his or her own hand or through an innocent agent.

Principal in the second degree: One who is actually present, aiding and abetting another in the commission of the deed. Accordingly: (1) The person must be present, actually or constructively; (2) The person must aid or abet the commission of the act; (3) There must be community of unlawful purpose at the time the act is committed; (4) Such purpose must be real on the part of the principal in the first degree.

Accessories before the fact: One who was absent when the act was committed, but who procured, counseled, ordered, or abetted the principal or actual perpetrator of the criminal act.

Accessories after the fact: One who receives, comforts, or assists another, knowing that the other person has committed a felony. Three things are necessary: (1) the felony must have been completed; (2) the person charged as accessory must have committed assistance to the felon personally; and (3) the person must have known when assisting the felon that he or she had committed a felony.

"Aider and abettor" and accomplice: The term *aider and abettor* applies to principals in the second degree. The term *accomplice* applies to all who take part in the commission of a crime, whether they are principals or accessories.

Principal's liability for acts of agents: As a rule, no person is criminally liable for the act of another unless he or she has previously authorized or agreed to it; and consequently a principal is not liable for acts of his or her agents or servants that the principal did not authorize or agree to, even if the crime is committed in the course of the employment.

Exceptions: (1) In the cases of libel, the principal is liable, under certain circumstances, for the acts of his or her agents upon the ground of negligence in failing to exercise proper control of them; and (2) Under some statutes, the principal is liable for prohibited acts, regardless that they are committed by his or her agents without authority or instructions.

Agent's liability for own acts: An agent of sufficient mental capacity, is criminally liable for his or her own acts, though they are ordered by a principal and in the course of the principal's business.

Overt act: An open act; a physical act, as distinguished from an act of the mind; an act done pursuant to a formed intent. To constitute assault, there must be an overt act or an attempt. In homicide cases, an overt act is an open act, indicating a present purpose to do immediate, great bodily harm.

Necessity for overt act: The law does not punish mere intention but requires some overt act in an attempt to carry the intention into execution. *Exception*: There is an exception to this rule in the case of conspiracy, unless the conspiring may be regarded as an overt act.

Attempts: An act done with intent to commit that crime but failing in the commission of the act. (1) The act must be connected with the completed crime; (2) There must be a possibility to commit the crime in the manner proposed; (3) There must be specific intent to commit the crime at the time of the act. Attempts to commit a crime, whether a felony or a misdemeanor, and whether at common law or by statute, are misdemeanors.

Exceptions: (1) In some states, attempts are entirely regulated by statute. (2) In most states, some attempts are felonies by statute. (3) Attempts to commit certain classes of statutory misdemeanors are not indictable.

Preliminary examination: An investigation by a magistrate of a person who has been charged with a crime and arrested, or of the facts and circumstances alleged to have attended the crime and to fasten suspicion upon the party so charged, in order to ascertain whether there is sufficient ground to hold the person to bail for trial by the proper court.

Cruel-and-unusual punishment: Such punishment as would amount to torture or barbarity, and any cruel and degrading punishment not known to the common law.

Negligence and recklessness: Neglect in the discharge of a duty, or indifference to consequences, is in many cases equivalent to a criminal intent. Upon the ground that everyone is presumed to contemplate the natural consequences of his or her acts, neglect and reckless conduct may be evidence of malicious intent, and negligent performance of a duty imposed by law or assumed by contract or by wrongful act may render the person guilty of such negligence criminally liable, except in cases in which a specific intent is essential to constitute the crime charged.

Act and intent must co-exist: The criminal intent or negligence must unite with the overt act, and they must concur in point of time.

Marshals: Officers belonging to the executive department of the federal government, who with their deputies have the same powers of executing the laws of the United States, in each state, as the sheriffs.

Provost marshal: An officer of an army whose duties correspond to those of a chief of police.

Probation officer: An officer whose duty it is to investigate and report to the court upon an application for probation and to supervise persons placed on probation by a court.

Sheriff: The chief executive and administrative officer of a county, being chosen by popular election. The sheriff's principal duties involve aiding the criminal courts and civil courts of record, such as serving process, summoning juries, executing judgments, holding judicial sales, and the like. This officer also serves as the chief conservator of the peace within a territorial jurisdiction.

Deputy: A person duly authorized by an officer to exercise some or all of the functions pertaining to the office, in the place and stead of the latter.

Deputy sheriff: One appointed to act in the place and stead of the sheriff in the official business of the latter's office. An *undersheriff*, by virtue of appointment, has the authority to execute all the ordinary duties of the office of sheriff. A special deputy, who is an officer appointed for one particular occasion or a special service (such as to serve a writ or assist in keeping the peace when a riot is expected or in progress), acts under a specific authority.

36

Legal Terminology

The records of federal and state courts contain considerable information of value to the federal investigator. To accurately check court records, it is essential to understand the terminology. On the following pages are selected terms from a glossary prepared by the Institute of Judicial Administration.

Abandonment: The relinquishment of a claim or privilege. In marine law, the relinquishment by the insured to the underwriters of what may remain of the property insured.

Abandonment of Wife: Desertion of his wife by a husband without reasonable cause, or negligence in providing for her support.

Abate: To terminate; to decrease; to quash, beat down, or destroy.

Abduction: Unlawfully taking a female or child by fraud or violence.

Abductor: One who carries away a child or female by fraud, persuasion, or open violence.

Abet: To knowingly and with criminal intent, aid, encourage, or advise another to commit a crime.

Abettor: One who aids, abets, or instigates.

Abeyance: A state of suspension; being undermined. In expectation.

Ab Inconvenienti: A forced and sometimes specious argument arising out of the difficulty of the case.

Ab Initio: From the beginning.

Abjure: To renounce or abandon by or upon oath.

Abortion: The act of miscarrying or producing young before the natural time.

Abscond: To avoid the process of the court by hiding or leaving the jurisdiction.

Abuse: To treat improperly or ill use; to injure.

Abut: To border on; to reach or touch with an end.

Accessory After the Fact: Every person who, after a felony has been committed, harbors, conceals, or aids a principal in such felony, with the intent that said principal may avoid or escape arrest, trial, conviction, or punishment, having knowledge that said principal committed or was charged with such felony. One who, knowing a felony to have been committed, receives, relieves, comforts, or assists the felon.

Accessory Before the Fact: One who, though absent at the time of the crime committed, procures, counsels, advises, encourages, or commands another to commit it.

Action In Personam: An action against the person, founded on a personal liability.

Action In Rem: An action for a thing; an action for the recovery of a thing possessed by another.

Administrative Offices of the State Courts: The business offices of state courts, established in several states; they supply information on judicial business and court personnel to the highest court or its chief justice. The powers and duties of these offices are not uniform.

Advisory of Opinion: An opinion rendered by a court to a lower court, or in some cases, to the legislative or executive branch of government, which is neither binding nor decisive of a controversy.

Amicus Curiae: A friend of the court; one who volunteers information upon some matter of law.

Arraign: In criminal practice, to bring a prisoner to the bar of the court to answer to a criminal charge.

At Issue: Whenever the parties to a suit come to a point in the pleadings that is affirmed on one side and denied on the other, they are said to be *at issue*.

Bail: A guaranty that a person arrested on criminal charges will appear for trial or examination when required if he or she is temporarily released. The guaranty may take the form of a bond, a deposit of money, or a deed to property, which is forfeited if the accused does not appear when required.

Calendar: A list of cases to be heard by a court during the court term.

Case: A suit in law or equity. In appellate procedure, the trial record made in the lower court, including the papers and the testimony.

Cases and Controversies: Word appearing in Section 2, Article III of the United States Constitution, limiting the exercise of judicial power by the federal courts to actual cases between parties with adverse interests, as compared to hypothetical or friendly disputes.

Certification: The submission of questions of law arising in a particular case by a lower court to a higher court.

Certiorari: A writ issued by a higher court requiring the record of a case in the court below to be sent up to itself for redetermination.

Challenge to the Array: Questioning the qualifications of an entire jury panel, usually on the grounds of a partiality or some fault in the process of summoning the panel.

Chancellor: Chief advisor of the king of England. By issuing writs, the office eventually became the Court of the Chancery in the fourteenth and fifteenth centuries. In some states, the chancellor is the chief judge of the equity courts.

Change of Venue: The removal of a suit that is in progress from one county or district to another for trial, or from one court to another in the same county or district.

Chief Judge or Justice: The presiding judge of a court. In addition to judicial functions, this judge may have administrative tasks.

Circuit: A division or territory for judicial business.

Civil Action: An action that seeks the establishment, recovery, or redress of private and/or civil rights. Civil suits relate to and affect only individual rights, whereas criminal prosecutions involve public wrongs.

Common-Law Pleading: A system of pleading and procedure in force in England until 1852, and until 1848 in most of the United States. Opposition to its extreme rigidity and technicality led to the adoption of code pleading in most American jurisdictions, fashioned after the Field Code adopted in New York in 1848.

Concurrent Jurisdiction: Occurs when two courts have the power to determine the same issues.

Constitutional Court: In the federal system, a federal court established by Congress pursuant to Article III of the Constitution of the United States. Judges of constitutional courts serve during good behavior and cannot have their compensation reduced while in office. The United States Supreme Court, the United States Courts of Appeal, and the United States District Courts are constitutional courts. In the states, a court provided for under the Constitution.

Corporation Court: A court of limited civil jurisdiction, usually exercising its authority in a city or borough. In some American colonies, the corporation court also heard criminal cases. These courts still are in existence in some states.

Court-Martial: A court convened to hear an offense committed by a person in the military. Under the 1950 Uniform Code of Military Justice (UCMJ), court-martial courts have jurisdiction to try any military person or civilian serving with the armed forces for an offense against military law. There is no jury.

Court of Appeal: A court in which appeals from a lower court are heard.

Courts of Equity: Courts that administer remedial justice according to the system of equity, as distinguished from courts of common law. Equity courts are sometimes called *courts of chancery.*

Court of First Instance: A court in which a case must originally be brought. Usually a trial court.

Court of General Jurisdiction: The largest jurisdiction a court of first instance can have in a given political unit (i.e., state, federal, district, circuit, county).

Court of General Sessions: Criminal courts of general jurisdiction existing in some American cities (e.g., New York).

Court of Intermediate Appeal: A court of appeal established in several states to lessen the workload of the highest reviewing tribunal. Ultimate review can still be had in the highest court by its permission, or, in limited cases, as a matter of right.

Court of Jail Delivery: A colonial court trying all persons accused of crime and held in jail until the court's arrival, and having the power to deliver, i.e., discharge those who are acquitted. The name is still retained for criminal courts in some states.

Court of King's Bench: Formerly the highest English common-law court, now a department of the High Court of Justice. It is also referred to as the "King's Bench," or the "Queen's Bench" when the Queen is the highest royal authority.

Court of Last Resort: A court from which no appeal lies to a higher court in the same jurisdiction. This may sometimes not be the highest court in the jurisdiction.

Court of Record: A court whose proceedings are permanently recorded, and that has the power to fine or imprison for contempt. Courts not of record are those of lesser authority whose proceedings are not permanently recorded.

Court of Special Sessions: A court of limited jurisdiction in criminal cases in some states, e.g., New York.

Court Session: The time during which a court sits and may exercise its judicial power.

Court Term: A division of the year during which the court holds its session.

Defendant: A person who is being sued in a civil action, or is prosecuted in a criminal action.

Direct Appeal: An appeal from a lower court to an appellate court.

Discovery: A proceeding whereby one party to an action may be informed as to facts known by other parties or witnesses.

Dismissal Without Prejudice: Permits the complainant to sue again on the same cause of action. Dismissal *with prejudice* bars the right to bring or maintain an action on the same claim or cause.

Dissenting Opinion: An opinion by a judge of an appellate court indicating his reason for disagreeing with the result reached by the majority.

Double Jeopardy: Charging an accused with a crime for which he or she has already been tried.

En Banc: A judicial bench. The term is usually applied to a court of appeal when all of its judges sit together and jointly issue a decision or opinion.

Ex Post Facto: After the fact; an act or fact occurring after some previous act or fact, and relating thereto.

Exhibit: A paper, document, or other article produced and exhibited to a court during a trial or hearing.

Felony: A more serious crime, usually carrying with it a sentence in the state penitentiary.

General Court: A common term for a colonial legislature that acted as court.

Good Behavior: An office held during *good behavior* is one from which the incumbent may not be removed except on proved charges of misconduct.

Grand Jury: A body of persons, the number of whom varies in different jurisdictions, sworn to inquire into crimes within the jurisdiction of the county or district.

Habeas Corpus: Literally, "You have the body." A writ that requires an officer having custody of a prisoner to bring that prisoner before the court or judge for the purpose of determining if the prisoner is being unlawfully detained.

Impeachment Trial: The hearing of charges of misconduct against a public official, conducted by a legislative body.

In Camera: In the judge's chambers; in private.

Indictment: A formal accusation made by a grand jury charging a person with having committed a crime.

Inquest: Judicial inquiry.

In Forma Pauperis: A proceeding whereby a court may absolve a poor person of certain legal costs upon appropriate application. These proceedings constitute a large number of the cases filed in the United States Supreme Court.

Information: A formal accusation made by an official prosecutor, without presentment to a grand jury, charging a person with committing a crime.

Inns of Court: Societies of barristers in England.

Injunction: Writ by a court forbidding a person to perform a certain act.

Instruction: A direction given by a judge to the jury concerning the law of the case.

Judgment: Official determination by a court.

Judicial Administration: The organization and procedures of the judicial branch of the government.

Judiciary: The branch of government that has judicial power. Also, the name for all the courts of a jurisdiction taken collectively.

Jurisdiction: The authority of a court to exercise its judicial power in a specific case.

Justice of the Peace: A public official with minor civil and criminal jurisdiction. In more serious crimes, this person may be authorized to conduct preliminary hearings and hold the accused for trial by a higher court.

Legislative Court: A court created by Congress pursuant to a constitutional power other than Article III of the United States Constitution. Judges of legislative courts, as contrasted to those of constitutional courts, are not automatically appointed for good behavior, nor are their salaries automatically subject to nonreduction during their appointment. The legislative courts are the United States Court of Claims, the United States Court of Customs and Patent Appeals, the United States Emergency Court of Appeals, the United States Customs Court, the territorial courts, and the local courts for the District of Columbia.

Local Court: A court whose jurisdiction is limited as to a specific place.

Magistrate: Title of a judge of an inferior court with limited criminal, and sometimes limited civil, jurisdiction.

Majority Decision: A decision by an appellate court by more than one-half of those judges hearing a case.

Mayor's Court: An inferior court whose jurisdiction is limited to a city or town.

Misdemeanor: A crime less than the grade of felony.

Mistrial: An erroneous or invalid trial; a trial that cannot stand in law because of lack of jurisdiction, wrong drawing of jurors, or disregard of some other fundamental requisite.

Municipal Courts: In the judicial organization of some states, courts whose territorial authority is confined to the city or community.

Nisi Prius: Courts for the initial trial of issues of fact, as distinguished from appellate courts.

Nolle Prosequi: A declaration by the plaintiff in a civil suit, or the prosecuting officer in a criminal case, that states that he or she "will no further prosecute" the case.

Nolo Contendere: A pleading, usually used by defendants in criminal cases, which literally means, "I will not contest it"; a plea similar to "Guilty."

Notary Public: A public officer whose function it is to administer oaths; to attest and certify by his or her hand and official seal, certain classes of documents in order to give them credit and authenticity in foreign jurisdictions; to take acknowledgments of deeds and other conveyances, and certify the same; and to perform certain official acts chiefly in commercial matters, such as the protesting of notes and bills, the noting of foreign drafts, and marine protests in cases of loss or damage.

Official Report: A report of decided case, generally in courts of appellate jurisdiction, containing statements of the facts, judgments, and opinions published by a government body. Several states publish such reports officially for selected trial courts.

Per Curiam: An opinion rendered by the court as a whole, rather than by one judge with whom others concur.

Petit Jury: A body usually of twelve or fewer persons selected to hear and find the facts in a trial at law, so called to distinguish from the grand jury.

Plaintiff: A person who brings suit.

Pleadings: Statement by litigants that specify the allegations upon which they base their own claims or challenge the claims of their opponents.

Police Court: A court for the trial of minor criminal offenses, and which controls the adoption and guardianship of minors; a surrogate court.

Recorder: A county officer in charge of public records. In some towns, *recorder* is the name of a local court with limited civil jurisdiction.

Rule of Court: An order made by a court having competent jurisdiction.

Stare Decisis: The doctrine that, when a court has once laid down a principle of law as applicable to a certain set of facts, it will adhere to that principle and apply it to future cases where the facts are substantially the same.

Supersedeas: A writ containing a command to stay proceedings at law, such as the enforcement of a judgment pending an appeal.

Surrogate: A judge or judicial officer who has administration of probate matters.

Trial De Novo: A new trial or retrial held in an appellate court, in which the whole case is gone into as if no trial had been held in a lower court.

Venue: The place designated for trial.

Voir Dire: "To speak the truth." The phrase denotes the preliminary examination the court may make of one presented as a witness, or a prospective juror, as to his or her qualifications.

Writ: An order issued by a court or judge directing a public officer or private person to do a specific act.

37

Evidence

Evidence: Any type of proof legally presented at trial, by the act of parties and through testimony of witnesses, presentation of records, documents, concrete objects, etc., for the purpose of inducing belief in the minds of the court or jury as to their contention.

Classification: Evidence is either *judicial* or *extrajudicial*. *Judicial evidence* is the lawful means of ascertaining, in a judicial proceeding, the truth respecting a question of fact. *Extrajudicial evidence* is that which is used to satisfy persons as to facts requiring proof.

Primary Evidence: Evidence that, under every circumstance, affords the greatest certainty of the fact in question. A written instrument is itself the best possible evidence of its existence and contents; original or firsthand evidence. The best evidence that is required in the first instance, and that must fail before secondary evidence can be admitted.

Secondary Evidence: That which is inferior to primary evidence; thus, a copy of an instrument, or oral evidence relating to the instrument, is secondary evidence of the instrument and its contents.

Direct Evidence: Direct evidence is that means of proof which tends to show the existence of a fact without the intervention of proof of any other fact, and is distinguished from circumstantial evidence, which is often called *indirect evidence.*

Indirect or Circumstantial Evidence: That which tends to establish the issue by proof of various facts, sustaining by their consistency the hypothesis claimed. *Indirect evidence* consists of both inferences and presumptions.

Intrinsic Evidence: That which is derived from a document without anything to explain it.

Extrinsic Evidence: External evidence, or that which is not contained in the body of an agreement, contract, or the like.

Adminicular Evidence: Auxiliary or supplementary evidence, such as is presented for the purpose of explaining and completing other evidence.

Circumstantial Evidence: Evidence directed to the attending circumstances: evidence that is inferential by establishing a condition of surrounding and limited circumstances, a premise from which the existence of the principal fact may be concluded by reasoning. When the existence of the principal fact is only inferred from one or more circumstances, the evidence is circumstantial. All presumptive evidence is circumstantial because it is derived from or made up of circumstances. All circumstantial evidence, however, is not presumptive, as it leads to necessary conclusions instead of probable ones.

Competent Evidence: That which the law considers admissible.

Conclusive Evidence: That which is so strong and convincing that the law considers it beyond contradiction; that which establishes beyond any doubt.

Corroborative Evidence: Strengthening or confirming evidence. Additional evidence of a different character in support of the same fact or proposition.

Cumulative Evidence: Additional or corroborative evidence to the same point, used to prove what has already been established by other evidence.

Documentary Evidence: That which is supplied by writings and documents of every kind.

Evidence Aliunde: Evidence from outside, from another source. In certain cases, a written instrument may be explained by evidence aliunde, the testimony of a witness to conversations, admissions, or preliminary negotiations.

Expert Evidence: Testimony given in relation to some scientific, technical, or professional matter by experts, i.e., persons qualified to speak authoritatively by reason of their special training, skill, or familiarity with the subject.

Extraneous Evidence: Refers to a contract, deed, will, or any writing. Extraneous evidence is not furnished by the document itself, but from outside sources, the same as evidence aliunde.

Fair Preponderance of Evidence: Evidence weighed against that which is offered to oppose it and is found more convincing in the minds of the jury.

Hearsay Evidence: Evidence not proceeding from the personal knowledge of the witness, but from the mere repetition of what the witness has heard others say. The very nature of the evidence shows its weakness, and it is seldom admitted as evidence or accepted by the court.

Incompetent Evidence: That which is not admissible under the established rules of evidence; that which the law does not permit to be presented because of lack of originality or of some defect in the witness, the document, or the nature of the evidence itself.

Inculpatory Evidence: Evidence that without a specific or particular fact cannot be proved.

Legal Evidence: A broad, general term meaning all admissible evidence, including oral and documentary, but with a further implication that it must be of such character as to reasonably and substantially prove the point, not merely raise a suspicion or conjecture.

Material Evidence: That which is relevant and goes to the substantial matters in dispute. Evidence that has a legitimate and effective influence or bearing on the decision of the case.

Mathematical Evidence: Demonstrative evidence, such as establishes its conclusions with absolute necessity and certainty. It is used in contradistinction to moral evidence.

Moral Evidence: As opposed to *Mathematical* or *Demonstrative* evidence, it denotes that kind of evidence that, without developing a necessary certainty, generates a high degree of probability, founded upon analogy or induction, experience of the ordinary course of nature or the sequence of events, and the testimony of human beings.

Newly Discovered Evidence: Evidence of a new and material fact, or new evidence related to a fact in issue, discovered by a party to a cause after the rendition of a verdict or judgment.

Opinion Evidence: Evidence of what the witness thinks, believes, or infers, rather than personal knowledge of the facts themselves. Not admissible except (under certain limitations) in the case of experts.

Oral Evidence: Evidence given by word of mouth.

Original Evidence: An original document, writing, or other material object introduced in evidence, as distinguished from a copy.

Parol Evidence: Oral or verbal evidence given by word or mouth.

Partial Evidence: That which goes to establish a detached fact, in series tending to the fact in dispute. It may be received, subject to be rejected as incompetent, unless connected with the fact in dispute by proof of other facts.

Positive Evidence: Direct proof of the point in issue; evidence that, if believed, establishes the truth or falsehood of an issue, and does not arise from any presumption.

Preponderance of Evidence: Greater weight of evidence, or evidence that is more credible and convicing to the mind. In criminal cases, guilt must be established in the minds of the jury, based on the evidence presented to them, beyond any reasonable doubt and to a moral certainty (and the jury must be unanimous in its decision), whereas civil cases are decided on the basis of a preponderance, or weight, of the evidence presented, to a reasonable degree of certainty (and only a majority, usually two-thirds, of the jury must agree).

Presumptive Evidence: This term has several meanings in law: (1) Any evidence that is not direct and positive: the proof of minor or other facts incidental to or usually connected with the fact sought to be proved, which, when taken together, inferentially establish or prove the fact in question to a reasonable degree of certainty. (2) Evidence that must be received and treated as true and sufficient until rebutted by other testimony; as where a statute provides that certain facts shall be presumptive evidence of guilt of title. (3) Evidence that admits of explanation or contradiction by other evidence, as distinguished from conclusive evidence.

Prima Facie Evidence: That which is good and sufficient on its face; such evidence as, in the judgment of the law, is sufficient to establish a given fact, or the group or chain of facts constituting the party's claim or defense, and which if not rebutted or contradicted will remain sufficient.

Prima Facie Case: One in which the evidence in favor of a proposition is sufficient to support a finding in its favor, if all the evidence to the contrary be disregarded.

Probable Evidence: Presumptive evidence, based on its foundation in probability.

Proper Evidence: Such evidence as may be presented under the rules established by law and recognized by the courts.

Real Evidence: That which is furnished by things themselves, on view or inspection, as distinguished from a description of them by word of a witness, e.g., the physical appearance revealed to the jury of marks, scars, wounds, fingerprints; weapons or implements used in the commission of a crime; the place or scene of the crime or accident.

Rebutting Evidence: Evidence given to explain, repel, counteract, or disprove facts given in evidence by the opposing side.

Relevant Evidence: That which relates to, or bears directly upon, the point in issue, or conduces to prove a pertinent theory in a case.

Satisfactory Evidence: Satisfactory proof; credible evidence in respect to its amount or weight, sufficient to justify the court or jury in adopting a conclusion.

Scintilla of Evidence: Any material evidence that, if true, would tend to establish the issue in the mind of a reasonable jury.

Secondhand Evidence: Hearsay evidence.

State's Evidence: A term for testimony given by an accomplice or joint participant in the commission of a crime, tending to criminate or convict the others; usually given under actual or implied promise of immunity.

Substantive Evidence: Evidence used to prove a fact, as opposed to evidence given for the purpose of discrediting a witness.

Substitutionary Evidence: That which is admitted as a substitute for what would be the original or primary instrument of evidence, as where a witness is permitted to testify to the contents of a lost document.

Sufficient Evidence: Adequate evidence in character, weight, or amount, as will legally justify the judicial or official action demanded. It may be *prima facie* or *satisfactory* evidence, according to the definitions of those terms given above.

Traditionary Evidence: Evidence derived from tradition, reputation, or statement formerly made by persons since deceased, regarding pedigree, boundaries, etc., where no living witnesses having knowledge of the facts can be produced.

Weight of Evidence: The preponderance of credible evidence, offered in trial to support one side of the issue.

Evident: Clear to the understanding and satisfactory to the judgment; manifest; plain; obvious; conclusive.

Ex Facie: "From the face"; apparently; evidently. A term applied to what appears on the face of a writing.

ADMISSIBILITY OF EVIDENCE IN CRIMINAL CASES

Facts in Issue: Facts in issue include all facts that are in dispute or that tend to establish the guilt or innocence of the accused, or tend to support or disprove any special defense, such as former jeopardy or legal capacity of the accused to commit the crime charged.

Facts Relevant to the Facts in Issue: Evidence of any fact that, though not itself in issue, has a bearing upon any fact in issue, is admissible.

Facts Necessary to Explain or Introduce Relevant Facts: Facts are admissible: (1) If necessary to be known to explain or introduce a fact in issue, or relevant to the issue. (2) If they support or rebut an inference suggested by any such fact. (3) If they tend to establish or disprove the identity of any thing or person whose identity is an issue or is relevant to the issue. (4) If they fix the time or place at which any such fact happened. (5) If they show the relation of the parties by whom any such fact was transacted. (6) If they afforded an opportunity for its occurrence or transaction. (7) If they are necessary to be known in order to show the relevancy of other facts.

Motive: Any fact that shows a motive or lack of motive to commit the crime charged is admissible.

Preparation for Act: Any fact or evidence tending to show preparations by the defendant to commit the act charged is admissible.

Subsequent Conduct or Condition of Defendant: Any conduct or condition of the defendant, subsequent to the act charged, that influenced the act, and any act done in consequence of it by or by the authority of the defendant, may be shown. But self-serving statements or acts cannot be shown by the defendant.

Statements Accompanying Acts: Statements accompanying and explaining an act made by or to the person doing it may be proved if they are necessary to understanding the act.

Statements in the Presence of Defendant: When the defendant's conduct is in issue or is relevant, statements made in his or her presence by which his or her conduct can be affected are admissible when the defendant makes no denial.

Conduct and Complaint by Person Injured: In prosecutions for rape, the conduct of the victim, and particularly the fact that he or she made complaint after the crime was committed, may be shown, but the particulars of the complaint are not admissible.

Other Crimes: During the time a person is being tried for one crime, the state cannot prove the commission by that person of another crime that is not connected with the crime charged. If, however, the other crime was committed as part of the same transaction, and tends to explain or qualify the fact in issue, it may be shown. When the existence of intention, knowledge, malice, or other state of mind is in issue, and the commission of another crime tends to prove its existence, the other crime may be shown. The evidence is admitted for this purpose only, and not to show that the defendant was likely to commit the crime in question.

Acts and Declarations of Conspirators: When two or more persons conspire to commit any offense, everything said, done, or written by one of them in the execution or furtherance of their common purpose is admissible as against each of them.

Hearsay: *Hearsay evidence* is the testimony given by a witness who relates, not what the witness knows personally, but what others have told him or her; it is admissible only in exceptional cases.

Declarations by Persons Other Than Defendant: Declarations by persons other than the defendant cannot be proved unless: (1) they are part of the resgestae; (2) they are admissible as dying declarations; (3) they are admissible as declarations by authority of the defendant; or (4) they are admissible as evidence given in a former proceeding.

Dying Declarations: In prosecutions for homicide, a statement made on behalf of the deceased as to the cause of death, and as to the circumstances which resulted in death, is admissible if it appears to the judge that when the statement was made, the person had given up all hope of recovery. The deceased must have been competent as a witness, and the facts stated must be such that he or she could have testified to them. To be competent to testify to dying declarations, a witness must be able to state the substance as it was made, though the witness need not state it verbatim.

Admissions and Declarations by Defendant: Declarations made by the defendant, or by a third person by the defendant's authority, if relevant, are admissible against him or her, but they are not admissible in the defendant's favor.

Confessions: A *confession* is an admission made at any time by a person charged with a crime, and is admissible against him or her if voluntary. No confession is deemed voluntary if it was caused by any inducement, threat, or promise from a person in authority and if it made reference to the charge against the accused.

Silence When Accused of a Crime: The silence of a defendant when accused of a crime may be shown as an implied admission of guilt.

Against Whom Confessions are Admissible: A confession is admissible only against the person who made it. A confession by one defendant is not competent evidence against that person's codefendant.

Evidence Given in a Former Proceeding: Any evidence given in a former proceeding is admissible for the purpose of proving the matter stated in a later stage of the same proceeding, under the following circumstances: (1) When the witness is dead; (2) When the witness is insane; (3) When the witness is out of the jurisdiction; (4) When the witness cannot be found within the jurisdiction; (5) Provided the person against whom the evidence is to be given had the right and the opportunity to cross-examine the witness during the former proceeding.

Opinion Evidence: This evidence is admissible only in exceptional cases. A witness must testify to facts, not state a personal opinion or conclusion.

Expert Testimony: Testimony with respect to science or art may be given by persons specially skilled in any such matter. The words *science or art* in the above rule include all subjects on which a course of special study or experience is necessary. Where a witness possesses knowledge, not of the facts of the case but of a trade or science art beyond that of the average person, he or she may give an opinion based upon such special knowledge so that the jury may have this knowledge in arriving at a verdict.

Character Evidence: Evidence of the character of a person is admissible in the following cases: (1) The fact that the defendant of the crime charged has a good character may be shown, but the state cannot show that he or she has a bad character, unless the individual's character is at issue, or unless evidence has been given that he or she has a good character, in which case evidence disputing that testimony is admissible; (2) In prosecutions for homicide, the character of the victim as a violent and dangerous person may be shown when addressing the question of whether the defendant acted in self-defense; (3) A witness may be impeached by proof of his or her bad character for truth and veracity; (4) In crimes where character is an element—for example, in *some* sex crimes—the prosecution must prove that the female was of previous chaste character.

Evidence Wrongfully Obtained: Where no objection is made at the trial to the introduction of evidence wrongfully or illegally obtained, error cannot be claimed for the first time on appeal. And where the record is silent as to whether the officers had a search warrant or warrant of arrest, the seizure is presumed to be lawful.

Presumption of Innocence: The defendant is presumed to be innocent, and the burden is on the state to prove guilt beyond a reasonable doubt and to a moral certainty.

Competency of Witnesses: There is little difference between civil and criminal cases as regards the competency of witnesses and the mode of examining them. All persons are deemed competent to testify except those types described below. If, in the opinion of the judge, the witness is prevented by extreme youth, disease affecting the mind, or any other cause of the same kind, from: (1) recollecting the matter on which he or she is to testify; (2) understanding the questions put to him or her; (3) giving rational answers to those questions; or (4) knowing that he or she ought to speak the truth, the individual is deemed to be incompetent to testify.

A witness unable to speak or hear is not incompetent, but may give evidence by writing or by signs, or in any other manner in which he or she can make it intelligible, but such writing must be written and such signs must be made in open court. Evidence so given is deemed to be oral evidence.

Generally a husband or a wife cannot be a witness against his or her spouse, except for a crime committed against him or her by that spouse, but the laws on this subject vary in the different states. In most states by statute, the accused is now allowed to testify in his or her own behalf, but he or she cannot be compelled to testify.

Privileged Communications: (1) No husband is compelled to disclose any communication made to him by his wife during the marriage, and no wife is compelled similarly. (2) No one can be compelled to give evidence relating to any affairs of state, as to official communications between public officers upon public affairs, except with the permission of the officer at the head of the department concerned. (3) In cases in which the government is immediately concerned, no witness can be compelled to answer any question, the answer to which would tend to disclose the names of persons by or to whom information was given as to the commission of offenses. (4) No legal advisor is permitted, whether during or after the termination of employment as such, unless with his or her client's expressed consent, to disclose any communication, oral or documentary, made to him or her as such legal advisor. The expression *legal advisor* includes lawyers, their clerks, and interpreters between them and their clients.

Self-Incrimination: Under the constitutions and at common law, no one is bound to answer any question if the answer would have a tendency to expose the witness to any criminal charge, or to any penalty or forfeiture that the judge regards as reasonably likely to be preferred or sued for. However, no one is excused from answering any question only because the answer may establish, or tend to establish, that the person owes a debt or is otherwise liable to any civil suit. If a defendant offers to be a witness, he or she cannot refuse to answer proper questions on cross-examination.

When Corroboration is Required: In some states, a conviction cannot be had in a criminal case on the testimony of an accomplice unless corroborated by other evidence. In some states, in prosecutions for abortion, seduction, rape, and similar crimes, there can be no conviction on the uncorroborated testimony of the woman.

Number of Witnesses Necessary: In trials for treason, no one can be convicted unless he or she pleads guilty except upon the oath of two lawful witnesses to the overt act. If, upon a trial for perjury, the only evidence against the defendant is the oath of one witness contradicting the oath on which perjury is assigned, and if no circumstances are proved that corroborate such witness, the defendant is entitled to be acquitted.

Examination, Cross-Examination: Witnesses examined in open court must be first examined in chief. They may then be cross-examined and subsequently re-examined. The examination and cross-examination must relate to facts in issue or relevant thereto; and in most states, the cross-examination must be confined to the facts to which the witness testified on his or her examination in chief. Re-examination must be directed to the explanation of matters referred to in cross-examination, and if new matter is, by permission of the court, introduced in re-examination, the adverse party may further cross-examine upon the matter.

Leading Questions: These are questions put or framed in such a form as to suggest the answers that are sought to be obtained by the person interrogating. Questions are leading that suggest to the witness a desired answer, or that embody a material fact and may be answered by a mere negative or affirmative, or that involve an answer bearing immediately upon the merits of the cause.

Questions Lawful in Cross-Examination: When a witness is cross-examined, he or she may be asked any questions that tend: (1) to test accuracy, veracity, or credibility; or (2) shake the witness's credit by injuring his or her character. However, the court has a right to exercise its discretion and to refuse to compel such questions to be answered when, in the opinion of the court, it would not affect the credibility of the witness as to the matter to which he or she is required to testify.

Exclusion of Evidence to Contradict Answers to Questions Testing Veracity: When a witness under cross-examination has been asked and has answered any question that is relevant to the inquiry only so far as it tends to shake the witness's credit by injuring his or her character, evidence can be given to contradict the witness in the following cases: (1) If a witness is asked whether he or she has been previously convicted of any felony or misdemeanor, and denies it or does not admit it, or refuses to answer, evidence may be given of a previous conviction. (2) If a witness is asked any question tending to show that he or she is not impartial, and answers it by denying the facts suggested, he or she may be contradicted.

Statement Inconsistent with Present Testimony: Every witness under cross-examination in any proceeding, civil or criminal, may be asked whether he or she has made any former statement, relative to the matter of the action, that is inconsistent with the present testimony.

Impeaching the Credit of a Witness: A witness may be questioned on cross-examination as to bias, motive, and interest in the case. His or her credit may be impeached by the adverse party by the evidence of persons who are able to swear that they know the general reputation of the witness for truth and veracity. In some states, the inquiry may be made to the witness's general moral character, but in all states, the inquiry is confined to general reputation. Specific acts by the witness sought to be impeached cannot be shown.

Offenses Against Women: When a man is prosecuted for rape, in some jurisdictions, it may be shown that the woman against whom the offense was committed was of a general immoral character, although she is not cross-examined on the subject. In some states, the woman may be asked if she has had sexual relations with other men, but her answer cannot be contradicted. She may also be asked whether she has had sexual relations on other occasions with the accused, and if she denies it, she (probably) may be contradicted. In a prosecution for seduction, the unchastity of the woman may be shown.

38

Criminal Procedure

Criminal Procedure: The method fixed by law for the apprehension and prosecution of a person who is supposed to have committed a crime, and for that person's punishment if convicted. The term includes pleading, evidence, and practice.

Jurisdiction: The authority by which the court acts, and the territory over which its authority extends. Unless extended by statute, a state has jurisdiction over only those crimes committed within its territorial limits and crimes committed by its own citizens abroad. A crime must be prosecuted in the county in which it was committed (unless a change of venue is ordered by the court by virtue of evidence to show that a fair trial cannot be obtained within the venue in which it was committed).

Where a blow is struck in one county and death ensues in another, the offense is generally held to have been committed in the latter. When a person in one county commits a crime in another by means of an innocent agent, such as the U.S. Postal Service, the latter county has jurisdiction. Several states have special statutes governing the subject of jurisdiction, such as provisions for prosecuting homicides in the county where the body is found (even though the homicide took place in another county); giving jurisdiction to either county when the crime is committed partly in one county and partly in another, or to either state when the crime is committed partly in one state and partly in another.

State courts: The courts in the various states are created, and their jurisdiction is conferred and defined, by statutes. In some states, crimes committed on public conveyances may be prosecuted in any county through which the conveyance passed on the trip during which the crime was committed.

Change of venue: Changing the place of trial from one county to another in the same state, or from one local jurisdiction to another similar jurisdiction within the same county. In exceptional cases, the place of trial may be changed from one state to another if the nature of the crime being charged, or reportage of the circumstances surrounding the offense, are so inflammatory as to provoke intense public sentiment across the state, thus rendering a fair trial within that state improbable.

Federal courts: Federal courts of criminal jurisdiction include the U.S. Commissioners Courts, U.S. District Courts, U.S. Circuit Courts of Appeal, and the U.S. Supreme Court. The jurisdiction of the federal courts arises solely out of the Constitution and the acts of Congress.

United States Commissioners are charged generally with such functions in the federal government as devolve upon justices of the peace in state government. They are appointed and removable by the district courts.

The U.S. District Courts have jurisdiction exclusive of the state courts of all offenses against the United States committed within their respective districts or on the high seas.

The circuit courts of appeal have appellate jurisdiction of crimes on writ of error to the District Courts.

The U.S. Supreme Court has appellate jurisdiction in the following cases: (1) to review a decision of the circuit court of appeals in a case certified to it by the latter, or caused by the Supreme Court to be certified; (2) where the judges of a district court certify the case to the Supreme Court; (3) on writ of error to the state court of highest resort in certain cases; and (4) by writ of habeas corpus, aided by writs of certiorari, where a person is, without authority, detained in custody under color of the authority of the United States.

Locality of crime against the United States: The Constitution and the acts of Congress provide the right to be tried where the offense was committed. A trial shall be held in the state where said crime was committed. Should the crime not be committed within any state, the trial shall be at such place or places as Congress may, by law, have directed; those accused of a crime shall have the right to trial by a jury of the state and district wherein the crime shall have been commited. There are various provisions by act of Congress of crimes committed on the high seas, or elsewhere out of the jurisdiction of any particular state or district, to be tried in the district where the offender is first found, or into which the offender is first brought.

39

Arrest

Arrest: The taking of a person into custody in a manner provided by law for the purpose of holding or detaining him or her to answer a criminal charge or civil demand. It may be made: (1) by virtue of a warrant issued by a competent authority; or (2) under some circumstances, without a warrant.

What constitutes an arrest: The restraint of the person arrested, or submission to the custody of the officer or arresting person.

Duty after arrest: After making an arrest, the officer must, without unnecessary delay, take the prisoner before a magistrate for examination. A private person has the option of delivering the prisoner to an officer instead of the magistrate.

Authorized arrest in unauthorized manner: The fact that an authorized arrest is made in an unauthorized manner may render the officer or arresting person liable but will not affect the state's right to detain the accused if lawful cause exists.

Rights and liabilities of parties (lawful arrest): If an arrest is authorized and is attempted or made in a proper manner, the person making it, whether an officer or a private person, merely performs a duty, and that person incurs no liability, as the law throws its protection around him or her.

If the person sought to be arrested resists, he or she is criminally liable for the resistance. If the resist involves force, the person is civilly and criminally liable for assault and battery. If the individual, or someone assisting him or her in resisting, kills the person making the arrest, the homicide is murder.

If a person unlawfully departs from custody after having been legally arrested, he or she is guilty of a misdemeanor known as *escape*. If the person breaks from or forcibly escapes from the place of imprisonment, he or she is guilty of *prison breach*, which is either a misdemeanor or a felony, depending on circumstances.

If third persons interfere in aid of the person sought to be arrested, the bare interference constitutes a misdemeanor or a felony, and if they use force, they are also guilty of assault and battery. If the force used results in the killing of the person attempting to make the arrest, they are guilty of murder. If they procure the escape of the person after his or her arrest, they are guilty of rescue, which can be either a misdemeanor or a felony.

Rights and liabilities of parties (unlawful arrest): If an arrest or attempt to arrest is illegal, either because there is no authority to arrest at all or because the arrest is made in an unlawful manner (as for instance, by the use of unnecessary violence), the person arresting, whether he or she is an officer or a private person, and whether the arrest or attempt to arrest was made with or without a warrant, is guilty of false imprisonment or of assault and battery or both (as the case may be), and is both civilly and criminally liable therefor. An unlawful attempt to arrest or a false imprisonment may be lawfully resisted by any necessary force short of taking life or inflicting grievous bodily harm. Even when life is taken in resisting an unlawful arrest, the attempt to arrest or the false imprisonment is generally deemed sufficient provocation to reduce the homicide to manslaughter. Within certain limits, third persons, particularly relatives, may interfere to prevent an unlawful arrest or imprisonment.

Arrest by officer without warrant, when lawful: A peace officer may, without a warrant, arrest a person when: (1) the person to be arrested has committed a felony or misdemeanor in the officer's presence. In the case of such arrest for a misdemeanor, the arrest shall be made immediately or on fresh pursuit; (2) the person to be arrested has committed a felony, although not in the presence of the officer; (3) a felony has in fact been committed and the officer has reasonable grounds to believe that the person to be arrested has committed it; or (4) the officer has reasonable grounds to believe that the person to be arrested has committed or is committing a felony.

Arrest by private person, when lawful: A private person may make an arrest when the person to be arrested has, in his or her presence, committed a misdemeanor amounting to a breach of the peace or a felony, or when a felony has been committed and there are reasonable grounds to believe that the person to be arrested has committed it.

Method of arrest by officer by virtue of a warrant: When making an arrest by virtue of a warrant, the officer shall inform the person to be arrested of the cause of the arrest and that a warrant has been issued for his or her arrest, except when the subject to be arrested flees or forcibly resists before the officer has opportunity to so inform him. The officer need not have the warrant in his or her possession at the time of the arrest, but after the arrest the warrant shall be produced as soon as possible.

Method of arrest by officer without a warrant: When making an arrest without a warrant, the officer shall inform the person to be arrested of his or her authority and the cause of the arrest, unless the person to be arrested is then engaged in the commission of an offense, or is pursued after its commission or after an escape, or forcibly resists before the officer has opportunity to so inform him or her.

Method of arrest by private person: A private person, when making an arrest, shall inform the person to be arrested of the intention to arrest and the cause of the arrest, unless the person to be arrested is then engaged in the commission of an offense, or is pursued after its commission or after an escape, or forcibly resists before the person making the arrest has opportunity to so inform him or her.

Reasonable cause, probable cause: *Reasonable cause* or *probable cause*, or good reason to believe, have been believed to exist when: (1) the person resembles the one accused and fails to identify himself or herself as a person who did not commit the felony; (2) the person's movements or actions are similar to those of the suspect; (3) it becomes known that the person to be arrested committed a felony or was in the company of the perpetrator before or after commission of same; or (4) the person to be arrested has some of the proceeds of the felony in his or her possession or has been seen leaving the place where the felony was committed.

Arrest by warrant: A *warrant* is a writ issued by an authorized magistrate to an officer, requiring the officer to arrest the offender or suspect therein named, and bring him or her before a proper magistrate to be dealt with according to law.

Issuance of a warrant: To authorize the issuance of a warrant before indictment, there must be made before a magistrate a proper complaint showing that a crime has been committed and that there is probable cause to suspect the accused. After indictment, the usual practice is to issue a bench warrant. An arrest under an insufficient warrant, or without any warrant if a warrant is necessary, is illegal.

Complaint: A charge, proferred before a magistrate having jurisdiction, that a person named (or an unknown person) has committed a specified offense, in order that a prosecution may be instituted. To enable a magistrate to issue a warrant, it is necessary that a proper complaint under oath be brought before the magistrate in order that he or she may determine that a crime has been committed and that there is probable cause to suspect the accused.

Admissions: In cases where conspiracy is charged, the admission of one of the accused may become, by reason of the other proof in the case, admissible against the other. By themselves and without other proof, however, such admissions are not admissible against the other. But if the proof shows the existence of the conspiracy, statements made by one of the parties as to details of the crime charged become admissible against the other. In cases of joint crime, such as fornication or adultery, which cannot be committed except by the concurrent act of two parties, the rule is the same as in cases of conspiracy.

There is no distinction between civil and criminal cases in respect to the use of admissions. The rules of evidence are the same.

Confessions: Where a confession is used against an accused person, the whole confession must be introduced. A confession, like an admission, is always open to explanation by the person against whom it is used.

Confession under the influence of intoxicating substances: Confessions made by the accused when under the influence of any intoxicating substance are thereby rendered inadmissible. Any condition of mind that renders a person temporarily incompetent while in such condition thereby renders his or her statements valueless.

Credibility and weight of the testimony of police officers, private detectives, and experts: Even though it may be in the interests of certain witnesses to procure a conviction against the accused, there is no rule of law that their testimony is to be weighed by any other method than that employed in the case of other witnesses. It has been held improper for the court as invading the province of the jury to instruct that the testimony of police officers who labored to bring the accused to justice should be received with caution or with distrust, although the jury may take into consideration the fact of the interest of such witnesses in securing a conviction. Similarly, the fact that a witness was paid for gathering evidence against the accused or for testifying as an expert against the accused does not necessarily invalidate his or her testimony.

Footprint and fingerprint evidence: Footprint evidence is admissible, but no one can lawfully compel another, against the person's consent, to place a foot in a shoe track for the purpose of using the evidence obtained thereby against him or her. The condition upon which footprint testimony is admissible is that, so far as the defendant is concerned, he or she shall not have involuntarily contributed to its production, so as to cause him or her in legal effect to serve as a witness against his or her will to furnish testimony to convict himself or herself.

Records of fingerprints taken at penal institutions or by police departments are admissible in evidence for the purpose of proving former convictions or for proving identity, under such circumstances that the evidence would be admissible of itself. Such records should not be admitted, however, where they will show, or expose to the jury, memoranda or other information placed upon the record, unless such memoranda or information is removed or covered so as to keep it from the view and inspection of the jury.

40

Homicide

Homicide is the killing of a human being, and the circumstances of the homicide determine whether or not the taking of that life is criminal or innocent.

A criminal homicide is neither excusable nor justifiable and falls into two categories: murder and manslaughter.

In order to charge *murder*, it must be proven that there was premeditation, that the person or persons accused of the murder intended to commit bodily harm or kill, or that the person or persons accused were engaged in a dangerous act and had shown wanton disregard for human life, or that the accused was engaged in a felony such as a robbery, burglary, rape, or aggravated arson. And in order to prove a murder was indeed committed, it must be proven that the victim is dead, that the death was at the hands of the accused, and that the act was a result of premeditation to kill or inflict bodily harm, or that the accused was perpetrating a crime such as rape, robbery, burglarly, or aggravated arson.

The charge of *manslaughter* indicates neither murder nor an innocent homicide took place, indicating it was the unlawful taking of a human life without premeditation or malice aforethought. The terms "voluntary" and "involuntary" demonstrate whether or not the killing was intended. Taking a human life during the heat of passion, even though there was an intent to kill, is considered voluntary manslaughter. The taking of a life without the intent to kill is considered involuntary manslaughter.

MOTIVES FOR HOMICIDE

Revenge
Sadism
Self-defense
Gain
Employed for the purpose
Mental deficiency
Rage
Mercy
Sex
Cover another crime
Jealousy
Blackmail
Fear
Debt
Love
To frame another
Feud
Ambition
Rivalry
Thrill
Protecting something or someone

TYPES OF HOMICIDES

Shooting
Knifing
Suffocation
Poisoning or gassing
Beating to death
Vehicular
Strangulation
Hanging
Electrical shock
Burning

INVESTIGATOR'S ARRIVAL ON SCENE:

(1) Determine identity of perpetrator or possible suspect(s); (2) Note time of arrival; (3) Prevent anyone touching body or disturbing scene pending arrival of Medical Examiner and Crime Lab. Prevent unauthorized people from entering the crime scene and anyone that is present from leaving; (4) Locate and preserve weapon and check for prints; (5) Take names of all present and description of any possible suspect(s); (6) Separate witnesses to prevent any conversation between them; (7) Note position of the body, clothing. Position of body marked; (8) Check for bullet holes, shell casings, bloodstains; (9) Search for clues; (10) Preserve evidence discovered; (11) Check with Medical Examiner for time of death, cause, wounds, if death occurred at location where body was discovered. Await pathology report for toxicology; (12) Have Crime Lab photograph scene; (13) Have sketch made of location, body position; (14) Take statements of any witnesses; (15) Attempt to learn motive; (16) Run make on victim to see if prior record exists; (17) Have Crime Lab dust for prints, look for fibers, blood samples; (18) Check for datebooks, diary, letters, addresses, and phone numbers belonging to victim; (19) Learn identity of friends, relatives, enemies, etc.; and (20) Escape route of perpetrator.

Bibliography

Alison, H.C. *Personal Identification.* Boston: Holbrook Press, 1973.

Blum, Richard H. *Deceivers & Deceived: Observations on Confidence Men & Their Victims, Informants & Their Quarry, Political & Industrial Spies & Ordinary Citizens.* Springfield, Illinois: Charles C. Thomas, 1972.

Chapman, Robert L., ed. *New Dictionary of American Slang.* New York: Harper & Row, 1986.

Guttmacher, Manfred S. *The Mind of the Murderer.* Salem, New Hampshire: Ayer Co. Pubs., 1960.

Hall, J. *Inside the Crime Lab.* Englewood Cliffs, New Jersey: Prentice Hall, 1974.

Hendrickson, R. *Ripoffs.* New York: Viking Press, 1976.

Hilton, O. *Scientific Examination of Questioned Documents.* New York: Elsevier Science Publishing, 1984.

Kahaner, Larry. *Cults that Kill: Probing the Underworld of Occult Crime.* New York: Warner Books, 1988.

Kotter, J.C. *Criminal Evidence,* 4th ed. Cincinnati: Anderson Pub., 1987.

Lewin, Esther and Arthur. *The Thesaurus of Slang.* New York: Facts on File, 1988.

O'Hara, Charles. *Fundamentals of Investigation.* Springfield, Illinois: Charles C. Thomas, 1962.

Reinhardt. *The Psychology of Strange Killers.* Springfield, Illinois: Charles C. Thomas, 1962.

Roland, Desmond and Bailey, James. *The Law Enforcement Handbook.* New York: Facts on File, 1985.

Rubenstein, Jonathan. *City Police.* New York: Farrar, Straus, and Giroux, 1973.

Saperstein, R. *Forensic Science Handbook,* vol. I. Englewood Cliffs, New Jersey: Prentice Hall, 1982.

———. *Forensic Science Handbook,* vol. II. Englewood Cliffs, New Jersey: Prentice Hall, 1988.

Svensson, A., and B.A. Fisher. *Techniques of Crime Scene Investigation,* 4th ed. New York: Elsevier Science Publishing, 1986.

Thorwald, J. *Crime and Science.* New York: Harcourt, Brace & World, 1967.

Index

A

Addiction, definition of, 164
Alcohol, Tobacco, and Firearms, Bureau of, 69-70
Ammunition, centerfire, 142
  rimfire, 141-142
The Anarchist Cookbook, 140
Arrest, 286-290
  definition of, 286
Arson, 156
  definition of, 118
  establishing evidence for, 118
  and inhabited structure, 118
  motives for, 118, 119-120
  oxidizing agents used in, 119
  proving malice or criminal intent in, 118
  and pyromania, 118, 119

B

Barbiturates, 172
Bloods, 16
Bureau of Land Management, 74
Burglary, 157
  and "commuter" burglars, 124
  definition of, 123
  from delivery truck, 124
  elements of, 123
  investigation of, 123-124
  vs. housebreaking, 123
  from loft, 124
  of residence, 124
  of safe, 123-124
  of store, 124
  and "supper" burglars, 124
  types of, 123-124

C

California Correctional Center (CCC), 233-234
California Correctional Institution (CCI), 231
California Department of Corrections, 224-225
  and conservation camp program, 237
California Institution for Men (CIM), 228-229
California Institution for Women (CIW), 227
California Medical Facility (CMF), 231-232
California Men's Colony (CMC), 230-231

California Rehabilitation Center (CRC), 232-233
California State Prison, Avenal, 234-235
The Camorra, 11, 12
Characters, 3
Cincinnati Police Division, 41, 51
  Central Vice Control Section of, 51
  Intelligence Section of, 51
  Investigations Bureau (I.B.) of, 41, 51
  Narcotics Liaison Section of, 51
  Office of Coordination, Planning and Budget of, 51
  Operations Bureau of, 41
  Personnel Resources Bureau of, 51
  Technical Services Bureau of, 51
Closed Story, 3
Cocaine, 165-172
Code cutter, 127-128
Common law, 241-252
Computer criminals, crimes commited by, 7-8
  methods of working of, 8
Confidence games, 128-130
  use of bereaved relatives in, 130
  computer scams as, 129-130
  and hot merchandise, 128-129
  and the inheritance, 128
  and just-a-few-dollars-more scam, 129
  mail-order ads used in, 130
  and phony airline tickets, 129
  See also Cons, dupes, and trickery; Individual names; under Piracy Cons, dupes, and trickery, devices used to aid in, 163
  list of, 162-163
  See also Confidence games
Correctional Institutions, 224-237
  of California, 224-225
  See also individual names; Prisons; United States Penitentiary
Correctional Training Facility (CTF), 226-227
Los Angeles County Sheriff's Department, 28-41
Courtroom, 83-86
  arrangement of, 84
  characters in, 83-84
  crime dramas in, 83
  crime dramas in, Perry Mason as example of, 83
  types of, 83
  See also Juries, special
Courts, 85-86
  federal, 284
  juvenile, 255
  state, 284
  types of, 85-86, 265-266, 267, 268, 269
  See also Juries, types of
Crack, 172
Crime, 213-217
  acts of violence, torture, cruelty used in, 215-217
  classification of, 255
  committed by U.S. military personnel, 92-93
  definition of, 249
  domestic, 154
  internal, by employees, 8-9
  kinds of, associated w/business and professions, 153-154
  kinds of, associated w/politics, 153

kinds of, associated w/racketeering, 154-155
kinds of, glossary of, 156-161
kinds of, list of, 151-155
means of execution used in, 214
methods of escape used in, 213-214
scene of, 103-105
scene of, discovery of suspect at, 103
scene of, importance of caution at, 104
scene of, personnel present at, 104-105
scene of, witnesses at, 103
unusual means of disposing of body in, 214-215
vs. tort, 250
weapons used in commission of, 138-139
See also Criminal procedure; under Investigators; Organized crime

Crime lab, 113-115
divisions of, 113
functions of, 114-115
police, 113-115
police, areas of crime solving covered by, 113
police, biological services, 114
police, chemical examinations conducted by, 114
police, divisions of, 113-115
police, documents-section functions of, 114-115
police, firearms-identification functions of, 114
police, markings, identification functions of, 114
police, photographic services of, 115
police, technological equipment used in, 115

Criminal law, 248-261
definition of, 249-261
procedure for handling infractions of, 248-249
purpose of, 249
sentencing in cases involving, 249
substantive, 252

Criminal procedure, 253, 283-285
definition of, 283

Criminals, 2-9
amateur, 4
computer, 7-8
identification of, by investigators, 100-101
locating, 101, 102-103
professional, 3-4
proving guilt of, in court, 102
proving guilt of, in court, role of malice in, 102
white-collar, 6
See also under Crimes; Serial killers

Crips, 16

D

Defense Criminal Investigating Service, and white-collar criminals, 6

Defense Criminal Investigative Service, 74-75

Defense Investigative Service (DIS), 75

Department of Corrections, and substance-abuse treatment programs, 246
work furlough centers of, 242

Devel Vocational Institution (DVI), 229-230
Doe, Jane or John, 121
  Jane or John, identifying, 121-122
Richard J. Donovan Correctional Facility (RJD), 235-236
Drug Enforcement Administration (DEA), 69
Drugs, of addiction and intellect-influence (list), 175-177
  dealers of, 173
  dealing in, 173
  dependency on, 165
  Golden Triangle and, 13
  means of administering, 165
  and motorcycle gangs, 17
  possession of, 172
  and street gangs, 15-16
  and tolerance, 165
  traffickers in, 173
  trafficking in, 165
  See also individual drug names

E

Evidence, admissibility of, in criminal cases, 276-282
  classification of, 271
  footprint and fingerprint, 290
  glossary of, 271-282
  kinds of, 271-276
  and prima facie case, 275
Explosives, 140

F

Federal Air Marshals (FAMS), 73-74
Federal Bureau of Investigation, 63-67
  Automated Identification Division System of (AIDS), 64-65
  case classifications of, 65-67
  Criminalistics Laboratory Information Systems (CLIS) of, 63-64
  files of, 64-65
  and fingerprint information, 63, 64
  and white-collar criminals, 6
Federal Bureau of Prisons, 87-88
  and American Federation of Government Employees (AFL-CIO) council of Prison Locals, 87
  Central Office of, 87
  Central Office of, functions of, 87
  telephone number of, 87
Federal Trade Commission, and white-collar criminals, 6
Firearms, 141-150
  See also Ammunition; Weapons
Firearms identification, 146
  terms used in, 144-150
Flying Dragons, 15
Folsom State Prison (FOL), 227-228
Foreign-Fugitive File, 77
Forensic and police sciences, 51-55
  equipment and technology in, 54-55
  sections of, 53
14K Triad, 13

G

Ghost Shadows, 15

H

Handguns, 141
  list of kinds of, 142-143
Hip Sing, 15
Hip Sing Tong, 15
Homicide, 291-93
  defined, 291
  investigating, 293
  manslaughter, 291-92
  motives for, 292
  murder, 291
  types of, 292
Hop Sing, 13
House arrest, 246-247

I

Identification, sources of, 116-117
Immigration and Naturalization Service, Investigations Division, 68-69
  Field Service of, 68
  Investigation Program of, 68-69
Institute of Judicial Administration, 262
intent, 102, 256-257, 261
Internal crimes, motives for, 9
Internal Revenue Criminal Investigations IRS, 72
Internal Revenue Service, and white-collar criminals, 6
INTERPOL, 63, 77
Investigation, for arson, 118-120
  authenticity of, in writing, 19-20
  of burglaries, 123-124
  federal law-enforcement agencies involved in, 75
  first twenty-four hours of, 102-103
  personnel involved in, 104-105
  and scene of crime, 103-105
  by United States Army, 78, 80
  by United States Navy, 79
  See also under Suspect
Investigator, 3
  importance of caution for, at scene of crime, 104
  as character, 3
  checklist for, 105
  checklist for, in rape cases, 126
  and computer crime, 8
  duties of, at scene of crime, 103-105
  informational sources for, 105-108
  objectives of, 100
  people providing clues to, 106
  places providing clues to, 106-108
  reasons of, for visiting scene of crime, 103-104
  six questions of, at scene of crime, 103
  See also under Criminals

J

Juries, special, 86
  types of, 86
Jurisdiction, 283-284

L

Lansky, Meyer, 12
Larceny, 127-130, 159
  bunco squad and, 130
  and confidence games, 128-130
  definition of, 127
  and temporary appropriation, 127

types of criminals who commit, 128
Law enforcement, 18-75
agencies of, 85
agencies of, federal, 20, 21
agencies of, local, 20-21, 21
authenticity in presentation of, 18-20
developing contacts in, for research, 20, 20-21
federal, 56-75
jurisdictional area of, 18
local, 20-21
military, 21
See also Forensic and police sciences; Individual agency names
Lawyers, types of, 84
Legal terminology, 259-267
Los Angeles Office of City Attorney, 56
Los Angeles Office of District Attorney, 55
Los Angeles Police Department (LAPD), 21-41
Administrative Office—special duties of, 25
Administrative Vice Division, 27
Anti-Terrorist Division of, 28
Bank Robbery, Hijack-Cargo Theft Section of, 23
Bureau of Special Investigations of, 26-28
Burglary/Auto Theft Division of, 23
Commercial Auto Theft Section of, 23
Criminal Conspiracy Section of, 22
Detective Support Division of, 22
Fugitive Section of, 22
Gaming Section of, 27
Gang Activities Section of, 22
Headquarters, Detective Services Group, Juvenile Division of, 24
Headquarters Detective Services Group, Robbery/Homicide Division of, 22
Homicide Special Section of, 23
Internal Affairs Division of, 25
investigative branches of, 21-24
Labor Relations Division of, 28
Major Crimes Investigation Section of, 23
Narcotics Division of, 26-27
Office of Operations of, 24
Office of Special Services of, 25-26
Officer-Involved Shooting Section of, 23
organizations and functions of, 21-24
Organized Crime Intelligence Division of, 25-26
Pawn Shop Section of, 23-24
Pornography Section of, 28
Prostitution Section of, 27-28
Public Affairs Section of, 28
Rape and Domestic Violence Section of, 23
Robbery Special Section of, 23
Special Investigations Section of, 22
vs. Cincinnati Police Department, 21
vs. New York Police Department, 21
L.A. County Sheriff's Depart-

ment, Administrative Division of, 35-36
administrative organization of, 34-35
Area Bureau of, 39-40
Court Services Division of, 36
Custody Division of, 36
departmental organization of, 35-37
Detective Division of, 36
duties and responsibilities of, 28, 34
Emergency-Services Detail of, 37
Field Operations Regions of, 36
Harbor Patrol of, 40-41
Justice Data System (JDS) of, 37, 38-39
and paramedics, 37
Radio Communications Center of, 37, 38
Specialized Investigations Bureau of, 36-37
Technical Services Division of, 36-37

M

Machine gun, list of kinds of, 143
Mafia, the boss and, 11
other names for, 11, 12
Marijuana, 172
Mescaline, 172
Military Justice System, 92-99
description of, in *United States Army Command and General Staff*, 94-99
Military Police Corps (MP), 79-80
Missing-children file, 76-77
Missing persons, 121-122
definition of, 121
locating, 122
vs. wanted persons, 121
Missing Persons Bureau, 121
and juvenile runaways, 121
Modus operandi (M.O.), 4
Money-making machine, 128
Motive, 276
vs. intent, 102, 256
role of in proving guilt of criminal, 102
shown by evidence, 276
Mule Creek State Prison, 235

N

Narcotics, 164-171
as area of crime, 164
definition of, 164
packaging of, methods used in, 173-174
possession of, 172
See also Drugs; Synthetic analgesics; Addiction
National Crime Information Center, 76-77
Advisory Police Board of, 76
and FBI director, 76
records of, 76
users of, 76
Naval Security and Investigative Command, 79
New York Police Department (NYPD), 21
vs. Cincinnati Police Department, 21
vs. Los Angeles Police Department, 21
Northern California Women's Facility, 236-237

O

On Leong Tong, 13
Open Story, 3
Opium, 172
Organized crime, 10-17
  and drug dealing, 173
  Mafia and, 10-13
  motorcycle gangs and, 16-17
  street gangs and, 15-16
  Triads and, 13, 15

P

Parole, 241-247
  Board of Prison Terms and, 242
  categories of, 243
  conditions of, 243-244
  definition of, 241
  duration of, 241-242
  for lifers, 242
  for nonlifers, 242
  offices furnishing information on, 247
  reentry programs used with, 245-247
  revocation of, 244-245
Parole agent, 243, 244, 247
Parolee, placement of, 244
Peyote, 172
Piracy, 160
  of films, records, home videos, 130
Pleadings, 253-254
Police, services of, 112
  codes, 218-223
  See also individual names of police departments
Ponzi Scam. *See* Pyramid
Postal Inspector's Office, and white-collar criminals, 6
Prisoner-mother programs, 245
Prisons. *See* Correctional institutions; Federal Bureau of Prisons; Individual names; United States Penitentiary
Private Investigators, 81-82
  real-life vs. fictional image of, 81-82
Probation, 254
  officer of, 261
Pyramid, 129

R

Rape, 160
  assault with attempt to commit, 125-126
  definition of, 125
  statutory, 125
Red herrings, 3
Restitution center, 246
Return-to-custody facilities, 245
Revolver, 141
  list of kinds of, 142
Rifles, carbines, and shotguns, list of kinds of, 143-144
Rights of individuals under U.S. Constitution, 250-251
  of parties under arrest, 286-287
Robbery, 131-132
  crimes committed in addition to, 132
  methods used in, 132
  objects of, 132
  types of, 131
  weapons used in, 132

S

San Quentin State Prison, 225-228
Securities and Exchange Com-

mission and white-collar criminals, 6
Serial killers, 4-6
characteristics of, 4-5
and episodic aggressive behavior, 5-6
patterns of, 5
pleasure-seeking type of, 5
sociopath as, 5
visionary type, 5
Sex offenses, 125-126
kinds of, 125
See also Rape
Shadowing. *See* Trailing
Sierra Conservation Center, 234
Slanguage, 178-212
general crime, 203-212
on-the-road, 203
police, 199-203
prison, 198-199
street gang, 194-198
of underworld, 178-194
Smugglers, characteristics of suspected, 134-135
Smuggling, 133-137
clues to at airfields, 135-136
clues to at checkpoints, 136-137
clues to at marinas, 136
of cocaine, 173-174
hiding places, 134
of individuals, 134
of objects, 133-134
SOFA (Status of Forces), 92-93
Street gangs, address for information on in Los Angeles, 198
slanguage of, 194-198
See also Individual names
Substance-abuse treatment centers, 246
Surveillance, 109-112
electronic equipment used in, 111
forms of, 111
objectives of, 109
police criminalistics laboratory used in, 112
police identification section used in, 112
police photographic laboratory used in, 112
police vehicles used in, 111
use of telephone taps in, 110-111
See also Tailing, techniques of; Telephone taps
Suspect, clues to at scene of crime, 103
discovery of at scene of crime, 101-102
identification of, 101-102
picking up trail of, 102-103
Syndicate, 12
Synthetic analgesics, 165
as narcotics, 165

T

Tailing, 109-110
techniques of, 109-110
Telephone tap, 110
bug as, 110
means of using, 110
roaming wired bug as, 110
wireless, 110
Triad, 13

U

United States Air Force Office of Special Investigations, 79
United States Army Command

and General Staff College Student Text 27-1 excerpt from, 94-99
United States Army Criminal Investigative Command and Army Crime Records Center, 78
U.S. Attorney's Office, and white-collar criminals, 6
United States Central Bureau of the International Police Organization (INTERPOL), 77
United States Coast Guard, 72
U.S. Customs Special Investigative Division, 70
United States Department of Justice, 56-69
organizations of, 56, 63
U.S. Marshal's Service, 67
United States Military and Naval Law Enforcement, 78-80
United States Naval Investigative Service, 79
United States Penitentiary, 238-240
address of, 238
visiting instructions of, 238-240
See also Correctional institutions; Prisons
U.S. Postal Inspection Service, 72-73

V

Victim of crime as character, 3

W

Weapons, 138-139, 161. *See also* Firearms; Handgun; machine gun
Weapons, automatic, 141
kinds of used by criminals, 142
kinds of used by law-enforcement agencies, 142
nonautomatic, 141
Work furlough centers, 242

Y

Ying On Tong, 13

Other Books of Interest

Annual Market Books

Children's Writer's & Illustrator's Market, edited by Lisa Carpenter (paper) $17.95
Guide to Literary Agents & Art/Photo Reps, edited by Robin Gee $15.95
Humor & Cartoon Markets, edited by Bob Staake (paper) $16.95
Novel & Short Story Writer's Market, edited by Robin Gee (paper) $19.95
Photographer's Market, edited by Sam Marshall $21.95
Poet's Market, by Judson Jerome $19.95
Songwriter's Market, edited by Brian Rushing $19.95
Writer's Market, edited by Mark Kissling $25.95

General Writing Books

Beginning Writer's Answer Book, edited by Kirk Polking (paper) $13.95
Discovering the Writer Within, by Bruce Ballenger & Barry Lane $17.95
Freeing Your Creativity, by Marshall Cook $17.95
Getting the Words Right: How to Rewrite, Edit and Revise, by Theodore A. Rees Cheney (paper) $12.95
How to Write a Book Proposal, by Michael Larsen (paper) $10.95
Just Open a Vein, edited by William Brohaugh $15.95
Knowing Where to Look: The Ultimate Guide to Research, by Lois Horowitz (paper) $16.95
Make Your Words Work, by Gary Provost $17.95
Pinckert's Practical Grammar, by Robert C. Pinckert (paper) $11.95
12 Keys to Writing Books That Sell, by Kathleen Krull (paper) $12.95
The 28 Biggest Writing Blunders, by William Noble $12.95
The 29 Most Common Writing Mistakes & How to Avoid Them, by Judy Delton (paper) $9.95
The Wordwatcher's Guide to Good Writing & Grammar, by Morton S. Freeman (paper) $15.95
Word Processing Secrets for Writers, by Michael A. Banks & Ansen Dibell (paper) $14.95
The Writer's Book of Checklists, by Scott Edelstein $16.95
The Writer's Digest Guide to Manuscript Formats, by Buchman & Groves $18.95
The Writer's Essential Desk Reference, edited by Glenda Neff $19.95

Nonfiction Writing

Creative Conversations: The Writer's Guide to Conducting Interviews, by Michael Schumacher $16.95
How to Do Leaflets, Newsletters, & Newspapers, by Nancy Brigham (paper) $14.95
How to Sell Every Magazine Article You Write, by Lisa Collier Cool (paper) $11.95
How to Write Irresistible Query Letters, by Lisa Collier Cool (paper) $10.95
The Writer's Digest Handbook of Magazine Article Writing, edited by Jean M. Fredette (paper) $11.95

Fiction Writing

The Art & Craft of Novel Writing, by Oakley Hall $17.95
Best Stories from New Writers, edited by Linda Sanders $5.99
Characters & Viewpoint, by Orson Scott Card $13.95
The Complete Guide to Writing Fiction, by Barnaby Conrad $17.95
Cosmic Critiques: How & Why 10 Science Fiction Stories Work, edited by Asimov & Greenberg (paper) $12.95
Creating Characters: How to Build Story People, by Dwight V. Swain $16.95
Creating Short Fiction, by Damon Knight (paper) $10.95
Dialogue, by Lewis Turco $13.95
The Fiction Writer's Silent Partner, by Martin Roth $19.95
Handbook of Short Story Writing: Vol. I, by Dickson and Smythe (paper) $10.95
Handbook of Short Story Writing: Vol. II, edited by Jean Fredette (paper) $12.95
How to Write & Sell Your First Novel, by Collier & Leighton (paper) $12.95
Manuscript Submission, by Scott Edelstein $13.95
Mastering Fiction Writing, by Kit Reed $18.95
Plot, by Ansen Dibell $13.95
Spider Spin Me a Web: Lawrence Block on Writing Fiction, by Lawrence Block $16.95
Theme & Strategy, by Ronald B. Tobias $13.95

The 38 Most Common Writing Mistakes, by Jack M. Bickham $12.95
Writer's Digest Handbook of Novel Writing, $18.95
Writing the Novel: From Plot to Print, by Lawrence Block (paper) $11.95

Special Interest Writing Books

Armed & Dangerous: A Writer's Guide to Weapons, by Michael Newton (paper) $14.95
The Children's Picture Book: How to Write It, How to Sell It, by Ellen E.M. Roberts (paper) $19.95
Comedy Writing Secrets, by Mel Helitzer (paper) $15.95
The Complete Book of Feature Writing, by Leonard Witt $18.95
Creating Poetry, by John Drury $18.95
Deadly Doses: A Writer's Guide to Poisons, by Serita Deborah Stevens with Anne Klarner (paper) $16.95
Editing Your Newsletter, by Mark Beach (paper) $18.50
Families Writing, by Peter Stillman (paper) $12.95
A Guide to Travel Writing & Photography, by Ann & Carl Purcell (paper) $22.95
Hillary Waugh's Guide to Mysteries & Mystery Writing, by Hillary Waugh $19.95
How to Pitch & Sell Your TV Script, by David Silver $17.95
How to Write Action/Adventure Novels, by Michael Newton $4.99
How to Write & Sell Greeting Cards, Bumper Stickers, T-Shirts and Other Fun Stuff, by Molly Wigand (paper) 15.95
How to Write & Sell True Crime, by Gary Provost $17.95
How to Write Horror Fiction, by William F. Nolan $15.95
How to Write Mysteries, by Shannon OCork $13.95
How to Write Romances, by Phyllis Taylor Pianka $15.95
How to Write Science Fiction & Fantasy, by Orson Scott Card $13.95
How to Write Tales of Horror, Fantasy & Science Fiction, edited by J.N. Williamson (paper) $12.95
How to Write the Story of Your Life, by Frank P. Thomas (paper) $11.95
The Magazine Article: How To Think It, Plan It, Write It, by Peter Jacobi $17.95
Mystery Writer's Handbook, by The Mystery Writers of America (paper) $11.95
The Poet's Handbook, by Judson Jerome (paper) $11.95
Powerful Business Writing, by Tom McKeown $12.95
Successful Scriptwriting, by Jurgen Wolff & Kerry Cox (paper) $14.95
The Writer's Guide to Conquering the Magazine Market, by Connie Emerson $17.95
Writing for Children & Teenagers, 3rd Edition, by Lee Wyndham & Arnold Madison (paper) $12.95
Writing Mysteries: A Handbook by the Mystery Writers of America, Edited by Sue Grafton, $18.95
Writing the Modern Mystery, by Barbara Norville (paper) $12.95

The Writing Business

A Beginner's Guide to Getting Published, edited by Kirk Polking (paper) $11.95
Business & Legal Forms for Authors & Self-Publishers, by Tad Crawford (paper) $4.99
The Complete Guide to Self-Publishing, by Tom & Marilyn Ross (paper) $16.95
How You Can Make $25,000 a Year Writing, by Nancy Edmonds Hanson (paper) $14.95
This Business of Writing, by Gregg Levoy $19.95
Writer's Guide to Self-Promotion & Publicity, by Elane Feldman $16.95
Writing A to Z, edited by Kirk Polking $22.95

To order directly from the publisher, include $3.00 postage and handling for 1 book and $1.00 for each additional book. Allow 30 days for delivery.

Writer's Digest Books
1507 Dana Avenue, Cincinnati, Ohio 45207
Credit card orders call TOLL-FREE
1-800-289-0963

Prices subject to change without notice.

Write to this same address for information on *Writer's Digest* magazine, *Story* magazine, Writer's Digest Book Club, Writer's Digest School, and Writer's Digest Criticism Service.